The Resistance Network

TEXTS AND STUDIES IN ARMENIAN HISTORY, SOCIETY, AND CULTURE

Texts and Studies in Armenian History, Society, and Culture (TSAHSC) is a project of the Armenian Research Center (ARC) at the University of Michigan-Dearborn. The series was created to expand English-language academic publishing of Armenian Studies. In addition to secondary sources based on original research, the series will also publish anthologies of historical documents pertaining to Armenia and the Armenians; annotated memoirs, both original and translated, of personalities influential in Armenian life; translations of medieval Armenian historical and literary texts as well as works of modern Armenian literature; other topical anthologies; bibliographies; and college textbooks, all related to Armenian Studies.

The Resistance Network

THE ARMENIAN GENOCIDE AND HUMANITARIANISM IN OTTOMAN SYRIA, 1915–1918

Khatchig Mouradian

MICHIGAN STATE UNIVERSITY PRESS | *East Lansing*

♾ The paper used in this publication meets the minimum requirements
of ANSI/NISO Z39.48-1992 (R 1997) (Permanence of Paper).

Michigan State University Press
East Lansing, Michigan 48823-5245

LIBRARY OF CONGRESS CATALOGING-IN-PUBLICATION DATA
Names: Mouradian, Khatchig, author. Title: The resistance network :
the Armenian genocide and humanitarianism in Ottoman Syria, 1915–1918 / Khatchig Mouradian.
Description: East Lansing : Michigan State University Press, 2021.
| Series: Texts and studies in Armenian history, society, and culture
| Includes bibliographical references and index.
Identifiers: LCCN 2020021791 | ISBN 9781611863857 (cloth) | ISBN 9781609176600 (PDF)
| ISBN 9781628954197 (ePUB) | ISBN 9781628964202 (Kindle)
Subjects: LCSH: Armenian massacres, 1915-1923. | Humanitarian assistance—Syria.
| Concentration camps—Syria. | Armenians—Syria.
Classification: LCC DS195.5 .M677 2021 | DDC 956.6/20154—dc23
LC record available at https://lccn.loc.gov/2020021791

Book design by Charlie Sharp, Sharp DesIgns, East Lansing, Michigan
Cover design by Shaun Allshouse, www.shaunallshouse.com
Cover art: Administrators of the largest orphanage sheltering Armenians
in Aleppo during the genocide, Nora Altounyan (seated)
and Aharon Shirajian (standing next to her) among them.
Image courtesy of AGBU Nubar Library, Paris.

Michigan State University Press is a member of the Green Press Initiative and is committed to developing and encouraging ecologically responsible publishing practices. For more information about the Green Press Initiative and the use of recycled paper in book publishing, please visit www.greenpressinitiative.org.

Visit Michigan State University Press at *www.msupress.org*

To my mother,
Marie Gharibian-Mouradian

"I believe in the resistance
as I believe there can be no light
without shadow; or rather,
no shadow unless there is also light."

MARGARET ATWOOD,
The Handmaid's Tale

"You look at the network,
and then it starts to look back at you."

MERLIN SHELDRAKE IN ROBERT MACFARLANE,
Underland: A Deep Time Journey

Contents

xi ACKNOWLEDGMENTS

xv INTRODUCTION

PART ONE. Genocide and Urban Resistance

3 CHAPTER ONE. Before the Storm: Deportation and Humanitarian Relief

25 CHAPTER TWO. Aleppo: Urban Resistance to Redeportation

PART TWO. From the City to the Desert

57 CHAPTER THREE. Wartime Civilian Internment: Concentration Camps in Ottoman Syria

69 CHAPTER FOUR. Gateways to the Desert: The Sebil, Karlık, and Bab Camps

89 CHAPTER FIVE. Along the Euphrates: The Meskeneh Concentration Camp

PART THREE. Der Zor Bound

105 CHAPTER SIX. Death and Resilience: The Military Supply Line

121 CHAPTER SEVEN. Zor: That Immense Graveyard of Our Martyrs

139 CHAPTER EIGHT. Surviving Talaat: The Network's Legacy

149 NOTES

217 BIBLIOGRAPHY

227 INDEX

Acknowledgments

Writing this book would have been bumpier, lonelier, and far less rewarding without the tremendous encouragement and support I received over the years.

Taner Akçam, Debórah Dwork, and Raymond Kévorkian were a dream team of a dissertation committee, and I also relied on their support as I ushered the manuscript from dissertation to book. Akçam's deciphering of the Ottoman state's machinery of destruction, Dwork's conceptualization of agency and resistance, and Kévorkian's engagement with the second phase of the Armenian genocide and the importance of Armenian sources, alongside Henry Theriault's explorations of power dynamics during genocide, have influenced my thinking. I am indebted to them for their mentorship, council, and critique of my work—and, knowing them, I know the best way to pay it back is by paying it forward!

Margaret Anderson, Hans-Lukas Kieser, and Marc Mamigonian offered valuable feedback on parts of the manuscript at different stages of writing. Nancy Eskijian and Jennine Jackson provided me with access to their family archives, helping shed further light on the humanitarian work of Rev. Hovhannes Eskijian and U.S. Consul in Aleppo Jesse B. Jackson respectively. Vahé Tachjian, Garo Derounian, and Ani Boghikian-Kasparian provided me with scans of primary sources, book pages, and newspaper clippings, while George Aghjayan and Nurhan Becidyan looked the other way as I carried away dozens of books from their private libraries. I thank them for their generosity.

Although many documents and books consulted in this book came to me, I had to go after most. My thanks go to the staff of the Prime Minister's Ottoman Archives in Istanbul, Turkey; the National Library of Armenia in Yerevan, Armenia; the library of the Mkhitarist Congregation in Vienna, Austria; the archives of the Catholicosate of Armenians of the Great House of Cilicia in Antelias, Lebanon; the Derian Library at Haigazian University in Beirut, Lebanon; the AGBU Nubarian Library (BNu) in Paris, France; the Armenian Research Center (ARC) at the University of Michigan-Dearborn; the Library of Congress in Washington, DC; the National Association for Armenian Studies and Research (NAASR) in Belmont, MA; the Armenian Museum of America, the Armenian Revolutionary Federation Archives, and the Hairenik Association library in Watertown, MA; and the Rockefeller Archive Center in Sleepy Hollow, NY. BNu director Boris Adjemian, Associate Librarian Vera Gosdanian at Haigazian, and Research Assistant Gerald E. Ottenbreit Jr. at ARC were of tremendous help. I am grateful to the Arts & Sciences Faculty Research Allocation Program at Columbia University, the Armenian Missionary Association of America, and the Knights of Vartan Fund for Armenian Studies administered by NAASR for travel and research grants that allowed me to work in these archives and libraries.

I embarked on the dissertation-to-book journey in the fall of 2016, while serving as the Kazan Visiting Assistant Professor at California State University–Fresno. I thank the university's Armenian Studies Program for that opportunity. Since 2017, Columbia University has been my home, and it is here that that this manuscript came of age. I thank the Department of Middle Eastern, South Asian, and African Studies (MESAAS) and the Armenian Center at Columbia University for their faith in my work.

I consider Ara Sanjian a mentor since my days as an undergraduate at Haigazian University. I thank him for his continued mentorship and for serving on my comprehensive examination committee alongside Cemal Kafadar and Akçam. It gives me great joy that my first book is published under Sanjian's editorship.

Special thanks to the three reviewers whose comments and suggestions I took to heart, and the manuscript is all the better for it! I would also like to express my appreciation to the editorial board of the series "Texts and Studies in Armenian History, Society, and Culture" and Michigan State University Press.

Words of gratitude go to Julia Salem for meticulously editing the book manuscript and offering invaluable feedback. Anne Osherson translated from German, and Bria-Hardin Boyer and Joshua Aaron Levendosk Nacht at MESAAS provided research help.

I thank Julie Loehr, Anastasia Wraight, Kristine Blakeslee, Terika Hernandez, and Elise Jajuga at MSUP for ushering the book to publication.

I would be remiss if I did not acknowledge the support and encouragement I received over the years from George Aghjayan, Ara Araz, Nayiri Arzoumanian, Stephan Astourian, Levon Avdoyan, Movses Babayan, David Barsamian, Nanore Barsoumian, Becky Berberian, Gaby Bitarian, Chris Bohjalian, Antranig Dakessian, Maggie Goschin, Rev. Paul Haidostian, the late Bill Hausrath, Kim Hekimian, Alex Hinton, Nora Hovsepian, Osman Kavala, Zaven Khanjian, Olga Litvak, Marc Mamigonian, Taleen Mardirossian, Edvin Minassian, Mark Momdjian, Eric Nazarian, Lara Nercessian, Razmik Panossian, James Sahagian, Ani Tchaghlasian, Khachig Tölölyan, Nicole Vartanian, Johanna Vollhardt, Vera Yacoubian, Amberin Zaman, and my colleagues at the Armenian Center and MESAAS at Columbia.

I thank my mother, Marie Gharibian-Mouradian, and my sisters, Suzanne and Knarik, for always being there for me, though we now live on different continents.

I owe much to the survivors whose accounts shape the backbone of this book, and to their descendants who published their memoirs or opened family archives and shared unpublished manuscripts with me. Their words allowed me to navigate through the abattoirs of the Ottoman Empire during World War I and witness unyielding resistance where scholarship and public discourse have often seen only victimhood.

Publication Credits

Shorter versions or parts of the introduction and chapters 1, 3, and 5 have been previously published as journal articles or book chapters.

Parts of the introduction and chapter 1 have appeared in "The Very Limit of Our Endurance: Unarmed Resistance in Ottoman Syria during WWI," in *End of the Ottomans: The Genocide of 1915 and the Politics of Turkish Nationalism*, ed. Hans-Lukas Kieser, Margaret Lavinia Anderson, Seyhan Bayraktar, and Thomas Schmutz (London: I. B Tauris, 2019), 247–261; and in "Genocide and Humanitarian Resistance in Ottoman Syria, 1915–1916," *Études arméniennes contemporaines* 7 (2016): 87–103.

Parts of chapter 3 and chapter 5 have been published in "Internment and Destruction: Concentration Camps during the Armenian Genocide, 1915–1916," in *Internment during the First World War: A Mass Global Phenomenon*, ed. Stefan Manz, Panikos Panayi, and Matthew Stibbe (London: Routledge, 2018), 145–161.

A version of chapter 5 has been published as "The Meskeneh Concentration Camp, 1915–1917: A Case Study of Power, Collaboration, and Humanitarian Resistance during the Armenian Genocide," *Journal of the Society for Armenian Studies* 24 (2015): 44–55.

I would like to thank I. B Tauris, Routledge, *Études arméniennes contemporaines*, and *Journal of the Society for Armenian Studies* for permission to reprint these sections.

A Note about Currency, Dates, and Transliteration

One *mecidiye* was equivalent to 23.5 *kuruş*. One *lira* was equivalent to 127 *kuruş* or US$4.4 (with an approximate purchasing power of US$100 today). One *metalik* was equivalent to ⅓ *kuruş*. In Aleppo in 1915, a kilogram of bread cost 3.5 *kuruş* (12 cents), yogurt 4.5 *kuruş* (16 cents), and cheese 12 *kuruş* (42 cents). All dates are according to the Gregorian calendar, unless specified otherwise. I use Library of Congress transliteration systems with some simplification (for example, without diacritics for Armenian transliteration), and do not transliterate from Arabic, Turkish, and Armenian personal and place names that have commonly employed versions (for example, Altounyan instead of Alt'unean).

Abbreviations

Aram Andonian Archives at the Bibliothèque Nubar, Paris (BNu/Andonian)
Armenian Revolutionary Federation (ARF)
Committee of Union and Progress (CUP)
Directorate for the Settlement of Tribes and Emigrants (İskân-ı Aşâir ve Muhacirîn Müdüriyeti, IAMM)
German South-West Africa (GSWA, modern-day Namibia)
Prime Minister's Ottoman Archives (Başbakanlık Osmanlı Arşivi, BOA)
Provisional National Administrative Assembly (PNAA)

Introduction

"My dear *Badveli* [Reverend], barely out of bed from his sickness, disregarding the personal hardships and peril to his own life, relentlessly labored day and night to save other lives. Together we pressed ourselves to the very limit of our endurance. All our time, energy, effort, sleep, food, clothing, and other material possessions we put on the line on behalf of this wretched, miserable mass of torn and battered humanity," wrote Gulenia Danielian Eskijian in a letter in 1919.[1] Until his death in March 1916, her husband, Rev. Hovhannes Eskijian, provided food, shelter, and medication to Armenian deportees arriving in Aleppo. The pastor's health was failing, and the Ottoman Turkish authorities were tracking his movements. The disease got to him first. He died at thirty-four from typhoid contracted from the deportees he served.

Rev. Eskijian was part of an informal, unarmed resistance network in Ottoman Syria during World War I that saved thousands caught in the maelstrom of genocide by securing safe houses and provisions, helping them evade or escape redeportation, internment, forced labor, and sexual slavery, and recruiting them to help with the resistance effort. The scholarly and public discourse on the Armenian genocide have long emphasized armed resistance—or the lack thereof—and

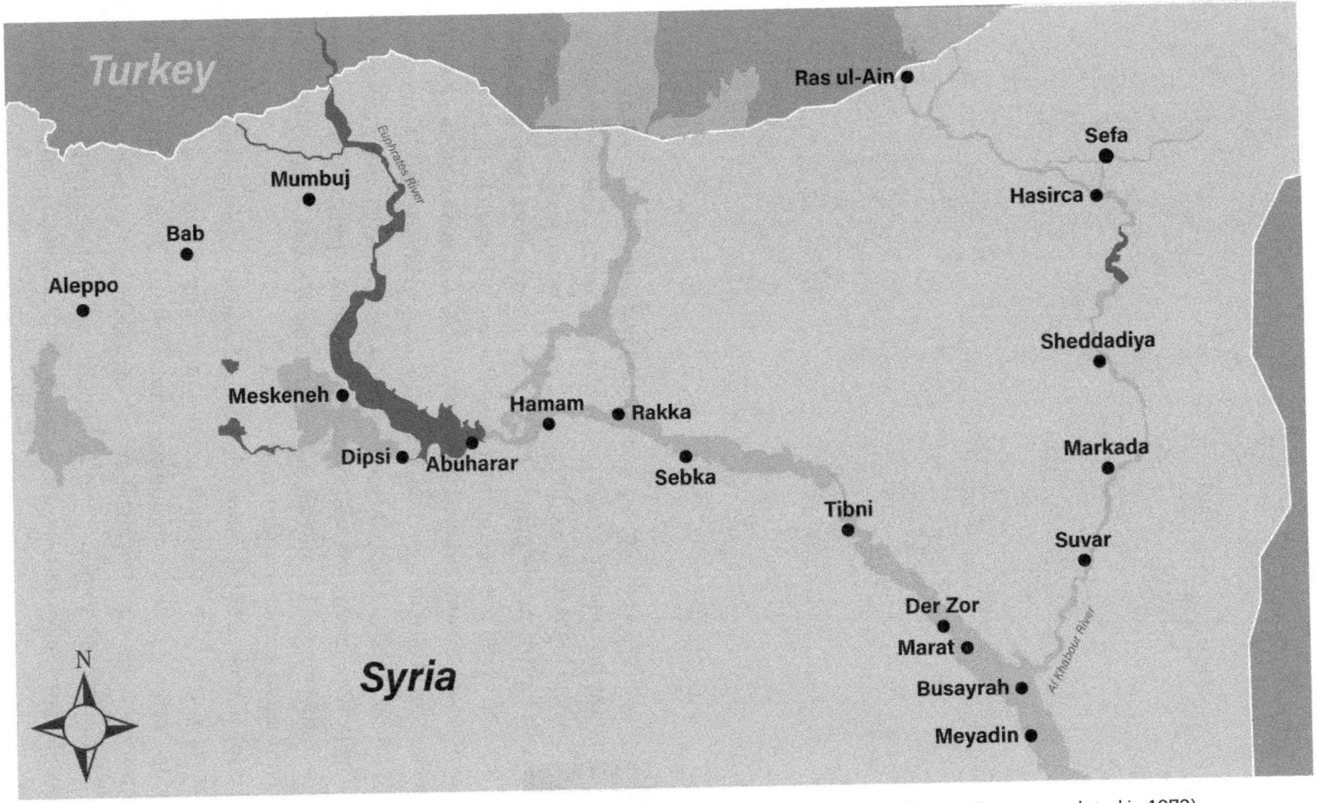

MAP PREPARED BY GEORGE AGHJAYAN.

Main locations under study in this book, on a modern map of Syria (after the construction of the Euphrates Dam, completed in 1973).

neglected the less conspicuous yet more common civilian resistance.[2] In this book, I challenge explicit and implicit depictions of Armenians as passive recipients of violence on the one hand and of Western humanitarian assistance on the other, arguing for expanding our conceptualization of resistance to include subtler, more common forms of organized opposition and humanitarian action. I do so by exploring the genocidal process and unarmed defiance to it from urban settings like Aleppo, Rakka, and Der Zor to transit and concentration camps in rural and desert areas of Syria. I examine in tandem the policies of the local, regional, and central authorities of the Ottoman state, and the self-help efforts of Armenians aided by locals and Western missionaries. I outline how a series of wartime decisions culminated in massacres in the Syrian Desert in the summer of 1916, and how thousands of Armenians survived the carnage through the efforts of a loosely connected resistance network that stretched from Aleppo to Der Zor and beyond. I argue that despite the violent and systematic mechanisms of control and destruction in the cities, concentration camps, and massacre sites in the geographic triangle stretching between Aleppo, Ras ul-Ain, and Der Zor, the genocide of the Armenians did not progress unhindered: resistance proved an important factor, saving many lives.

Although Holocaust scholarship has made great strides in recent decades toward broadening the conceptual spectrum of actions that constitute resistance, the literature on other instances of mass violence has been slow to catch up. The Armenian genocide is a case in point. The scholarship and the public discourse largely define the perpetrators and Western humanitarians—but not the targeted group—as actors, focusing on how the former killed and the latter saved. Yet our understanding of the dynamics of mass violence would be flawed, or at best incomplete, without fully integrating the targeted group's resistance into the narrative. Although the genocidal machine aims to maximize the very power asymmetry that propels it, it cannot erase the opposition of the victims as individuals and as a group. Zooming in on one region of the Ottoman Empire during the Great War, I demonstrate in this book how Armenians coordinated a massive, robust humanitarian resistance effort, which helped save the lives of thousands. To piece together this blow-by-blow narrative of destruction and resistance, I stand on the shoulders of survivors who told their stories. Hundreds of published and unpublished accounts, supplemented by a plethora of archival documents and secondary literature, sustain the narrative and support the arguments presented here.

The Allure of the Sword

A gradual shift "from an examination of the mechanics of death to an exploration of the dynamics of survival" has occurred in Holocaust historiography, and the literature on anti-Nazi resistance in general, over the past half century.[3] In a compelling essay on Jewish resistance, historian Robert Rozett notes that most scholars had converged in an inclusive definition of resistance by the 1970s, and by the end of the 1990s they had begun "considering Jewish resistance less and less as a special category of behaviour, and started to discuss it in the context of a broader exploration of the life of Jews under the Nazi domination."[4] These scholars were challenging what historian Vesna Drapac refers to as the "entrenched fixation of historians with the 'warrior element' of resistance, an inflexible, individualized and masculinist view of what it takes to win a total war and the fronts on which one fights an ideological war," which "has led to an impasse (or revisionism in certain contexts) in resistance studies."[5]

Ignoring unarmed forms of defiance or ascribing them a supporting role diminished the importance of women's contributions. "For decades, most scholars have in fact shared a stereotype of the resistance, presenting it almost exclusively as an armed action and almost entirely masculine. . . . Later, references began to appear to the unarmed actions and those of women, but only rarely did such mention go beyond an emotional homage," offers the historian Anna Bravo.[6] While scholars have gradually succeeded in dispelling, in the words of historian Paul Bartrop, "one of the greatest myths of the Holocaust . . . that the Jews made little or no effort to defend themselves against their Nazi oppressors,"[7] Armenian genocide scholarship and public discourse continue to suffer from it. This myth has been exacerbated and amplified by the Turkish state's aggressive genocide denial campaigns, in the face of which scholars have focused on studying the victimization and destruction of Armenians, often ignoring the historical record on Armenian mobilization and resistance. It is as if by granting perpetrators absolute power, the case for asserting the veracity of the genocide were strengthened. The literature of the second best-studied case of genocide tells us that in those rare instances when Armenians resisted, it was by taking up arms, especially in Van, Urfa, Musa Dagh, and Shabin Karahisar.[8] The scarcity of armed opposition has even perplexed some scholars. The oral historians Donald E. Miller and Lorna Touryan Miller remark:

> In the course of our interviews, we often wondered why there was so little resistance to the deportations. This is a complex question. . . . First, the Armenian leadership had been imprisoned or killed; second, weapons had been confiscated; and, third, the young men most capable of defending their communities had been drafted into the Turkish army.

The authors also attributed Armenian passivity to an engrained receptiveness to authority that had developed over centuries, and to the fact that "they could not perceive the master plan of extermination that was unfolding."[9] In his authoritative history of the genocide published in 2015, historian Ronald Suny agrees: "Most Armenians did not resist, hoping that they would survive by obeying the authorities, not imagining that arbitrary and massive killing was occurring daily."[10] Yet, as we broaden our analytical aperture to include nonviolent forms of defiance, the argument for Armenian passivity crumbles.[11]

Defining Resistance

Armenians did indeed resist as soon as the Committee of Union and Progress (CUP) enacted the empire-wide arrests, deportations, and massacres in the spring of 1915. Shavarsh Misakian, an Armenian Revolutionary Federation (ARF) leader and intellectual in Istanbul who had escaped arrest, organized a clandestine chain of communication between the Ottoman provinces, Istanbul, and the outside world, smuggling reports of atrocities out of the country.[12] Others created groups that procured, transferred, and distributed funds, food, and medication to exiles, saved them from sexual slavery, created safe houses and underground orphanages, and upheld deportee morale as hundreds of communities were forcibly removed from their ancestral lands and marched in the direction of Syria.[13] These groups were loosely interlinked, operating out of cities where the population was only partly deported (Istanbul and Aleppo), and along railroad lines stretching from Istanbul to Konya, Aleppo, Ras ul-Ain, and Mosul.[14]

Focusing on this network's operations in Syria, I situate resistance within a range of victim responses, including the exploitation of and profiteering from fellow Armenians, corruption and misappropriation of humanitarian assistance, and collaboration with Turkish authorities, gendarmes, police, and even post office authorities in order to denounce, extort, deport, and, in rare cases, sexually abuse and even kill deportees. As such, this is not a hagiography of resisters, nor an attempt to glorify victims "by exaggerating resistance, which can imply a condemnation of those who did *not* resist," to quote historian John M. Cox.[15]

I view the Armenian genocide as the centrally planned destruction of organized Armenian life shaped by local particularities and ad hoc measures, with the center intervening when the process encountered hindrances, slowed down, or progressed too overtly. Spurred by an exclusionist ideology and a drive to homogenize a crumbling empire, and citing wartime security measures and military necessity, the ruling CUP codified into law its decision to uproot, dispossess, and destroy Armenian communities. Initially, local authorities implemented these laws, and parallel orders of massacres, with varying enthusiasm, resulting in reassignments, firings, courts martial (typically with charges of corruption or for harboring dangerous elements), and, in cases like that of the mayor of Lice Hüseyin Nesimi, the murders of recalcitrant officials.[16] In this environment, efforts to save Armenians were often conducted against the law or against the will of the authorities.

In the scholarship on anti-Nazi resistance, a broad, inclusive definition carrying symmetric components now stands as the norm. Sociologist Nechama Tec sees resistance "as a set of activities motivated by the desire to thwart, limit, undermine, or end the exercise of oppression over the oppressed."[17] Historian Bob Moore defines resistance to Nazis in Western Europe as "any activity designed to thwart German plans, or perceived by the occupiers as working against their interests."[18] Historian Yehuda Bauer once defined resistance to the Holocaust as "any group action consciously taken in opposition to known or surmised laws, actions or intentions directed against the Jews by the Germans and their supporters." More recently, he has argued for including individual acts of resistance and referring to the perpetrators as "Germans and their collaborators."[19]

I define resistance as actions carried out illegally, or against the sanction and will of the authorities, to save Armenian deportees from annihilation. I make the distinction between acts of humanitarian relief and those of humanitarian *resistance* because eliminationist policies, to borrow historian Daniel Jonah Goldhagen's formulation, are not implemented in unison and uniformly.[20] Mass violence unfolds in erratic, unforeseeable ways. Priorities and local dynamics generate lags in execution. While the destruction of Armenian communities was progressing in full force in the eastern provinces of the Ottoman Empire in the spring of 1915, local authorities in Aleppo were coordinating efforts with the local Armenian community to provide shelter and assistance to deportees arriving in the region. During that period, humanitarian activities aimed at saving Armenian lives in Van, a region fully caught in the vortex of genocide, constituted resistance, while similar actions in Aleppo did not. A few months later, however, when authorities cracked down on humanitarian efforts in Aleppo, many relief workers there were forced to go underground and form an unarmed resistance network.

Humanitarian Relief

Historian Yaron Ayalon argues that whenever disaster struck in the Ottoman Empire, one's community stood as the "primary venue for seeking and providing aid," all the more so for non-Muslims, for whom religious institutions "fulfilled some of the needs the state did for Muslims."[21] Indeed, the small Armenian community of Aleppo immediately organized relief committees to help the Armenian survivors who had arrived in Syria.[22] On 24 May 1915, within a week of the first convoys' arrival, the Armenian Apostolic Church formed the Council for Refugees (Kaghtaganats zhoghov in Armenian, henceforth, the council) and tasked it with "caring for the immediate financial, moral, and health needs" of the deportees.[23] Separately, the city's Armenian Evangelical and Catholic churches launched their own relief initiatives. Relying on their clerical hierarchy, lay representation, and congregations, these churches mounted an expansive humanitarian effort that received the tacit approval and sometimes even the support of the local authorities until fall 1915: they compiled detailed lists of deportees in Aleppo, Bab, Mumbuj, Idlib, Riha, Maarra, and Hama; prepared reports on the conditions of deportees and identified the pros and cons of settling deportees in each of the aforementioned areas; provided funds, food, shelter, medical assistance, and supplies to the thousands arriving in the region; dispatched priests and pharmacists to deportees who had been temporarily settled in camps in distant Der Zor to distribute funds, medication, and provide spiritual nourishment; organized fundraisers; established orphanages; and coordinated efforts with the Aleppo governorate as well as foreign consuls and missionaries residing in the city.

The Armenians were not newcomers to humanitarian work, nor were they the only community engaging in it during the Great War. During previous years, Armenian churches and other institutions empire-wide had established relief committees following the Hamidian massacres of 1894–1896 and the Adana massacre in 1909. As wartime blockades and closure of ports, plagues of locusts, and failures in government precipitated epidemics and starvation in Ottoman Syria, many communities organized to assist the needy.[24]

Ayalon rightly notes that in the Ottoman context, "the larger share of charitable acts took place within the community and in a faith-specific context, even when the people involved were only loosely connected to their religious group otherwise." In a work that covers centuries of Ottoman history, Ayalon notes only one example (also in Aleppo, in 1787!), where "Christians were involved in charitable endeavors of a denomination other than their own."[25] Yet the enormity of Armenian suffering and need necessitated, and galvanized, a more collaborative approach to relief. Many Aleppians eventually set confessional and even religious differences aside as they networked to assist deportees arriving in Ottoman Syria that, by early 1916, numbered around half a million.[26] The city's Armenian Apostolic, Catholic, and Evangelical congregations now coordinated efforts and received assistance and support from other Christians, as well as from leaders and members of the city's Muslim and Jewish communities.

This indigenous, organized, and sustained effort to help deportees, led by Aleppo's Armenian community, was in full swing four months ahead of the establishment of the Armenian Relief Committee in the United States in September 1915. Millions more would be raised in the United States and Europe and sent to the Ottoman Empire in subsequent years for Western diplomats and missionaries to administer relief. As asymmetric as this relationship between Western humanitarians and locals can appear in the scholarship and public discourse on the Armenian genocide, and informed as it was "by colonialism, paternalism, and ideas about ethnic and religious superiority," in the words of historian Keith Watenpaugh, it was also "a relationship in which forms of mutual respect, even friendship, could be established based on class and profession, but based on modern conceptions of shared humanity as well; and this sort of relationship was not just possible, but common."[27]

The scholarship on the wartime and interwar Western humanitarian efforts largely misses the connections it forged with local Christians and Muslims and arriving deportees, and the central role these Ottoman subjects themselves played in the humanitarian work. They not only launched an extensive effort months before relief funds started flowing from the United States and Europe, but also took upon themselves the task of distributing aid to deportees beyond the reach of consuls and missionaries, with Armenian couriers carrying funds or supplies to areas and encampments as far away as Idlib, Maarra, and Der Zor.

These interactions between local activists and Western humanitarians invite a rethinking of the dynamics of humanitarianism in the region where, as Watenpaugh argues, "much of modern humanitarianism was born."[28] Yet Watenpaugh's authoritative work on this genesis relies primarily on Western sources—a challenge he himself acknowledges, noting that "the amount of source material produced by humanitarian organizations and intergovernmental bodies is truly immense, and dwarfs that produced by the objects of humanitarianism themselves." He warns us that this imbalance, coupled with the inaccessibility of local archives, should make us "conscious of how that might skew the way we formulate basic historical questions."[29] Integrating into this book a wealth of sources hitherto difficult to access, which have been produced by the very objects of humanitarianism, I demonstrate that the latter were also *subjects* of humanitarianism.

Humanitarian Resistance

What set the humanitarian network under study apart from other wartime relief efforts (as well as earlier ones) were the increasingly hostile attitudes of Ottoman authorities toward it. When Armenians surviving the deportations and massacres began arriving in Syria in May 1915, local authorities scrambled for stopgap solutions in the absence of practicable guidance from the central government. The CUP leaders orchestrating the empire-wide deportations and massacres were initially paying little attention to the deportees who managed to arrive in Aleppo and its environs. This changed beginning in the fall of 1915, following a series of developments: a number of high-level meetings and consultations in the region, the formation of the Subdirectorate for Deportees in Aleppo, the dispatch of officials to the city to oversee the redeportation process, the replacement of the governor twice (and finally with an enthusiastic executor of Istanbul's policies),[30] the crackdown on the Aleppo Armenian community leadership, as well as the decision to remove all Armenian deportees from the city and ban the entry of new convoys. The central authorities exerted a sustained effort to neutralize organized Armenian responses to their policies and deal with what they perceived to be a demographic problem created by the arrival of a large number of survivors.[31]

The resistance network that pushed back at Istanbul's policies was, at its core, comprised of a few dozen dedicated Armenian religious and secular community leaders, Western missionaries and diplomats, and deportees who had arrived in

Syria beginning in the spring of 1915.[32] They included church leaders Catholicos Sahag II Khabayan (henceforth, the Catholicos), Vicar of the Armenian Apostolic Church of Aleppo Harutiun Yesayan, Rev. Eskijian, Rev. Aharon Shirajian, Dr. Asadour Aram Altounyan who owned a hospital bearing his name, his daughter Nora, the Mazloumian brothers who owned Hotel Baron, U.S. Consul Jesse B. Jackson, German Consul Walter Rössler, Swiss businessman Emil Zollinger, and Sister Beatrice Rohner.[33] They served as the glue connecting a much larger constituency of Armenians and, sometimes, local Muslim, Jewish, and Christian volunteers who helped in any way they could. Many others, like military hospital head nurse Elmasd Santoorian and military clothing workshop director Arika Amiralian in Aleppo, intellectuals Krikor Ankut and Garabed Kapigian in Rakka, and Levon Shashian and Mihran Aghazarian who worked for or had close ties with local authorities in Der Zor, were only loosely associated with the core group—typically through couriers or a personal connection with members of the network. Others engaged in acts of defiance without even the loosest form of coordination with, or even knowledge of, the network's existence.

Ottoman subjects in particular paid a heavy price for their resistance. Rev. Eskijian was an early victim, Shashian was killed during the Der Zor massacres in the summer of 1916, Father Yesayan was incarcerated from the fall of 1915 until the Ottoman withdrawal from Syria in October 1918, the Catholicos was exiled to Jerusalem in October 1915 and the Mazloumian brothers to Zahle in September 1916, and Rev. Shirajian was imprisoned on several occasions. Eliminating couriers was even easier for the authorities, particularly when they left urban areas to distribute aid and convey information to deportees in the desert. Many couriers, like Garabed, who worked with Rohner, disappeared on assignment in 1916. Another associate of Rohner's, Araxia Jebejian, who was based in Der Zor, was arrested and killed the same year. Locals who hid Armenians were arrested and tortured, while others, like George Soukkar, an Assyrian in Der Zor who helped deportees, died of diseases contracted from them.[34]

Assisting the deportees was also a source of tremendous stress for diplomats and missionaries. Even as they enjoyed diplomatic protection or held passports of countries allied to the Ottomans or neutral during the war, they were also pressured by their superiors to avoid conflict, surveilled by the Ottoman police and spies, and risked their physical and mental health. Jesse B. Jackson, the American consul in Aleppo, was watched and harassed.[35] Following the arrest, interrogation, and torture of one of her messengers, Swiss missionary Beatrice Rohner was forced to stop sending assistance to the camps along the Euphrates River in September 1916, and her orphanage was shut down by the authorities in February 1917. Devastated, she experienced a nervous breakdown and left Aleppo, returning only after the war had ended.[36]

The Network

A social network analysis of the humanitarian effort in Ottoman Syria during World War I allows for a deeper understanding of the dynamics of resistance. Great as the sacrifices of resisters were, what magnified their impact and sustained the effort for the duration of the war was the coordination between the network's nodes and their replaceability. When members were killed, arrested, exiled, burned out, or decided to withdraw for any reason, others assumed their responsibilities, and the work continued: upon the arrest of council chair Father Yesayan, Father Khachadur Boghigian replaced him; when council members resigned under duress, the Catholicos nominated others to serve on the board; when Rohner left Aleppo, she delegated her work to Zollinger and a committee of Armenians.[37]

Sensitivity to an approach that, in the words of sociologists Alexandra Marin and Barry Wellman, "conceptualizes social life in terms of structures of relationships among actors, rather than in terms of categories of actors," also problematizes the depiction of some Ottoman officials strictly as perpetrators and some Armenians as collaborators, and helps us explore overlaps. Examining structures that are not bound by categories allows us to discern "differing levels of group memberships, membership in multiple groups and cross-cutting ties between groups."[38] Minister of the Navy and the Commander of the Fourth Army Cemal Pasha reigned supreme in Syria during the war, and although he was advancing the genocidal policies of the central authorities, key network members like Dr. Altounyan leveraged favors from him that advanced the goals of the humanitarian resistance. Similarly, Armenians working for the local authorities, like Amiralian in Aleppo and Aghazarian in Der Zor, helped make the survival of many Armenians possible while serving the state that was annihilating their people.

Had it not been for the existence of organized community structures and key connectors in Aleppo prior to the arrival of deportees in the spring of 1915, such an expansive network would have been difficult to establish. The Armenian Apostolic, Catholic, and Evangelical churches were institutions with deep roots, sizeable congregations, and experience with humanitarian work. Dr. Altounyan's hospital and the Mazloumian brothers' hotel were the best Aleppo had to offer, placing their owners among the elite long before the war, and necessitating their continued service as it was waged. The tacit support of key local authorities for the Armenian community's humanitarian work in the spring of 1915 offered a window of opportunity for Armenians to mobilize and allowed for the unhindered organization of committees and subcommittees. When the tides turned, it was often the same people who went underground and continued the work.

What is striking is how fast some deportees arriving in Syria took on the mantle of resistance despite the risks involved and, in many cases, their unfamiliarity with the region. Rev. Shirajian knew what it meant to challenge the authorities. He had been imprisoned and tortured in 1895.[39] Yet soon after his convoy arrived in Aleppo from Marash in the spring of 1915, he took the helm of an orphanage that sheltered thousands of children and did not give in despite harassment and repeated arrests. Marzbed (Ghazaros Ghazarosian), an intellectual who had barely escaped the 24 April purges in Istanbul, played a leadership role in the network, disguised as a Jewish soap seller named Bokhor Efendi, and later as a Kurdish merchant selling sheep named Haji Hiuseyin. Dr. Khachig Boghosian, yet another member of the network, was among those arrested in Istanbul in April 1915. He was imprisoned for several weeks in Çankırı before being deported and ending up in Aleppo. As resourceful as these deportees were, their feats were accomplished with critical support from a number of institutions and key figures and, ultimately, stood as testament to the infrastructure that was already in place in the city.

The Urban Dimension

Venturing beyond the obvious argument that the Ottoman state's eliminationist policies, and the efforts to counter them, necessitated the utilization of Aleppo as an operations hub, the first part of this book demonstrates that the resistance effort was an urban phenomenon through and through: it did not just take place *in* Aleppo—it was *of* Aleppo. This approach not only sees the city as a vessel for state-sanctioned violence but, as historian Nelida Fuccaro observes, "entails a shift in emphasis from the macrolevel of the institutional setting of the state to the microlevel of its spaces of encounter with residents: streets and neighborhoods, workplace and home, urban peripheries and public buildings."[40] In recent years, scholars have increasingly engaged with the urban "microlevel" to understand conflict, war, and social mobilization in the late Ottoman era and the modern Middle East.[41] This book aims at expanding this theoretical aperture to examine an urban network of resistance to genocidal policies.

In her essay surveying the state of the art of the scholarship on "violence and the city," Fuccaro observes, "Intimate knowledge of the built environment was not only the prerogative of surveyors, bureaucrats, and police, but also a tool in the hands of rioters, protesters, and urban gangs."[42] The resistance network, too, maximized the use of the built environment as it worked to save deportees. Armenian churches, schools, and institutions became focal points of community mobilization and deportee support. Hospitals, hotels, and other businesses owned by local Armenians or others sympathetic to the plight of the deportees doubled as hideouts, shelters, makeshift orphanages, gathering places, and venues for the network's meetings. By the summer of 1915, as conglomerating in churches and schools made it easy for the authorities to round up and deport Armenians to the desert, deportees used false papers to rent rooms or commandeered abandoned buildings and street corners. It is from such urban hideouts that members of the resistance network often planned operations that stretched to other cities, rural areas, and the desert. In the early months of 1916, Ghazar Charek and Marzbed prepared a report for Misakian's underground committee in Istanbul on the empire-wide deportations in a room Marzbed had rented out in an elderly Jewish couple's house in Aleppo.[43]

Outside of urban areas, the villages and tent towns near concentration camps that authorities used to establish telegraph stations and gendarmerie outposts often also harbored a safe house for the network, thanks to local Muslims collaborating with the latter. Some of these Armenians and their Muslim associates had established relationships that predated the war.[44] Still most couriers hid in the very network of camps they were secretly traversing. This allowed them to exchange information, distribute funds and medication, and engage in smuggling operations. The second part of this book examines destruction and resistance in this complex web of rural outposts and particularly the world of transit, concentration, and labor camps in the Syrian Desert, beginning with a comparative overview of the global and Ottoman trajectories of civilian incarceration.

Taken in its entirety, and as it demonstrates how much is lost from the historical narrative when the actions and words of the targeted groups are not front and center, this book is a memorial to up to half a million Armenians who died in the region under study alone, and to tens of thousands of others who survived in no small part thanks to the efforts of the resistance network, reconstituting after the war Armenian community life outside the boundaries of the Turkish Republic that blocked their return home.

PART ONE

Genocide and Urban Resistance

CHAPTER ONE

Before the Storm

Deportation and Humanitarian Relief

> A royal treasury is needed to alleviate these pains.
>
> —Catholicos Sahag II Khabayan on the plight of Armenian deportees

The city of Aleppo constituted a major hub for deportation routes during the Armenian genocide.[1] Convoys that survived the treacherous journey reached the area beginning in May 1915. Three hundred twenty-two deportees arrived in Bab, north of the city, as early as 18 May.[2] Consul Jesse B. Jackson explained:

> There is a living stream of Armenians pouring into Aleppo from the surrounding towns and villages, the principal ones being Marash, Zeitun, Hassanbeyli, Osmania, Baghtche, Adana, Dörtyol, Hajin, etc. They all come under a heavy armed escort, usually from 300–500 at a time, and consist of old men, women and children. . . . No animals are provided by the Government, and those who are not fortunate enough to have means of transport are forced to make the journey on foot.[3]

Often, deportees from a particular village or town conglomerated in a specific neighborhood or site in Aleppo before authorities broke them up. Those arriving from the village of Shar, north of Hajin, for example, mostly gathered in the Jemileh neighborhood.[4] Authorities generally allowed deportees from the same town to cluster in transit and in camps, but orders stipulated breaking them up when settling them in Syria and Mesopotamia, with the explicit aim of destroying Armenian community life and assimilating the settled population. A June 1915 telegram from the Directorate for the Settlement of Tribes and Emigrants (*İskân*-ı Aşâir ve Muhacirîn Müdüriyeti, IAMM) outlines this policy; it requires preventing Armenian deportees from any region from conglomerating in one settlement area, prohibiting the creation of schools and forcing the children into government schools, and ensuring that the distance between settlement areas is at least a five-hour journey (twenty-two kilometers according to one estimate).[5]

The ten-thousand-strong Armenian community in Aleppo mobilized to assist the deportees when the first convoys arrived.[6] The Prelacy of the Armenian Apostolic Church in the city, operating under the jurisdiction of the Catholicosate of Cilicia, took ad hoc measures to support the new arrivals for a few days. Between 19 and 24 May, the church assisted nearly four hundred deportees, providing them with funds, food (bread, cheese, eggs, bulgur, yogurt, onions, and oil), and wood.[7] On 24 May, the church launched a more coordinated effort, inviting a group of community leaders to form the Council for Refugees (Kaghtaganats zhoghov in Armenian, henceforth, the council), tasked with "caring for the immediate financial, moral, and health needs" of the arriving Armenians.[8] The council held daily meetings.[9] The city's Armenian Evangelical and Catholic churches also launched their own relief initiatives and synchronized their work as needed.[10] Rev. Eskijian, the pastor of the Emmanuel Armenian Evangelical Church in Aleppo, was an important partner in these efforts. In addition to providing assistance and shelter to deportees in his own home and establishing a small orphanage for destitute children, Rev. Eskijian assisted the council in its initiatives.[11] The Armenian Catholic Church of Aleppo cared for three thousand deportees, "who are lodged in different localities and fed by the local church community" at the nadir of suffering in Aleppo.[12] Jackson noticed this groundswell of support from the community early on, reporting to his superiors on 5 June that the deportees are being "taken care of locally by the sympathizing Armenian population of this city." In another report, he noted, "Each religious community has a relief committee to care for its own."[13]

The council exercised caution as it launched its humanitarian effort in an extremely tense environment. The Ottoman military had entered the war on the side of the Central powers seven months earlier. Its military campaigns had failed in the Sinai Peninsula, Basra, and Sarıkamış, and now a massive Allied armada was attacking the Dardanelles Strait, not far from Istanbul. Aleppo Province had felt the impact of the mobilization for the Sinai in particular, as it contributed thousands of soldiers to the attack on the Suez Canal.[14] "Taking into account the current sensitive political situation," the council's first order of business was to secure approval for its relief work from the governor of Aleppo Province, Celal Bey, who would be removed from his position in June 1915. Thus, the group resolved "to inform [the governor] of the formation of the council, provide a list of members, and to start work only with the permission of the governorate."[15] On 10 June, more than two weeks after it had begun its activities, the council received local government authorization.[16] For as long as it proved possible, the council coordinated its efforts with the provincial authorities and appealed to them for help.

The council set to work preparing lists of deportees in the city and neighboring towns and villages, and thus ascertaining housing, food, and medical needs. It hired a full-time employee to assist in the day-to-day work.[17] Within a day, a list was compiled: in total, 781 people from four towns and villages had arrived in Aleppo by that point.[18] They were to receive bread and four *metalik*s per person per day.[19] The council had already paid some eighty-two deportees 1,927 *kuruş* each, their share for fifteen days. In subsequent days, hundreds of others were disbursed the same sum.[20] The council noted that several dozen families were well-to-do in their home towns but had left with precious little, so it resolved to loan them one *mecidiye* per person. The financial situation of deportees back home factored into the decision to provide loans because, at this early stage, the community leaders in Aleppo were operating on the assumption that the deportees would soon have access to the assets they had left behind. Moreover, Aleppo Armenians did not suspect that within weeks scores of deportees would flood the area, exerting such a strain on the community's resources that even providing basic relief for their survival would constitute a major challenge. By 31 May, the council had come to the realization that it could not handle the problems alone. It petitioned the Armenian Patriarchate of Constantinople—the primary Armenian religious authority in the empire—for five hundred Ottoman liras, in view of the large influx of deportees and the "insufficient means" available.[21]

In the meantime, the Armenian Apostolic Church of Aleppo allocated large sums of money to meet deportee needs. On 23 May, the council withdrew one hundred Ottoman liras (12,700 *kuruş*) from the bank to tackle the exigency. Two days later, a significant sum (three hundred Ottoman liras) from the Catholicosate of Cilicia was placed at the council's disposal. Donations from the Armenian community and other locals constituted another source of income. Between 18 and 20 May alone, nearly ten donations were made, only one of which was sizeable (one thousand *kuruş*).[22] The council regulated the process of collection as much as possible: "Taking into account the fact that many individuals are handing their donations to this or that [random] person, it was decided to make announcements in church that donations be given only to the council's treasurer, Sarkis Jiyerjian."[23]

From the beginning, Aleppo Armenians did not confine their efforts to the city or even the province of Aleppo, sending aid and dispatching missions all the way to Der Zor. As the Armenian Apostolic Church did not have a presence there, it partnered with Aleppo's Armenian Catholic Prelacy, which communicated via telegram with its counterpart in Zor. This triangle of coordination proved useful for aid efforts. Already in its meeting on 27 May, the council resolved to send forty Ottoman liras through the Catholic Prelacy in Aleppo to Zor, earmarked for deportees from Zeytun.[24]

The council formed committees and subcommittees to expand the relief network and maximize its reach. The first committee comprised six deportees from Hasanbeyli and Dörtyol "to facilitate the process of receiving, directly from the deportees, daily updates about their needs."[25] A women's auxiliary subcommittee was formed shortly thereafter, and by 28 May it had already prepared two reports for the council.[26] The council appointed (24 May) two community members to a body for distribution of relief aid and allocated a room for its operations in the Prelacy building.[27] The council established yet another committee in early June, made up of deportees from Hajin, to assess the needs of their fellow townspeople arriving in Aleppo, in order to provide assistance accordingly.[28] Finally, the council formed a subcommittee (7 July), headed by Father Hovhannes Etmekjian, to find proper housing for young girls and widowed women who had no support or providers in the city. This body was tasked with the preparation of a list of these women, who soon received temporary shelter in the hall of the Armenian school.[29]

Deportation orders soon encompassed Armenian communities empire-wide, with most columns moving in the general direction of Syria. Yeghishe Hazarabedian, deported from Marash on 15 May as part of a group of seven families, arrived in Aleppo later in the month.[30] He remembered:

> We spent about ten days as the guests of my sister and brother-in-law, the Apraham Chorbajians, and then rented a house in the Jideidi section, near Aleppo's Sourp Karasoon Mangantz Church [Forty Martyrs Cathedral]. We took over two rooms in that house and Melkon Babikian occupied the third.[31]

Yeranuhi Simonian, a deportee from Adana, stayed at a *khan* (inn) near Aleppo for a day before a chance encounter with relatives. "The next morning, my brother and uncle come out of the *khan* and—what joyful surprise!—on the road of death they meet their cousins, the brothers Haji and Manug Sinanian," she recalled years later. "They all return to the khan immediately, place everything we have on a cart, and transport us to their house. Being government employees, they were safe."[32]

The humanitarian network sought to provide shelter to deportees who lacked connections in the city. Centers of thriving community life (including most schools and churches) were transformed into refugee shelters for the duration of the war. In a memoir he wrote years later, John Minassian, a deportee from Sivas, revealed that he found refuge for a short time in the courtyard of Rev. Eskijian's house in Aleppo, where "some twenty families had been crowded . . . all were in tatters, and were slowly dying of hunger and lack of care. Barely alive, they had little protection here, but they did have a friend in the Reverend."[33] Survivor Ghazar Charek recalled:

> Aleppo in those days was a life raft towards which scores of Armenian deportees converged every day, every hour. The city's Christian neighborhoods flooded with Armenian residents. Those houses, providing shelter, and full of hideouts, offered a newfound safety to arriving Armenians. . . . All around, people worked like ants to get their families, relatives, and friends to safety in Aleppo. In all this, the local Armenians of Aleppo and those who had settled there a long time ago made extreme sacrifices.[34]

The community leadership sought other strategies, too, and did its best to find host families for the arriving deportees "to get them away from the eyes of the police officers so that they would not be redeported to the interior," as Jackson explained to the U.S. secretary of state. This effort resulted in thousands of Armenians, "practically all women, girls, and boys under 14 years of age," being placed in the homes of Christians, Jews, and Muslims, and avoiding redeportation at least temporarily.[35] Still, many had no shelter. According to eyewitness Hayg Toroyan, an Aleppo Armenian serving in the Ottoman Army, his fellow townspeople "generally accepted the deportees with open arms. They opened their homes to them. . . . Yet the streets, the fields, and forgotten corners of the city were full of thousands of desolate people whose nests had been destroyed."[36]

The Armenian community supported the new arrivals even in such thankless tasks as complying with the government's redeportation orders. The plight of these deportees, continually herded from one location to the next, had caught the attention of the Western diplomats stationed in Aleppo. In a report to the U.S. ambassador to the Ottoman Empire Henry Morgenthau, Jackson explained that after "[a] few days rest in churches and schools, where they fill all rooms, courts, balconies, and even cover the roofs; [the deportees] are forced to continue the journey to some out of the way place where there is neither shelter, food nor means of possible existence."[37] German consul Walter Rössler was equally concerned. He cabled his embassy in Istanbul on 6 June urging them "to raise a protest." He noted that the deportees comprised mostly women and children who "would be defenseless and liable to be violated during transport and in the villages." He requested that only the men be redeported, while the women and children remain in Aleppo.[38] As redeportations continued, the council's intervention made a difference. Gendarmes accompanying the columns were bribed in hopes of securing the safety of the deportees. The council's ledgers abound, week in week out, in entries documenting "gifts" up to seventy *kuruş* to gendarmes accompanying the deportees.[39] But for how long could protection be bought? Many deportees realized full well the perils ahead. "Some women who were transported through Aleppo hid their young children under blankets here and left them behind in order not to lead them to their probable deaths or certain misery," Rössler observed in a report.[40]

Hygiene and health claimed the community's attention too. Early on, it arranged for soap distribution to families upon arrival.[41] Within a few weeks, more pressing needs emerged. Thousands of exhausted, undernourished deportees packed in the city were falling prey to disease and epidemics at an alarming rate. The physicians serving deportees were overwhelmed, the council noted on 21 June. It asked a local doctor by the name of A. Shmavonian, to allocate two hours a day to the new arrivals and tasked pharmacists to vaccinate as many children as resources allowed.[42] Such vaccination campaigns took place in the city as well as in the camps. The council also asked its subcommittees to prioritize the cleanliness of the deportees and their living spaces "by conducting the most serious oversight." The situation was so dire that they could not be satisfied with merely demanding hygienic practices, but had to pay surprise visits to the deportees to monitor compliance.[43] "Since the cleanliness and discipline of deportees have become increasingly important," the commission established a subcommittee to focus on these matters alone, and the council frequently purchased cleaning supplies for deportee use.[44]

Appeals for Help

As resources dwindled, talk about donations and fundraising dominated the meetings. The council launched a broad fundraising effort in early June.[45] The Catholicos, who had arrived in Aleppo from Adana on 28 May, donated two hundred liras to the effort, and a mailing campaign in Khabayan's name targeting affluent Armenians in the community also proved successful.[46] By 22 June, this effort had raised 25,400 *kuruş*, but the push continued.[47] The council "happily" reported in the minutes the next day that the president of Aleppo Province's Abandoned Properties Commission (Emvâl-ı Metruke Komisyonu), Hamid Bey, had promised to attach his name to the fundraising work and write an introduction for the donation collection books. As a gesture of his commitment to the effort, he had given ten liras.[48] Ironically, the Abandoned Properties Commission was the very institution through which the Ottoman authorities confiscated the properties Armenians were forced to leave behind.[49]

Noting the importance of looking beyond Armenians for support, the council secured a permit from the local government (17 July) to fundraise among other religious communities, and proceeded to engage in discussions with the respective leaders of these groups about the format of such an effort.[50] Soon, small donations trickled in from these communities as well. Many Muslims assisted Armenian deportees arriving in the city, according to Celal Bey.[51] Jackson tells of "kindnesses extended by good Muslims who pitied these sufferers" and a Muslim soldier giving two *mecidiye* to the deportees.[52] The council ledgers confirm that Greeks, Assyrians, Christian Arabs, Jews, and Muslims contributed to the fundraising campaign.[53] Such intercommunal solidarity points to a realization among locals of the plight of utterly dispossessed deportees forcibly strewn across foreign lands at a time of wartime economic hardship and epidemics that spared no family or community.

The number of deportees arriving in the city rose exponentially in the period between May and July 1915. Seven hundred eighty-one people (forty-two families) from four towns and villages had reached Aleppo city by 24 May, when the council began keeping a record. Ninety-two deportees (twenty families) arrived on 27 May, and 279 on 5 June. Between 9 and 15 June, 1,219 deportees (196 families) from Hajin (495), Hasanbeyli (347), Dörtyol (204), and nearby villages flocked to the city. On 17 and 20 June, 183 people (thirty-two families), and from 30 June to 6 July a whopping 3,064 deportees (417 families) arrived in the city.[54]

Forced to move the deportees to provincial towns, the Armenian Prelacy in Aleppo communicated regularly with local authorities. Responding to the governor's decision to transfer twenty-six Dörtyol families (around ninety people) from Aleppo to Mumbuj, the council "handed the deportees to the official and provided each with half a *metalik* for travel and other expenses."[55] Two other groups of deportees, a total of 229 people (thirty-eight families) were sent to Bab and Maarra, southwest of Aleppo, on 23 and 24 May, again with financial support from the council.[56] Eight convoys of deportees (a total of 347 people, fifty-one families) were sent to Bab, Maarra, and Mumbuj that next week.[57]

Authorities also demanded information about the deportees from the council. In response to one such request, the council provided (30 June) a list of orphans among deportees in the city.[58] It is unclear whether the council also provided the authorities with the lists it had compiled of deportees who arrived in Aleppo Province in May and June. These lists provided detailed information about each family, including the town they were deported from, their date of arrival in the region, the name of the head of the family, the number of its members, their gender, and their age.[59] Demands for lists and statistics from local officials and Armenian community institutions in Aleppo continued during the war and, when furnished, they often led to targeted arrests, deportations, or the shutting down of orphanages and the transfer of children to state institutions that implemented a policy of Turkification.

The authorities also sought to compile deportee lists of their own. They mandated that all Armenians arriving in Aleppo register their local address with the police. "Posters [were] glued to the walls, announcing that all Armenians must register at their local police station within a week. Those who disobeyed orders will be heavily fined and thrown into prison," wrote survivor Vahram Dadrian, who had taken refuge in the city, in his 23 September 1915 diary entry.[60]

A recurring theme in the community's appeals to the provincial and city authorities in these early months was the distribution of food. A small amount of food was indeed being disbursed, albeit irregularly, by the municipal authorities within the city. People in surrounding areas and beyond received nearly nothing. Even in the city of Aleppo, Catholicos Sahag II told Rössler in June that 2,500 deportees received a daily ration totaling 445 kilograms (and, for three days, going up to 1,346 kilograms), which was significantly less than the necessary amount for subsistence.[61] This amounted to 178 grams per person. For reference, Ottoman soldiers received a ration of up to 900 grams daily, although in areas far from grain production the amount sometimes was as low as 300 grams.[62] Despite interventions, the situation did not improve. "The government distributes an insignificant amount of food to all deportees, and this is given out regularly, but outside the city there are people crying out for bread," the Armenian patriarch in Constantinople was told in late July by "a reliable source in Aleppo."[63]

Deportee hunger drove the council to ask the municipality to increase the bread ration (26 May).[64] But a few days after this request, the bread distribution stopped altogether, and the council appealed to the municipality on 4 June for its resumption, as well as for three cases of oil so that the deportees would have light at night. The community's resources were "insufficient even to simply alleviate" the misery of the arriving caravans of famished and exhausted deportees, and it turned once again to the government for basic supplies.[65]

If the Aleppo Armenian community sought to tackle hunger, it looked, too, to effect radical change, pressing the government on deportation policy. It first appealed to Cemal Pasha, whose jurisdiction covered the council's area of operation. In an attempt to stop the routine redeportation to camps in the Syrian Desert, the council sent him a telegram on 31 May asking to spare the Armenian deportees who had found refuge in the city from the misery of being sent elsewhere.[66] When they received no response, the community leadership appealed to the Prime Ministry, the War Ministry, and the Interior Ministry on 3 June, "begging" them to stop the redeportation.[67] When no word came from the capital either, the council sent (5 June) a "heart-rending appeal" to the governor of the Aleppo Province.[68] Finally, chairman Father Harutiun reported to the council that Cemal Pasha replied through Governor Celal: "Advise Fr. Haroutyun to stay out of the government's affairs."[69] But the council did not give up. It promptly sent yet another appeal, signed by deportee women, to Sultan Mehmed V Reşâd, a figurehead.[70] The relocations continued. The government ordered fifty-one deportees, who had arrived in the city from Dörtyol, to be sent to Mumbuj on 21 July.[71]

Operating on the assumption that the intention of the central authorities was to settle the Armenians in Ottoman Syria, the council tried to match the skills of the deportees with the needs of particular districts in the province. To that end, it studied a report it had commissioned earlier about the demography and climate of the different districts of Aleppo Province to which deportees were shipped, in the hope that deportees would find work and thus be able to sustain themselves.[72] The central authorities did not seem to have any plans to support the deportees other than vague notions of settling them in towns and provinces around Aleppo. There were indeed orders to create new settlement areas for the arriving Armenians in this early stage, but no funds were allocated for such a purpose, and within a year, most of the deportees would be "settled" under the sands of the desert.[73]

The Demise of Governor Celal Bey

Aleppo Governor Celal Bey provided direct and indirect assistance to the Aleppo Armenians' relief effort. He advocated for the deportees in his communication with the central authorities as well. As caravans of deportees arrived in the province, he continuously pressed the Ministry of the Interior, asking for a concrete plan to ensure the dignified treatment of the deportees, beyond general and vague orders. In a telegram on 23 May, he explained that settling non-Muslims in Maarra and Rakka was "absolutely impossible," because most of the population in the region was nomadic, and the areas available for settlement were close to wasteland, and the deportees would be subject to attacks by bandits. Moreover, he inquired about the manner in which settlement would be realized, pointing out that while it would not be advisable to scatter the deportees in Muslim villages, financial constraints prevented the formation of separate villages for the new arrivals.[74] In a subsequent telegram, he posed a barrage of follow-up questions to the central authorities: Will new houses be built for the deportees, as there are no empty homes in these villages? Will the government provide the deportees with land? Will they receive assistance until they are settled? And how are these expenses going to be covered?[75] Celal Bey even lectured the central authorities, declaring it was unbefitting for a state to leave the deportees hungry and without shelter.[76] Although Celal failed to move the central authorities, he wielded significant sway over government officials within the province. Police chief Fikri Bey, for example, was influenced by him.[77] Together, they absorbed some of the pressure from central authorities that would have worsened the situation of the deportees in these early months.

Although Celal's actions emanated from his principles, they were also partly shaped by his relationship with the Armenian church leadership, as well as his friendship with Jackson and a number of influential local Armenians, including the Mazloumian brothers Onnig and Armenag, known as "the barons" for the hotel of the same name they owned in Aleppo.[78] Jackson described his own relationship with the governor as "brotherly": "During several years that Djelal Bey had been governor of Aleppo our weekly exchange of dinners, receptions and card parties had cemented our friendship until it had become almost brotherly, and was recognized throughout the province and even in all Syria."[79]

Celal Bey's sympathy for the plight of the Armenians did not earn him many friends in the capital. The minister of the interior removed him from his position as governor in late June 1915 for his moderate policies, and for refusing to deport Armenians in his province. Jackson explained that Celal "was and had been for many years very friendly towards the Armenians, and because of the tremendous influence brought to bear on him locally, he at first ignored the instructions he received [to deport the Armenians], and which were repeated several times, and finally flatly refused to be an instrument in such an atrocious proceeding. Naturally this could have but one result, and that was his removal."[80] In his memoirs, Celal Bey himself traced his dismissal to his resistance to deporting Armenians from Aleppo.[81]

Beirut governor Bekir Sami Bey replaced Celal Bey in Aleppo (24 June), while the latter was designated governor of Konya. The news of Celal Bey's removal sent shockwaves across the camps and settlement areas in the province, leaving the Armenian community leadership in despair. Prior to Celal Bey's departure for Konya, Catholicos Sahag met with him one last time and appealed to him to do his utmost to assist the five thousand to six thousand deportees in Konya. Celal Bey promised not only to help the deportees in Konya—a promise he kept—but to advocate for the deportees in general during his next visit to Istanbul.[82] The Catholicos mourned his departure:

> The transfer of Celal Bey to Konya compounded one more pain to all my pains. He was wholeheartedly against the policy of deportation. He suffered as much as we did about the unprecedented misery [of the deportees] but couldn't remedy it.
>
> In the end, *the military* made him a victim of his sentiments, as some proudly announced after his departure.

> The race of anguish and suffering [i.e., the Armenians] was afflicted with an irremediable loss with His Excellency's departure. During his last visit, he left almost in tears, and seeing deportees in the narthex of the church, he declared: I would have preferred to be sucked into the earth than see this suffering.[83]

The government's actions soon grew more aggressive, as the German consul reported: "As was to be expected after the dismissal of the local Vali Djelal Bey, the deportation has now been extended to the coastal strip of the Vilayet Aleppo. According to news from an Armenian source, the order for the clearance of Alexandretta, Antioch, Harem, Beilan, Soukluk, Kessab and other towns has been given, but only a short term of notice has been granted for carrying this out."[84]

The Catholicos in Aleppo

The arrival of the Catholicos in Aleppo city a few weeks prior to Celal Bey's dismissal had intensified efforts to intervene with the authorities on behalf of the deportees. In response to the Catholicos's appeals, Cemal Pasha sent him a telegram on 21 June asking whether there were violations of the property and honor of the deportees and, if so, requesting a report about these. Cemal also noted that efforts would be made to assist the deportees by whatever means possible.[85] The Catholicos had a copy of the telegram delivered to the council, requesting the preparation of "an extensive and elaborated report" on violations. The minutes of the council's seventeenth meeting note that additional reports about the needs of the deportees would also be included in the folder the Catholicos would hand to Cemal Pasha upon the latter's imminent arrival in Aleppo.[86] Chairman Father Haroutyun was entrusted with preparing the report on the difficulties faced by the deportees en route, as well as the inconsistencies in the distribution of aid by the local authorities.[87]

The Catholicos met with the deputy commander of the Fourth Army, Fahrettin (Fahri) Türkkan Pasha, on 26 June.[88] Lamenting the deplorable state of the deportees, he implored the deputy commander to consider what had been done so far as sufficient punishment and to halt the deportation of Armenians from other parts of Cilicia like Adana and Sis. Fahrettin Pasha told the Catholicos that Cemal Pasha "is categorically opposed to the ongoing deportation."[89] Three days later, the Catholicos met with Cemal himself, in the presence of Celal Bey, who was still in town.[90] He now got a very different message. After listening intently to the two men's reports, Cemal burst out in anger "lumping together Van, Dörtyol, and Zeytun":

> The government recognizes Armenians as Armenians; it does not differentiate between bandit, party-member, or Caucasian and Cilician; it considers all of them the enemy, as much of an enemy as the Russian, the British, and the French. . . . It is the final decision of the Council of Ministers to destroy the hearths of the political parties and to completely empty areas heavily populated by Armenians.[91]

As the conversation continued, Cemal was all over the map. He stated flatly that what Fahrettin Pasha had told the Catholicos about him being "categorically opposed to the deportations" was part of his earlier plan, which had not been accepted by the Council of Ministers. He added, "Had it not been for my explicit and threatening statements and had the agitated Muslims not been reined in, horrible massacres could have happened, just like they did in Diyarbakir," where tens of thousands were massacred.[92] The Catholicos met with Cemal again the following week, on 2 and 4 July, and discussions proceeded in a calmer manner.[93] The commander of the Fourth Army promised to investigate crimes committed against the deportees, and to punish by death those responsible. The Catholicos also received permission from Cemal to send priests to the various concentration camps and settlement areas for "spiritual needs."[94]

Having secured the relevant authorization documents from Cemal Pasha through the efforts of the Catholicos, the council dispatched Father Sahag, a priest from Kilis, and Iskender Efendi, a pharmacist, to the camps in and around Der Zor, providing the delegates with a check for sixty liras to be cashed upon arrival. The two were asked to make stops at Bab and Mumbuj on their way, and they were given ten liras to distribute among refugees in Bab and fifteen liras among those in Mumbuj. The council also sent Father Khachadur Boghigian to the deportees in Idlib, Maarra, and Riha, providing him with twenty-five liras to distribute, and an additional five liras for travel expenses.[95] In addition to bringing food and medicine, these visits to camps and settlement areas in remote towns and villages were an opportunity for the council to acquire firsthand information about the plight of the deportees and to address their problems. Going beyond the "spiritual needs" of the deportees, the council essentially engaged in illegal activities that undermined the central authorities' aims. If caught, the emissaries risked imprisonment, or worse. And indeed, the Ministry of the Interior sent a telegram to the Aleppo Governorate notifying them that Father Sahag and pharmacist Sarkis (Iskender Efendi), who carried documents from Aleppo authorizing them to visit Der Zor, were illegally distributing money to the deportees there.[96] This was followed by a telegram to Zor asking the authorities to send the two back to Aleppo immediately.[97] Father Sahag returned to Aleppo and reported his observations to the council.[98] The Catholicos reported food scarcity and hundreds of deaths to Rössler, who in turn passed the information on to the imperial chancellor. "In order to protect themselves from starvation, the deportees have had to sell more than 30 of their children," he wrote.[99]

This reconstruction of the incident involving Father Sahag and Iskender Efendi—by the triangulation of Ottoman, German, and, crucially, Armenian sources—offers a glimpse into the complex dynamics between the humanitarian network, local authorities, foreign diplomats, and the central authorities at a time when the tide was shifting, and Istanbul was demonstrating greater zeal in cracking down on relief efforts. Dispatching to Der Zor emissaries who sought to maintain the deportees' health constituted action that openly contravened the restrictions the central authorities imposed. Their reaction stood as an early indicator that they aimed to crack down on relief efforts throughout the region. The local actors took note. Within a few weeks, the relief network would begin conducting most of its activities clandestinely.

During his meetings with Cemal Pasha, the Catholicos also secured the resumption of government aid to deportees in Aleppo. The first entry in the minutes of the council on 7 July read:

> As a result of the persistent appeals to Cemal Pasha by His Holiness the Catholicos, we were happy to learn today that the government's Commission for Refugees [*muhacir komisyonu*] has ordered the distribution of five *metaliks* to adults and three *metaliks* to children among the deportees in the city, and the amount is being distributed regularly for three days now, in the presence of the council['s representative]. The Refugees Commission has already [acquired from us] the list of deportees.[100]

Rössler reported on this too. Writing to the imperial chancellor (Theobald von Bethmann Hollweg) on 27 July, he explained:

> At present in Aleppo, where the food supplied by the government was sometimes insufficient and after the Catholicos had intervened on behalf of the Armenians, 5 *metaliks* (20 pfennigs) is being paid for each adult, 4 *metaliks* (16 pfennigs) for each child at the order of Djemal Pasha. The number of those currently on the road in Aleppo alone is estimated at an average of several thousands. They are allowed to rest here for a while.[101]

These conditions, short-lived as they were, led the council to focus its aid elsewhere. "For now, the assistance being provided by the government on a regular basis can be considered sufficient," the council observed. Deportees outside the city needed the community's help more. As its financial resources were being depleted, the council also stopped providing aid and loans to deportees in the city "unless there are extraordinary circumstances."[102]

Trying desperately to alleviate the suffering of his flock and prevent further deportations and massacres, the Catholicos also appealed to Hans Freiherr von Wangenheim, the German ambassador in Istanbul. His letter, while cautious and overly laudatory of the "gracious" Ottoman Empire, aimed to disabuse Berlin of "the false opinion that is held here and there that the Armenians would not wish for Germany's success." He noted that "the good or bad opinion of the Armenians [about Germany] has no influence on the power and glory of the victorious German people. But the widespread suspicion which rests on the Armenians causes our unhappy, dying people one of its greatest griefs." The Catholicos's letter was, in essence, a petition for help, although he was careful to underline that "my letter is neither a complaint nor a plea . . . for as Turkish subjects we can only turn to the Ottoman government to handle our difficulties."[103] Thus, he concluded:

> In the hope that Your Excellency will believe the truth of my letter, I request that Your Excellency uses his great influence to direct this suspicion away from us, which is one of the greatest of our many griefs.
>
> We ask Your Excellency to continue intervening on our behalf as you have done in the past. We pray for Your Excellency's and your wife's precious life, for the Ottoman government and for the powerful empire allied with it.[104]

The much-needed interventions never came. The appeals of German consuls and the ambassador to Berlin were repeatedly silenced by the central government, so as not to jeopardize Germany's alliance with the Ottomans in wartime. In a response to the German ambassador who demanded that Berlin confront the Ottomans, the chancellor responded, "Our only aim is to keep Turkey on our side until the end of the war, no matter whether as a result Armenians do perish or not."[105]

The Hotel and the Hospital

While Berlin left the deportees to perish, two Armenian-owned businesses in Aleppo opened doors for them. The scholarship offers little more than a nod and a few footnotes to the role played by Hotel Baron and the Altounyan Hospital in saving lives, yet the two institutions were indispensable nodes in the humanitarian network during the Armenian genocide. The brothers Onnig and Armenag Mazloumian, known as "the barons," and Dr. Asadour Aram Altounyan and his daughter Nora tapped into their rich web of connections with Ottoman and Western elites, twisting arms when possible, currying favors when necessary, to channel assistance to deportees.

Before it became "the most famous refueling stop in the Middle East" in the interwar period, "believed to store as many memories of a glorious past as the Ritz in London or Raffles in Singapore,"[106] Hotel Baron was the place where decisions impacting the fate of Armenian deportees in Syria were made—and altered. Chronicler Aram Andonian likens the wartime Hotel Baron to a government building, where Cemal Pasha, German military commander Otto Liman von Sanders, and Mustafa Kemal stayed, and the governor, police chief, and other officials gathered.[107] For the entire duration of the war, the hotel had become "part of the Turkish Army, although it was run along the lines of a hotel," said Krikor, Armenag Mazloumian's son, in an interview decades later.[108]

Establishing the hotel in 1911, the Mazloumian brothers hosted, wined, and dined Aleppo's elite as well as Western diplomats, merchants, and adventurers arriving in the city.[109] The outbreak of the war may have affected profits, but not the access the brothers had to the Ottoman and Western elites. Ohannes Kuyumjian, the last governor of autonomous Mount Lebanon, provided a particularly astute depiction of the influence of the Mazloumians in his memoirs written right after the war:

> Baron, the hotelier, is certainly the most widely known and popular person in town. He is viewed favorably by the Muslims of the region and even by the Turkish authorities. All of the provincial governors and most of the high-ranking officials

> who were recently appointed to Aleppo or stop by, visit his hotel. Many leave having forgotten to settle the bill. But while Baron is a philosopher, he is also a shrewd administrator. He transfers the sum to the "insurance" account; does he not have to pay ransom in order to peacefully run his business? In return he exercised a real influence at the Conak [*konak* in Turkish, inn] which he uses, exclusively, to help the Armenian deportees as much as possible. But these measures are very feeble: he may well try, but he only succeeds in saving very few of them.[110]

Onnig Mazloumian's friendship with Cemal, Aleppo governors Celal Bey and his successor Bekir Sami, Corps commander Şevki Pasha, and others proved extremely helpful in the early months when many decisions related to deportee relief, redeportation, and settlement were taken locally.[111] As the repression intensified and the network went underground, the Mazloumians were caught between the secretive world of humanitarian resistance and the demands of a hotel turned to an officers' club or, in the words of historian Elizabeth F. Thompson, "a buzzing hive of war time intrigue much like Rick's Cafe in the movie *Casablanca*."[112] Chronicler Charek remembered "with great admiration" Baron Senior's (a reference to Onnig, the elder brother) willingness to help fellow Armenians:

> Impossible as it is to provide an account of all the assistance, and all the successful endeavors in preserving Armenianness, it is possible to say in a few words that in those difficult days of deportation and war, Baron Senior, his hotel, and his entourage, were anchors of safety for Armenian masses in Aleppo, and the greatest antidote to the brutalities and successive persecution campaigns of the Turkish central government.[113]

Payladzou Captanian, too, heaps praise on Baron Senior for taking great risks and did all he could to save deportees. "He had saved hundreds of girls from the claws of Turks."[114]

Ultimately, the local elite that shielded the brothers could not withstand the pressure from the central authorities to remove them from the Aleppian stage. Cemal Pasha, who in the words of Andonian "loved and protected" the Mazloumians, was able to change the destination of their exile, just like he had done earlier with Catholicos Khabayan.[115] The brothers were sent to Zahle—not to Der Zor or beyond as the Interior Ministry was demanding—in September 1916 and stayed there until the war's end.[116]

Getting rid of the Altounyans, on the other hand, was difficult to fathom. Aleppo's leading physician, Asadour Aram Altounyan owned and operated the best hospital in the region, serving a who's who of Ottoman and Western dignitaries and officers, including Cemal Pasha, who "was intelligent enough to see that the Armenian [Altounyan] and his hospital were irreplaceable in that particular time and place," in the words of the doctor's granddaughter Taqui.[117]

Born in 1854 to a family with a "tradition of medicine," Altounyan's education with missionaries and work for doctors in his home town of Sepasdia (Sivas) and then in Aintab helped pave his way to an MD from Columbia University in 1885.[118] He returned to Aintab in 1887 after a stint in Dr. Robert Koch's laboratory in Germany. He met and married Harriet Martha Riddall, the matron of the missionary hospital in Aintab, and two years later he settled in Aleppo with his wife and firstborn. It took Altounyan two decades to realize his dream of building a state-of-the-art hospital in Aleppo. The Great War broke out three years after its completion.[119]

During the war, Altounyan took on additional responsibilities at the military hospital, but he also provided personal care at his own hospital for Ottoman leaders and officers including Cemal and Mustafa Kemal. He also allocated a wing to Armenian deportees who had contracted typhus, made visitations free of charge to many who could not afford to pay, and provided all the medication needed at the largest orphanage for deportee children arriving in Aleppo, established by his daughter Nora. "The financial and moral assistance provided by Doctor Altounyan and his daughter Ms. Altounyan will forever remain in the memory of the hundreds who took shelter there. If they and Baron Senior had not helped cover the orphanage's expenses, it would have been impossible to save the lives of hundreds of children," noted Captanian.[120]

The Council's Internal Problems

Several incidents in June and July reveal the toll on those involved in the relief effort. Overwhelmed by his responsibilities, the council treasurer, Sarkis Jiyerjian, presented a letter of resignation (30 June), which the council unanimously rejected, promising instead to help him with his tasks.[121] On 4 July, chairman Father Harutiun Yesayan angered the council members by walking into their meeting and demanding that they leave the room. The only agenda entry of the meeting that day recounted what transpired:

> When the Council for Refugees was meeting today in the conference room reserved for it at the Prelacy . . . suddenly, without prior notification, chairman Father Harutiun Yesayan walked in, accompanied by a few people, and with an attitude that insulted the dignity of the council, declared, "Get out! We have work to do here!" The members of the council left the room without making a fuss.[122]

They may have left, but they did not let the matter go and, also noting earlier disagreements with Father Harutiun, collectively tendered their resignation to the Catholicos. The latter invited the council and its chairman to a meeting that very day, urging the members to continue their work. In turn, Father Harutiun told the Catholicos that his intention had not been to insult the council and apologized to him. "The members of the council, realizing the sensitivity and gravity of the circumstances, and especially the fact that its resignation risks disrupting the effort to assist the deportees, and prompted by feeling of the love of our nation, accepted the recommendation of His Holiness and decided to continue its work."[123] The available sources do not provide details of these tensions and their precipitating factors. Mounting pressure from the authorities and the overwhelming situation of the refugees eventually forced the council to write a second resignation letter on 21 September 1915, which the Catholicos reluctantly accepted. He then proceeded to appoint a new council immediately.

"The sensitivity and gravity of the circumstances" were gnawing on the Catholicos as much as anyone. In a letter to the Armenian patriarch of Constantinople, Zaven Der Yeghiayan, on 19 July, he wrote:

> What will become of God's temples? What will become of the monasteries and convents? What will become of the church properties, the sacred utensils and vestments? Give me counsel. I am alone. My eyes have no more tears; my heart is emptied of emotion. Day and night all around me, there is starvation, fainting, weeping, and wailing.[124]

The Catholicos appealed to the patriarch for help, asking him to petition the American and German embassies and missionaries. "Send money," he pleaded, for "five hundred liras here and there are not enough." He stressed that appeals to the Ottoman authorities were worse than futile:

> The [Armenian] people has lost its mind; it doesn't understand the enormity

> and nature of the pain. It thinks that the Catholicosate and the Patriarchate are indifferent. They push me to appeal to the sultan and the elite. They push me to telegram and ask for bread for the hungry, but I know that every appeal, every single act of begging is useless, and only opens the door to stricter measures and more evil.[125]

The Catholicosate had received a significant blow a month earlier: a telegram of 24 June had informed him that the bishops who until then had managed to remain in Sis, the seat of the Catholicosate, were also being deported. The Catholicos had paid yet another visit to Cemal Pasha the next day, begging him to spare the Armenian Church, the loyalty of which was firm and unequivocal. "This is the destruction—despite our genuine loyalty—of a spiritual center that has stood for centuries," he had told Cemal.[126] The latter had promised to allow a member of the Catholicosate's clerical entourage, Bishop Kiud, to remain in Sis. But the decision was reversed.[127]

From Bad to Worse

Thousands of survivors from the eastern provinces of the empire began to arrive in Aleppo in the second half of July. By 30 July, there were many more deportees than there were local Armenians in the city.[128] Province-wide, the number of deportees was estimated to have reached sixty thousand by early August.[129] More deportees, on foot or packed in trains, arrived in the weeks that followed. "Since August 1, the German Baghdad Railway has brought nine trains each of fifteen carloads of those unfortunate people to Aleppo. Each car containing from 35 to 40 persons," Jackson reported to Morgenthau.[130] The most recent arrivals, particularly those who were marched to Aleppo, constituted mostly older women and children under ten. Their convoys had been attacked, robbed, and subjected to massacres along the way. Families who were left intact were now a rarity.

The German consul reported on 7 August that a convoy of 212 deportees had left Adıyaman, only 120 of whom arrived in Aleppo; fifty-five men and eleven women had been killed, several people were missing, and several girls had been raped. Another convoy of 120 from the province of Kharpert (Harput) was broken up, with only thirty-two arriving in Aleppo. Thirty-six deaths (twenty-four men, twelve women) and twenty-nine cases of rape were registered.[131] Some six thousand widows and orphans had arrived in Aleppo in the three-week period of 20 July to 10 August from cities and towns like Erzerum, Kharpert, Sivas, Adıyaman, and Behesni, and remained there. The local authorities gave them nothing. Their only means of subsistence was the meager, 180 grams of bread distributed daily by the council. "These five thousand to six thousand widows and orphans are without clothing, do not have beds and sheets, and the majority stays in gardens in open air. Many are ill, and thirty to forty deaths occur daily," the council wrote to the Catholicos on 10 August.[132] The railway had brought 32,751 deportees to Aleppo by 31 August, in addition to upwards of 100,000 others who had arrived on foot.[133] Most were redeported. Aleppo governor Bekir Sami reported that 37,702 Armenians were deported from his province to the Syria Province and another 5,700 to the *kaza*s of Bab, Mumbuj, and Maarra by 3 September. He further noted that these Armenians would be redeported in convoys of five hundred to one thousand persons in the direction of Urfa, Zor, and Mosul.[134] An eyewitness wrote on 23 August, "During the past few months, the local Armenians and some friends have assisted . . . [the deportees] with money, pieces of clothing, beds, etc., as much as they could, and thus the sources of assistance for the new arrivals are drying up."[135] A humanitarian disaster of massive proportions was now looming over the region.

As we have seen, during the period between May and August 1915, the Armenian Apostolic, Evangelical, and Catholic churches of Aleppo waged an extensive humanitarian relief effort. In the specific case of the council and its committees, by 31 August, they had spent an average of 21 liras (2,652.62 *kuruş*) a day, amounting to a total of 2,464 liras (313,009.40 *kuruş*). These relief efforts had reached far and wide and had an impact on thousands of deportees from Aleppo Province to Der Zor. Chronicler Charek observed that "the most beautiful and inspiring [thing] was the camaraderie expressed by our people, regardless of class, religious denomination, way of thinking, and party affiliation." This, "combined with our people's great power to resist and stubborn will to live, worked miracles."[136]

If Armenian self-help initiatives grew apace, the support deportees received from local and regional authorities gradually eroded as the center succeeded in eliminating dissent by transferring, removing, or even imprisoning officials sympathetic to the plight of the deportees, and replacing them with hardcore loyalists with a proven record of brutality against Armenians. The transfer of Celal Bey was but the first of a series of such decisions. Other governors and district governors in the region would suffer a similar fate in the months leading to the closure of the camps in the province along the Euphrates and massacres in Ras ul-Ain and Der Zor in the spring and summer of 1916. Moreover, the series of new appointments, and new party delegates, would diminish the influence of Cemal Pasha.

Notwithstanding the humanitarian initiatives and lenient local authorities then in office, Aleppo was a disaster zone by September 1915. Unlike in earlier months, during which relief efforts improved the lives of many destitute deportees, the distributed aid could barely ameliorate the condition of the deportees. Hundreds were dying on the streets from disease and starvation. Most of those who survived were soon to be forced out of the city into camps and settlement areas in the province or along the Euphrates, where more misery awaited them. Yet, compared to those sent to settlement areas elsewhere in the province or to the camps along the Euphrates, the deportees who managed against all odds to remain in Aleppo could be considered fortunate. Many received assistance from different sources and eked out an existence until the end of war. They constituted a significant number of the survivor generation that rebuilt Armenian communities after the war.

Aleppo

Urban Resistance to Redeportation

> After Aleppo there were so many roads and deserts that awaited us.
>
> —Survivor Artin Kitabjian

Chronicler Yervant Odian refers to September 1915 as "the gravest days of Armenian martyrdom,"[1] and rightly so. Having deported most of the empire's Armenian population, the central authorities now focused their attention on the survivors who had managed to reach Syria and enacted a series of decrees. The formation of the Subdirectorate for Deportees in Aleppo, the dispatch of officials to the city to oversee the redeportation process, the replacement of the governor twice (ultimately with an enthusiastic executioner of the central government's plans), the crackdown on the community leadership (particularly the banishment of the Catholicos to Jerusalem), and the decisions to remove all Armenian deportees from the city and to ban the entry of new convoys were not disparate, unrelated actions crammed into a few weeks. They point to a sustained effort by the central authorities to neutralize organized Armenian response to their policies and deal with what they perceived to be a demographic problem created by the arrival of tens of thousands of survivors.[2]

However, it was circumstances on the ground, particularly the spread of typhus, that prompted military and civilian authorities to accelerate the redeportation process. The authorities saw the deportees as a serious health hazard both for the local population and for the military supply lines in the area. They had to be removed quickly. The argument of military necessity was now used once again to deport Armenians—who would not have been in that predicament had they not been deported from their homes in the first place, also under the pretext of military necessity. The reality was more sinister. As the German ambassador notified his chancellor on 17 June 1915, "it was very clear that the Armenian deportations were not being carried out simply for military purposes."[3] Thus, the redeportation of Armenians from Aleppo City picked up the pace in the fall of 1915.

Still, the network was successful in anchoring thousands of Armenian deportees in the city. Various strategies were used, most notably employing deportees without wages or with nominal pay in factories and hospitals that serviced the military and securing permission from local authorities to open and expand orphanages that sheltered thousands of Armenian children, both with Cemal Pasha's tacit approval. The stories of Elmasd Santoorian and Arika Amiralian are cases in point. The former was a "massacre widow" from Marash who lost her husband during the Adana massacres of 1909. She went on to study midwifery in Istanbul, before returning to her hometown in 1914. A year later, she was deported from her hometown. She came down with typhus in Aleppo, but recovered with the help of Dr. Khachig Boghosian, a respected physician who was deported from Istanbul and became a key figure in the resistance network.[4] Santoorian's skills as a nurse and her immunity to typhus propelled her, within a few months, to the position of head nurse at a top Ottoman military hospital in Aleppo's Azizieh quarter. There, she hired "Armenian refugee girls, some orphaned, but all hiding from the gendarmes," securing *vesikas* (documents) for them and anchoring them in the city.[5] Meanwhile, Amiralian ran a uniform production factory for the Turkish military. Survivor Loossin Chorbajian Najarian remembered how in 1917,

> In Aleppo, my father found a job in a Turkish military workshop called "Imaret Khaneh," the director of which was an Armenian lady from Marash, Mrs. Arika Amiralian. Military uniforms were made there. Shortly thereafter, my mother too started working there and soon was made a supervisor. The Arabs used to call her "moodira" (directoress). I was now old enough myself to work and so I became a salaried employee of the same place.[6]

Survivor Yeranuhi Simonian too worked in one such factory, if not the same one directed by Amiralian, until the end of the war.[7] So did Payladzou Captanian, who signed up to avoid redeportation as soon as she heard about the workshops. A red and white piece of cloth with the inscription "women of the Third Army" was sown on their outfits, allowing them to walk freely in the city. "The government gave three pieces of bread to each of us on a daily basis, in return for our labor. Rich and poor, all came to work here, only to avoid exile," she remembered.[8] Walter Rössler reported in November 1916 that "each of the indigenous church administrations has taken over such workhouses, so that in total about 4,000 women have temporarily been saved in this manner."[9] Odian recalled that by March 1918, more than five thousand deportees labored in these workshops.[10] It is unfathomable that so many deportees were allowed to stay in Aleppo without the tacit approval of some Ottoman officials, chief among whom Cemal Pasha.

The resistance network, the core of which constituted religious and civic leaders of the Armenian community, was bolstered by missionaries and other foreign nationals living in the area and supported by Western diplomats. Jesse B. Jackson reported:

> Hundreds of personal incidents can be related wherein the Consulate assisted certain individuals and families to escape redeportation. . . . Daily prominent persons sought for persistently and fanatically by the authorities were sheltered by the Consulate and conducted clandestinely at night by faithful consular employees to secret friends among the townspeople and even to the friendly Bedouin Arabs adjacent to the city.[11]

Beginning in late 1915, the focal point of the genocide moved to the concentration camps along the Euphrates River, where deportees arriving in Aleppo Province were sent. Still, until the end of the war, the humanitarian resistance network continued to support the thousands of deportees who had managed, one way or the other, to disappear into the fabric of the metropolis or to find refuge in orphanages, community centers, safe houses, and hideouts, escaping redeportation to the desert.

Reconfiguring Aleppo in Line with Talaat's Plans

The local, hastily improvised solutions to the humanitarian challenges in Aleppo continued to be the order of the day as thousands continued pouring into the city. Yeghishe Hazarabedian, a deportee from Marash, witnessed their plight:

> While we ourselves marked time in Aleppo, groups of Armenian women began arriving under guard in the city. Several old and unkempt buildings in our area [near the Forty Martyrs Cathedral] were assigned to house these deportees. We were struck by the fact that there were no children among the women. We learned that these unfortunate women came from the distant interior reaches of Turkish Armenia. They marched through the streets in never-ending lines, two-abreast, all gaunt and emaciated—the animated corpses they were. Every day the authorities brought out from these decrepit buildings the corpses of those women who had died overnight. These bodies were dumped into garbage wagons.[12]

Those who survived were soon marched to the desert:

> Hardly had they arrived in Aleppo than they were taken away without being given a chance to rest. These women were nameless, faceless persons. We could not speak to them and they just stared at us, mute, their saucer-like eyes dull—dead. We never did find out where really they came from, whither they were being driven.[13]

The Interior Ministry set up a Subdirectorate for Deportees in Aleppo in late July to better regulate these movements.[14] The subdirectorate operated under the Directorate for the Settlement of Tribes and Emigrants (IAMM), which in turn reported to the Interior Ministry.[15] Muftizâde Şükrü Kaya Bey, the head of IAMM, was dispatched to Aleppo at the end of August to put in motion the subdirectorate's operations. In a series of telegrams sent from the ministry following the dispatch of Şükrü Bey, local authorities were instructed to follow his lead and were notified of the appointment of Abdulahad Nuri as director of deportations. Nuri reported to Şükrü Bey. Certain officials, including the district governors of Zor and Urfa, were invited to a private meeting with Şükrü Bey in Aleppo on 18 September.[16] Another telegram Talaat Paşa sent to Aleppo instructed the governor to decide upon deportation and settlement matters with Şükrü Bey. It also asked for a report detailing where deportees had come from, and how many from each location, where they had been dispatched, and how many were settled in each new location.[17]

What followed proved to be a turning point. On 17 October, on the recommendation of the head of IAMM, the ministry instructed the provincial officials of Aleppo to deport all nonlocal Armenians in the province, "without exception," to Rakka, Zor, and Kerek.[18] This meant death for the exhausted, the starving, and the sick. Ohannes Kuyumjian, who had arrived in Aleppo on 7 September, observed, "There are multitudes of [Armenian deportees] in Aleppo. Indeed, for the past few days the new arrivals have been denied entry to the town. Contagious illnesses have broken out there, threating public health."[19] Notifying the German embassy in Istanbul of the decision, the embassy administrator wrote: "Yesterday orders were given to empty the city of deportees (20,000) within 14 days, presumably due to military considerations. [The deportees] are being gathered at a concentration camp [*Konzentrationslager*] outside the city."[20]

Ad hoc measures by the local authorities, loosely coordinated with the center, to settle deportees in houses, *khans*, or hastily established camps had to end. The Interior Ministry wanted to exert full, direct control over the process. The ministry replaced Aleppo governor Bekir Sami, less than three months after he had assumed office, with Talaat's brother-in-law and governor of Bitlis, Mustafa Abdülhalik (4 October).[21] Armenian sources and foreign diplomats in the city by and large portray Bekir Sami in a positive light. Jackson, for instance, held that "the new governor [Bekir Sami] turned out as passive in reference to the deportation of the Armenians as his predecessor had been, and for that and other reasons he was recalled about two months later."[22] Abdülhalik, on the other hand, had been a proactive perpetrator: he had proposed to his Committee of Union and Progress (CUP) colleagues the annihilation of Armenians—and then carried out the crime in his province—during his tenure as governor of Bitlis.[23] In Aleppo, Talaat could work directly with him knowing that regional and local influences had little sway over the new appointee.

Bekir Sami's replacement constituted a tactical move in what Armenian genocide scholars refer to as the "dual-track" mechanism. An official track employed government communication to convey (re)deportation orders, resettlement, and the liquidation of Armenian property, while an unofficial track ordered "extralegal acts of violence, such as forced evacuations, killings, and massacres" privately, through trusted party functionaries.[24] Historian Erik-Jan Zürcher argues, based on several case studies, that the modus operandi of the CUP leadership consisted of trying "to create facts on the ground first and . . . using a dual system of communication with built-in deniability. The evidence seems to show that at least from January 1913 onwards, that is the way the Unionists made decisions and executed them."[25] For this dual-track system to function, Talaat needed trusted individuals in key leadership positions, and the series of dismissals and new appointments beginning in fall 1915 can be seen within this context.

Cracking Down on the Religious Leadership of the Community

In a fashion consistent with—if not imitating—the orders of deportation and arrests of leaders in Istanbul on 24 April, a series of orders fired in the fall of 1915 signaled the launch of a massive wave of persecution and redeportation. Dozens of community and church leaders were placed behind bars or exiled. The Armenian Prelacy's vicar and council president Father Harutiun Yesayan was arrested and locked up in the central prison near the Aleppo citadel. We have some insights about the charges brought against him, and about his time in prison, from an account by the Armenian Catholic priest Pascal Harootune Maljian, who too was arrested and ended up in the same prison cell. He recounted:

> Another section of the [police station cell block] was referred to as the "large prison." It was separated from our "small prison" [referred to as "Nazareth"] by a simple partition. I had found that . . . [Yesayan] was being held in the "large prison." Allegedly, according to the Turks, he had been guilty of cutting military communications between Intilli and Iskenderoon. . . . Through the intercession of this saintly servant of God and several of my Catholic parishoners, I was transferred to the "large prison" and was placed in the same cell with [Yesayan].[26]

Yesayan and Maljian remained in prison from late summer 1915 until the end of the war. They managed to escape during the descent into "plain lawlessness" following the Ottoman authorities' withdrawal from Aleppo, as a mob tore open the prison gates and started looting.[27] In October 1915, weeks after Yesayan's arrest, the council allocated a pension of five liras to his mother, arguing that she had spared no effort to assist deportees from the very beginning of the relief effort.[28] It would not be the first nor the last time that the council intervened to support those engaging in humanitarianism.

Unable to withstand the mounting pressures, the entire council tendered its resignation to the Catholicos (21 September), soon after its vicar and chairperson's incarceration. The pontiff, adamant that the situation not spiral out of control, formed a new committee and appointed Father Khachadur Boghigian, the spiritual leader of the Forty Martyrs Cathedral, as the Prelacy's vicar and the council president, handing over to him Father Yesayan's duties. Boghigian served in these two capacities until the end of the war.[29]

But the unfolding calamity eventually took a toll on the Armenian spiritual leader as well. "The Catholicos of Sis had a physical breakdown," the German consul reported to the ambassador in late September. "The other few member priests are either busy easing the mass misery by distributing bread and other things, or they do not dare to carry out their duties. It also seems that the despair over the doom of their people has won a victory over their faith."[30]

In subsequent weeks, dozens of Armenian priests who had arrived in Aleppo were exiled to Mumbuj, which had a sizeable Circassian population perceived to be hostile to Christians,[31] and attempts were made to ship the Catholicos there, too. The Catholicos's ordeal began with a telegram from the Ministry of Interior to the vice governor of Aleppo Province (Governor Bekir Sami had already been removed from his post and his replacement had not yet arrived), ordering that the Catholicos be sent away from the city to a provincial district. Mumbuj was considered as a possible destination by the authorities. The Catholicos attempted to gain time and renegotiate by asking the provincial authorities to wait for the expected arrival of Cemal Pasha. But he received a telegram from the Ministry of Justice and Religious Sects (Adliye ve Mezâhib Nezâreti) demanding his immediate departure. The telegram reads: "To the Catholicosate of Sis, Aleppo: As it is deemed necessary for you to live in one of the districts of Aleppo [Province] until further notice, consult with the Aleppo governorate and convey to us your destination. [Signed] Minister [Pirizâde] İbrahim [Bey]; 15 [28] October 1915."[32] It is worth noting here that Talaat did not engage with Armenian church leaders directly as he was orchestrating the destruction of the Armenians, often delegating the job to the Minister of Justice and Religious Sects Pirizâde İbrahim Bey. Back in July 1915, Patriarch Der Yeghiayan's repeated requests with Talaat were ignored, and eventually, he was given an audience with İbrahim Bey. Historian Raymond Kévorkian sees this as a clear sign that the authorities wanted to engage with the patriarch "only in his capacity as a religious leader," at first refusing to discuss the deportations with him, only to eventually rehash the military necessity argument.[33]

The Catholicos informed the German consul in Aleppo of the developments surrounding his exile and asked him to intervene to ensure deportation to a city and not a Circassian village. The consul, in turn, sent a telegram to the embassy soliciting Patriarch Der Yeghiayan's help.[34] The patriarch did in fact try to intervene on behalf of the Catholicos, but by then the decision to send the Catholicos to Jerusalem had already been made. The patriarch recounts:

> I heard by chance about Catholicos Sahag's move to Idlib through travelers, and this troubled me. I made a personal appeal to Jemal Pasha, who was in Constantinople at the time, and requested that the Catholicos be allowed to go to Jerusalem because of his advanced age. Jemal Pasha informed me that several days earlier he had given orders for the Catholicos to be transferred by train to Jerusalem in full comfort and had already received news of the Catholicos' arrival. The report calmed my anxiety about Catholicos Sahag.[35]

The decision to send the Catholicos to Jerusalem was taken after a few days of back-and-forth. Following the central government's orders to pick a destination in the province of Aleppo, the Catholicos had chosen Idlib, despite the vice governor's attempt to send him to Mumbuj.[36] He had left Aleppo on 3 November accompanied by several bishops and priests and had arrived in Idlib only to be summoned back to Aleppo upon the orders of Cemal Pasha (6 November). The following day, a telegram from Talaat had notified the Aleppo Governorate and the director of IAMM Şükrü Bey that he and Cemal had reached an agreement to send the Catholicos and three priests to Jerusalem, while other religious leaders would be sent to Mumbuj.[37] The Catholicos left Aleppo on 9 November and arrived in Jerusalem a few days later.[38]

The Armenian patriarch in Constantinople argued in his memoirs that Jerusalem was indeed the preferred destination for the Catholicos and his entourage, particularly in view of the financial challenges the clergymen would face in districts where the Armenian Church did not have a presence. The patriarch believed that the decision to remove the Catholicos from Aleppo city may have been prompted by "a thoughtless act," the publication in the Tiflis (Tbilisi) daily newspaper *Mshag* of a confidential letter the Catholicos had sent to the patriarch on the "extremely decimated and moribund condition" of deportees arriving in Aleppo. The patriarch had shared the letter, in confidence, with Professor Asdvadzadur Khachadryan, from whom the Armenian Revolutionary Federation had taken the letter and sent it to Tbilisi.[39] There was also another possibility. The patriarch observed that "an equally important reason for this order may have been a telegram the Catholicos had sent from Aleppo to the Minister of Internal Affairs, the Minister of War, the Chairman of the Parliament, and Jemal Pasha," in which he had demanded that the authorities stop the deportations and settle the Armenians wherever they are "so that they will be spared the ordeal of spending the winter outdoors, exposed to the cold and the rain."[40] The historical record demonstrates that the Catholicos was a clear and present impediment to the CUP policies, so his removal from Aleppo was not necessarily prompted by an isolated incident and was likely due to his sustained resistance to the genocide.

The end result fulfilled Talaat's wishes, without undermining Cemal's social strategy of projecting himself as a humanitarian to diplomats, Armenian community leaders, and deportees alike. The regime removed the Catholicos from Aleppo, where he had been a leader of humanitarian efforts. The minor victory of exile to Jerusalem instead of Mumbuj, thanks to a series of appeals and Cemal's intervention, did not make it any less of a blow to the resistance effort. Despite his frailty at age sixty-six, the Catholicos had succeeded in mobilizing the community around the council's efforts and maintaining pressure on local and central authorities through his appeals to foreign diplomats in the city. His presence was a source of strength and resilience to the thousands of deportees in the city and the camps nearby, which he visited whenever he could.[41]

In spring and early summer 1916, when another round of radical policies was unleashed, the Armenian Church once again became a target. The authorities liquidated outright three of the four major Armenian Apostolic religious centers: the Patriarchate of Constantinople, the Catholicosate of Aghtamar, and the Patriarchate of Jerusalem. The decision to shut down these institutions, and to annul the Armenian National Constitution that defined the principles governing the community's internal affairs, had been taken as early as January 1916, but was rolled out in late July 1916.[42] The annulment decree appointed Catholicos Sahag Khabayan as the Catholicos-Patriarch of Ottoman Armenians, headquartered in Jerusalem.[43] Thus, the Ottoman authorities erased the historic Armenian Church from existence in Cilicia and Eastern Provinces, and severed its ties with the Holy See of Etchmiadzin, the mother church with its traditional headquarters in Russia. For a nation that had organized its community life for centuries almost entirely around the Armenian Church, this was as devastating as it was ominous.

Before he left for Jerusalem in early November 1915, the Catholicos met with the newly formed council and encouraged it to continue its work, despite the challenges, "to alleviate the misery as much as possible."[44] Indeed, the council and its network of committees, employees, and volunteers carried on amid chaotic circumstances. Several of the new members were not available in the fall, and the practice of holding daily meetings was discontinued. As the council's records explain, "due to the illness of Tavit Ef[endi] Jidejian, the departure of Roupen Ef. Ejghojian from the city, Hagop Barsoumian's busy schedule, and the absence of Dikran Pironian from meetings for a long period of time have caused the Council to not hold regular meetings with a quorum. Still, the day-to-day work has been done without any delays."[45] Few meetings held after September 1915 were recorded in the council's books, likely as a precaution after the government started to crack down on the resistance network.[46] In any case, the council continued to track income and expenses associated with deportee relief throughout the war.

The Specter of Typhus and "Disinfecting" Aleppo

I argue that epidemics had a significant impact on policy toward Armenian deportees in Ottoman Syria during World War I. Several key orders associated with accelerating the redeportation of Armenians in the fall of 1915 were taken as the scourge of typhus loomed large in the region—a development that the German, and soon thereafter Ottoman, command considered a problem that required immediate attention. As the authorities tried to avert a crisis that threatened military supply lines, they also weaponized diseases, isolating Armenians in repositories of typhus and dysentery: concentration camps. Having dealt with Muslim refugees pouring in from the Russian Empire and from European territories it had lost, the Ottomans had significant experience with epidemics and were well aware of the devastation communicable diseases would cause in camps deprived of basic supplies and medical care.

Jackson attributed the spread of typhus in the region to "the arrival early in August, 1915, of some 5,000 terribly emaciated, dirty, ragged and sick women and children . . . the only survivors of the thrifty and well to do Armenian population of the province of Sivas."[47] Several deportees came down with the disease in the *khans* and courtyards into which they were herded. Such ad hoc locations where Armenians were temporarily interned were particularly susceptible to the disease. Survivor Mgrdich Hairabedian was among those held in one such site, an abandoned factory where hundreds of people were crammed. He describes how agricultural lime (limestone powder) was spattered at the entrance and in the courtyard of the building to kill lice, the vectors of the disease. "It was as if it had snowed. Everywhere was white."[48]

German officers recognized that the disease made intervention a "military necessity," and they requested that Cemal Pasha visit the region. As German consul Rössler reported, "The conditions have become so bad that this stretch of military road from Bozanti to Aleppo is totally contaminated. Only after Colonel Baron von Kress had succeeded in pointing out the military necessity of hygienic measure for this stretch of road did [Cemal Pasha] arrange for a visit to Aleppo."[49] Authorities took urgent measures. "Medical martial law" (*sihhi sıkıyönetim*) was declared in Aleppo City on 5 November 1915.[50] Cemal issued a ten-point detailed decree outlining the measures to be taken. The first point concerned Armenian deportees. It stipulated that all deportees staying in the city for some time by then, both men and women, were to be deported within five days. Thus, the process of redeporting Armenians from Aleppo, which had already been accelerated on 17 October, now received another boost. The army also ordered the emptying of the French hospital building, still under construction, of deportees who were stationed there. Armenians who had contracted communicable diseases were to be transported there. Şükrü Bey was assigned the responsibility of implementing the order.[51]

With this decree, Cemal instituted sweeping changes and stringent measures aimed at disease control. He ordered the immediate publication and distribution of ten thousand flyers outlining preventive measures; reorganized municipal cleaning; decreed compulsory registration of the infected; assigned doctors who would inspect households in different neighborhoods for unregistered patients; appointed a public health overseer, a German expert, who would directly report to him; and arranged for the transport of the sick.[52] Cemal listed three hospitals where patients could receive treatment: the Altounyan Hospital (with a daily rate of three *mecidiye*), the military hospital (one *mecidiye*), and the municipal hospital (ten *kuruş*).[53] Two Armenian physicians, Khachig Boghosian and Toros Ovajikian, were selected to treat the patients.[54] These documents are testament to the key role Armenian doctors played in the city, and the degree of Cemal's reliance on them during the war. Following Cemal's "epidemic control" orders, local authorities tried to contain the disease by isolating those infected from the general population, disposing of the dead in a hygienic manner, burning their lice-infested clothing. [55] But it was too little, too late. According to Jackson they simply "could not cope with the situation."[56] Some who survived the disease or witnessed their family members succumb to it described the horror in accounts and memoirs. Survivor John Minassian contracted it from "the strongest and healthiest boy from Gurun" in the shelter where he was staying. "He would curl next to me for warmth, for the nights were chilly and the covers were light. A few days later I, too, was sweating uncontrollably and wanted just to sleep. I heard strange noises that irritated me as never before. I grew weaker and weaker. . . . At times I could hardly recognize people or things."[57] Hayganush Khubeserian was among those who contracted the disease and were taken to the French hospital. "The government had allocated the Saint Louis Hospital for this purpose [typhus patients among deportees], and there, the patients were under the dedicated care of Dr. Hovagimian," she recalled. "They took me there. My health continuously deteriorated and a week later I lost consciousness and was hallucinating, cursing the Turks. However, I recovered a month later."[58]

Father Dajad Arslanian, who survived typhus but lost his ailing father to the disease in Aleppo in November 1915, explained how the government opened quarantine hospitals to care for the infirm, but these were "abattoirs more than hospitals, where hundreds of deportees who entered every day in the most miserable of conditions did not receive medical treatment and even basic health requirements were not met." For days, the dead remained in their beds, next to the living, and the stench of corpses pervaded the hospitals.[59] These conditions were not a secret, even to officials in the capital. "A visit to these so-called hospitals, which I myself have not seen, is supposedly so shocking . . . that even the strongest nerves fail," the chairman of the Baghdad Railway wrote in a report.[60]

The authorities provided ox carts to collect corpses in the streets and ad hoc locations. The corpses were buried in mass graves. Every day, Jackson witnessed the procession of these wagons in front of the consulate on the way "to the nearby cemetery with their gruesome load of ghastly uncovered corpses, usually nude, with the heads, legs and arms dangling from the sides and ends of the open carts."[61] The carts had become an ominous symbol of the apotheosis of suffering for the survivors, who would long remember them with horror. In the factory where Mgrdich Hairabedian stayed, Armenians who ran the internal affairs of the site sprinkled lime on the dead and left them in the courtyard until the next morning, when the ox carts carried them to Sebil to be buried in mass graves.[62] It was in this period that Kerop Bedoukian's family arrived in Aleppo and settled in a *khan* where "typhus had struck every family." The nine-year-old Bedoukian too remembered the wagons transporting the dead, on certain days "making three trips, each trip taking away at least a dozen bodies. . . . These drivers became experts as time went on. They could almost tell how many bodies there would be the next day."[63] Writer Dikran Yeretsian recounted that "the garbage carts of the municipality collected from the streets half-dead toddlers and children up to eight to ten years old all day long."[64] Survivor John Minassian escaped from one such raid while he was still in a semicomatose state. "I jumped from the bed and together [with the boy next to me] we sneaked out of the gate [of the shelter]. A garbage wagon was waiting at the door; a few bodies, half dead and buried in lye, had been thrown there. We turned to the left, where the coppersmiths were, and we disappeared into the crowd."[65]

Minassian survived diseases ravaging the Armenians, but Rev. Hovhannes Eskijian, who had provided him with shelter and recruited him to help with the relief efforts, did not. He contracted typhoid fever (a disease with similar symptoms to typhus but caused by a different type of bacteria and transmitted by contaminated food or water) and was taken to Altounyan Hospital, where he succumbed to the disease on 25 March 1916 at the age of thirty-four. Despite the harsh conditions in Aleppo, hundreds gathered at and outside the reverend's church for the memorial service, where Minassian himself eulogized him. His words lamented the fate of the Armenian nation, asking that Eskijian tell God of the suffering of his people: "Talk to him on behalf of the Armenian nation, and who knows he may put an end to these carnages and ferocities, these exterminatory tribulations, these demolishing consternations, these horrible and frightful persecutions."[66]

A few days after Eskijian's death, two officials approached his wife, Gulenia, asking about his whereabouts. Skeptical of her response, they corroborated it with Altounyan Hospital. Accounts by family members and friends indicate that there was an order to arrest Eskijian. Araxia Jebejian, one of his associates based in Der Zor, met that fate in 1916. Assisting deportees with funds Eskijian and Rohner transferred to her, she was arrested under trumped-up accusations of spying, and killed in prison.[67]

Gulenia received letters of condolence from near and far in the following weeks. One writer described himself as "despondent" upon hearing the news as he was getting ready to leave Aleppo for Der Zor. He goes on to echo the sentiments expressed in most letters and obituaries professing faith in God's will: "What can I say? Our Heavenly Father knows what he is doing. His hand doesn't do anything unjust: he takes whom he wants and leaves whom he wants." But the letter also offers a snippet into how Eskijian's associates continued his work, picking up and delivering supplies and assistance. The author informs Gulenia that "Muharrem had left the *emanet* (Turkish for what's entrusted to someone) in Sebka. Now it's safely with me."[68]

Typhus quickly spread across the city and beyond, claiming the lives of tens of thousands of locals, "devastating whole towns and villages throughout the interior, and also causing great ravages in the army."[69] Elmasd Santoorian, an Armenian nurse who recovered from typhus in Aleppo and went on to become the head nurse of a military hospital in the Azizieh quarter of the city, later referred to the disease as the "offspring of the genocide," noting that it had "become a full-fledged epidemic, indiscriminately attacking the city and its inhabitants."[70] Ali Fuad Erden, an officer in the Ottoman Fourth Army, observed how hundreds of thousands of deportees marched thousands of kilometers in deplorable conditions on roads that connected three Ottoman armies on three fronts (the Caucasus, Iraq, and Syria), and spread diseases like typhus and typhoid fever along the way. The result? "There were as many, perhaps even more, deaths in the army and among the population as there were among the deportees."[71] Hüseyin Kazım Kadri, who chaired a committee to assist in the settlement process of Armenian deportees, estimated in his memoir that close to two hundred thousand deportees, soldiers, and locals died of typhus in the region during the war.[72] As we shall see, the association of the epidemic with the Armenian deportees created or heightened hostility toward the recent arrivals whom the locals blamed for bringing the disease to cities and villages. Attacks on the deportees and local civilian initiatives to force them out followed.

The atmosphere of resentment against the Armenians in the wake of the typhus outbreak provided impetus, cover, and local support for the authorities' efforts to crack down on and redeport all non-native Armenians in Aleppo City to the interior. Particularly telling is the account by Naim Efendi, an IAMM official, about the violence against Armenian deportees when measures to curb the epidemic were instituted: "[At that point] the redeportation from Aleppo became so brutal that the police tied up the Armenians like pigs and dragged them away from homes."[73] Naim Efendi noted that in one case, a man's entire family, all sick with typhus, was hauled into garbage carts and sent away to Karlık. The man pleaded with the local authorities for permission for his family to remain in the city a few days. "No one would pity him. During my tenure [as an official at IAMM], some ten thousand pleas were presented to our office by Armenian deportees: I didn't even see them take ten of those into consideration," he observed.[74]

Despite the best efforts of the humanitarian network in Aleppo, countless deportees were sick at this point, and the death rate had risen from 120 to 200 a day.[75] Eyewitness Walter M. Geddes noted that "in one vacant house which I visited, I saw women and children and men all in the same room lying on the floor so close together that it was impossible to walk between them" (September 1915).[76] Returning to Aleppo in September after a three-month absence, a German eyewitness, Dr. Martin Niepage, described the situation:

> In dilapidated caravansaries (hans) I found quantities of dead, many corpses being half-decomposed, and others, still living, among them, who were soon to breathe their last. In other yards I found quantities of sick and starving people whom no one was looking after. In the neighborhood of the German Technical School, at which I am employed as a higher grade teacher, there were four such hans, with seven or eight hundred exiles dying of starvation. We teachers and our pupils have to pass by them every day.[77]

The 17 October telegram ordering local authorities to send deportees stationed in Aleppo, "without exception," to Rakka, Zor, and Kerek meant certain death for the exhausted, starving, and sick. Although the decision to accelerate redeportation from Aleppo city and crack down on the community leadership was centrally coordinated, conditions on the ground, particularly the calls to disinfect the city and the ensuing medical martial law, facilitated and accelerated it. Moreover, the central authorities realized that they could turn the specter of typhus haunting Syria into a weapon of genocide if they separated the Armenian deportees from the general population and sent them away to die alone. In a telegram, Talaat informed Şükrü Bey that typhus and dysentery were killing seventy to eighty people a day among the twenty thousand deportees in Hama and ordered that they be redeported as soon as possible.[78]

Was the Aleppo Armenian Community Deported?

The Armenian community in Aleppo was by and large spared deportation. Yet this was not a forgone conclusion in 1915–1917. In fact, for months on end, local Armenian community leaders and influential figures such as the Mazloumian brothers (until their exile) and Dr. Altounyan knocked on Ottoman officials' doors, as well as those of consuls stationed in the city, appealing to them to halt any possible plans to deport them. "These days, the Armenians of Aleppo are also anxiously contemplating the possibility of being deported. Tomorrow we will appeal to Jemal Pasha and our Governor for their grace and mercy and will inform you of the result," the Prelacy of Aleppo notified the Armenian patriarch in Constantinople in a letter dated 17 March 1916.[79] An uncertain future cast a dark shadow over the community. It is *despite* this that the Aleppo Armenians mounted humanitarian assistance—and resistance—efforts.

Appeals to officials and consuls helped; so did economic considerations. Influential business circles in Aleppo had a vested interest in keeping the local Armenian community intact. As Hermann Hoffmann, the vice-consul at Alexandretta, explained in a report, "The Armenians in Aleppo seem to owe the fact that they are still here mainly to the resistance of those local circles who would suffer great financial losses if they disappeared."[80] Similar considerations saved hundreds of Armenian deportees settled in Rakka from being redeported to Der Zor in spring and summer 1916.[81]

Yet Aleppo Armenians were at continuous risk. Amid the glut of deportation orders, interventions by consuls, exemptions, and the reissuing of deportation orders, hundreds of Aleppo Armenians were sent to the desert. Particularly vulnerable were those who had moved into the city over the previous two decades and had not updated their documentation by registering as Aleppo residents. The German consul in Aleppo, who inquired about one such case, learned from a police commissioner that "orders have been given to deport every Armenian who is not in possession of identity paper [*teskere nufus*] issued in Aleppo, without taking into consideration the time already spent in Aleppo." This meant that Armenians who had been residents of Aleppo for many years but had not exchanged their *teskere* for a local one (only few had done so, it was not common practice) would be deported. The consul argued that "with this order, the government possesses an effective weapon with which to deport the majority of the local Armenians. Only those who are born here are safe."[82] A similar process was implemented in Istanbul on 24 April 1915 and during the weeks that followed.[83]

Scores were indeed deported from Aleppo. The German chargé d'affaires reported in August 1916 that although "the deportation of the 'non-resident' Armenians has not yet been effected on a large scale [in Aleppo City] . . . about 800 have fallen victim to this so far. People are being picked up in the streets ruthlessly."[84] Jackson, too, reported in mid-August 1916 that hundreds of Aleppo Armenians were being deported to Der Zor, where massacres were raging.

> There are about 8,000 in this neighborhood (Aleppo) and 200 were sent on the 12th [of August], 150 last night [31 August], and the collection goes on daily wherever they can be dragged from their hiding places. It is complete extermination. Some people living here for six to eight years have been sent, and it looks as though this is only the beginning on our local people. Everybody is in terror."[85]

Although intervention by German and U.S. diplomats seems to have put an end to this process by September 1916, fear of being deported continued to grip the Armenian community throughout the war. So much so that in March 1917, months after deportations had stopped, Talaat asked the provincial authorities of Aleppo to relieve the community from such worries and reassure it that deportation was now out of the question.[86] Still, the arrests and persecution of Armenians continued, and the fear of deportation lingered. When chronicler Yervant Odian returned to Aleppo in March 1918, the arrests and harassment had not ended. He wrote, "I'd often see groups of 20–30 young Armenians in the street who, tied together with rope, were going to the police station in a very sorry state, from where they were handed over to the military authorities."[87] Andonian, in turn, recalled, "Two weeks before the fall of Aleppo [to Prince Faisal's forces on 26 October 1918], the persecution of the Armenians was still an issue."[88]

While many Armenian residents of Aleppo were deported, some new arrivals managed to remain in the city by securing a *vesika* (document) or a job through the resistance network, personal connections, or bribes. The difference a *vesika* made becomes amply clear in the account of survivor Hovhannes Toros Doumanian, a deportee from Hajin:

> I met many Armenian woodcutters who were working for a Serbian contractor by the name of Sokolovich. He was very kind to the Armenians. All of his employees were Armenians whose families were in Aleppo with "certificates." Because of this, they were not deported to the desert.
>
> To get a "certificate" for myself was going to cost 10–20 Gold Coins, which was a great deal of money for me.
>
> I waited for a train that was transporting wood to Aleppo. I jumped onto one of the wagons, hid myself and managed to reach Aleppo. An Armenian at the station helped me. I went to a construction site that employed Armenians and was employed as a secretary for the Turkish Director. I had a big responsibility.
>
> After a month, I took five days off and returned to Aleppo with the permit. I

made five copies and stayed there for a month. Aleppo was full of refugees who were subsequently driven to the desert to perish.

At that time the Turks were building a cinema in Aleppo, and were paying the workers 1.5 kilos of bread daily as compensation. They were also giving the families of workers permits to stay there.

We got that permit by paying 15 Gold Coins. My brother became a worker and so my family could stay in Aleppo.[89]

The *vesika* figures prominently in accounts of survivors, and for good reason. These documents granting permissions, offering exemptions, or allowing safe passage gave temporary respite to thousands of deportees arriving in Aleppo, and helped a few thousand others anchor themselves in the city for the duration of the war.[90]

Placing women and children in the homes of Aleppians as servants proved a less successful effort in the long run, although it was a desperate attempt "to get them away from the eyes of police officials so that they would not be deported to the interior," in the words of Jackson. This effort offered hundreds of "boys and girls under 14 years of age" a respite of a few months in the summer of 1915, but most were dragged from these homes and deported in the fall.[91] Moreover, these households were not always a safe haven. Many suffered physical and sexual abuse, and some escaped their employ and joined deportation caravans.[92]

Western Humanitarian Efforts and Armenians

As Aleppo was systematically emptied of its deportees in fall 1915, a humanitarian effort to rescue the "starving Armenians" was launched across the Atlantic.[93] In the United States, the Armenian Relief Committee (ARC) was formed in September 1915.[94] A month later, ARC cabled $100,000 to the U.S. ambassador in Istanbul, Henry Morgenthau. By the end of 1915, the committee had raised $176,929.[95] The distribution of relief funds was entrusted to a committee of prominent Americans in Istanbul headed by the ambassador.[96] U.S. diplomats received pushback from Ottoman authorities as they tried to dispense money to the deportees in Istanbul, Aleppo, and other areas. The ministers of war and foreign affairs objected "to Americans distributing relief to Armenians because assistance by foreigners encourages such idealists as the Armenians to further resistance against the government, although the government has admitted at other times that Armenians are not in a position to effectively oppose the Government."[97] The ministers proposed the transfer of American funds to government accounts, with relief administered by the authorities. Morgenthau refused, citing the wishes of the American donors that the funds be administered by none other than the U.S. ambassador.[98] He continued to distribute relief money through U.S. consuls, and Ottoman Turkish authorities did not press further.[99] Still, they denied in December a request by the American Committee for Armenian and Syrian Relief (ACASR), the entity that took over relief efforts in the Ottoman Empire from ARC, to send a commission "to ascertain the exact conditions and needs of the Armenian refugees, and to reach them at the earliest possible moment with effectual relief."[100] The idea of sending a commission was abandoned, and sums continued to be transferred through the consuls to the Armenian survivors.

The monies allocated in Syria in fall 1915 were woefully insufficient. In a report to Morgenthau, Jackson noted that "in order to provide the barest existence for these people a most considerable sum is necessary, say $150,000 a month. This would be at the rate of only a dollar a head, which would hardly furnish bread, to say nothing of clothing, shelter, medical treatment, etc."[101] A month later, as Morgenthau informed Washington of allocating $65,000 to deportee assistance, he noted: "Aleppo Consul writes that in his district there are now one hundred and fifty thousand deported Armenians totally without means."[102] Despite the insufficient amounts trickling in, the effort broadened the scope of the humanitarian resistance and paved the path for much larger sums of U.S. aid channeled to Aleppo and beyond in the following years.[103]

Jackson's action stoked the ire of local officials, who fired off complaint after complaint to the Interior Ministry: deportees arriving in Aleppo are using the U.S. consulate as a return address when writing to relatives overseas requesting funds (20 September 1915); Jackson is acting as conduit for Armenians (5 October 1915); hundreds of Armenians are receiving funds from the U.S. consulate (8 March 1916).[104] Many deportees stopped by the consulate to receive money their relatives and friends sent from the United States.[105] The consul was not only distributing funds sent from relatives in the United States to Armenian deportees arriving in Aleppo, it was also safekeeping deportee possessions. "During those days many persons fearing trouble left money and valuables at the Consulate," Jackson wrote in a report.[106]

The scholarly literature on efforts to raise funds for Armenians and the humanitarian relief efforts of Western missionaries by and large depicts Armenians as passive recipients of humanitarian aid. Historians present a compelling narrative of the efforts to raise money in America and send it to U.S. officials in the Ottoman Empire for distribution to Armenian deportees in Aleppo and elsewhere. Yet there is hardly any mention of *how* these funds reached the deportees. Armenians distributed funds to tens of thousands of survivors, often covertly and under dangerous circumstances, with U.S. consuls and Western missionaries serving as intermediaries. It was Armenian committees, orphanage administrators, and humanitarian resisters who conducted these high-wire acts of relief distribution, risking imprisonment, and often raising funds from other sources as well. In his memoir, Armenian Patriarch of Istanbul Zaven Der Yeghiayan described the challenges and dangers of openly raising funds: "There was no possibility for raising funds, because every Armenian faced an uncertain future and wanted to keep for himself what he had. Even if they had been willing to donate money, it would have been impossible for the Patriarchate to engage in fund-raising because it would have been viewed as an anti-government project."[107] Still, funds were raised, and monies sent from the United States and elsewhere made their way to the deportees. In his memoir, survivor John Minassian offered one way in which money reached the Armenian relief network in Aleppo. "I began delivering messages in folded envelopes to Mr. Jackson, the American consul, who, when evening fell, would send his secretary to visit Reverend Eskijian to leave him a small canvas bag."[108] Eskijian would, in turn, disburse the funds in Aleppo and send a portion to his associates in other areas for distribution. Garabed, an Armenian man who served as an emissary to Beatrice Rohner, made forays into Der Zor handing out assistance to deportees in need.[109]

Orphan Care

As the number of deportees arriving in Aleppo skyrocketed, missionaries, diplomats, and local Armenians joined efforts to open orphanages in Aleppo, providing shelter and basic education to hundreds and, eventually, thousands of the parentless children from different corners of the empire now roaming the city streets.[110] The authorities shut down some of these institutions, while others outlasted the Young Turks. Chief among the latter was Shirajian's orphanage, opened on 31 July 1915 through the efforts of Nora Altounyan, who was just 22 at the time, and others and others in the humanitarian network.[111]

The orphanage could not have had a better location. Operating in an inn owned by Swiss businessman Emil Zollinger situated right next to the German consulate in the Al-Aqabah neighborhood, the institution enjoyed the tacit support, and sometimes the direct help, of the consulate. Just south of the Bab el-Faraj neighborhood, it was a ten-minute walk from the Armenian Holy Martyrs Cathedral, where the council met, and the Mazloumian Brothers' famed Hotel Baron.[112] As the orphanage expanded, some ten more buildings were rented around the neighborhood.[113]

The orphanage enrolled thirty children the day it opened and provided safe haven to 340 in its first month of operation.[114] In late September, there were 369 children and widows at the orphanage, only 139 of whom were Evangelical; the remaining children came from Armenian Apostolic families.[115] By October 1915, the number had risen to 393, making resources scant.[116] "Initially each orphan had two of each article of clothing, but with the increase in number, we were forced to take from one and give it to another," Shirajian explained in an interview.[117] "Food was scarce but the reverend used to say, 'Let the remnants of the Armenian nation not die on the street,'" remembered Elmas Boyajian, who worked at the orphanage.[118] And the number of children housed at the orphanage continued increasing until the end of the war. Four hundred and two orphans were sheltered there by the end of 1915; 548 in 1916; 1,003 in 1917; and 1,500 by September 1918 (a net increase of 500 orphans per year).[119]

Around eighty Armenians, each of whom pledged to donate half a lira a month, initially covered the bulk of the institution's expenses. But within weeks, the orphanage directors appealed to consul Jackson and a certain Dr. Fisher for assistance.[120] Armenian churches, the council, as well as individuals, most notably Nora's father, Dr. Altounyan, Swiss friends of Emil Zollinger, and American donors, supported the institution.[121] Jackson, Zollinger, the two Altounyans, and Shirajian received special acknowledgment for their efforts during the war in the orphanage report published in 1922.[122] The children were not passive recipients of help either. They worked in a bakery associated with the orphanage that produced good quality bread that sold well, and later in other facilities run by the orphanage as gardeners, shoemakers, ironsmiths, and in milk production. The home also purchased fruits for the orphans to resell.[123] Overall, thousands pitched in to cover the expenses of the orphanage, which reached 25,600 Ottoman liras from its establishment to the end of the war (three years and three months).[124]

The orphanage received political cover, and sometimes food and other supplies, from local and regional authorities, with the incoming Aleppo governor Bekir Sami

Bey allowing its operation, and Cemal Pasha blocking attempts from the central authorities to arrest its director, Rev. Aharon Shirajian, and shut it down.[125] Here too, Dr. Altounyan played a significant role, capitalizing on his friendship with Bekir Sami and Cemal Pasha, and his position as the director of a hospital that cared for officers of the Ottoman Fourth Army under the latter's command.[126] The orphanage survived despite Talaat's efforts to shut it down and deport the children. The story of this Armenian institution's survival throughout the war evokes comparisons from a better-known case, that of Berlin's Jewish Hospital during World War II. The hospital "outlasted the Nazis" thanks in large part to the efforts of hospital director Dr. Walter Lustig (a German Jew), including his relationship with Adolf Eichmann.[127]

According to American educator and Near East Relief volunteer Stanley Kerr, "Shirajian was continually in trouble with the deportation office in Aleppo, but he enjoyed a certain degree of immunity thanks to the support of Jamal Pasha. The general had formed a friendship with Dr. Aram Assadour Altounian after he had been a patient at this renowned physician's hospital in Aleppo. . . . Shirajian was in trouble with the police, a message transmitted through Nora [Altounyan] to her father brought immediate action."[128] Decades later, Dr. Altounyan's granddaughter remembered that Cemal Pasha "was a frequent visitor to my grandfather's house. He was persuaded by my father's sister, Norah, to divert Army rations to feed little Armenian children who were wandering about everywhere in a most pitiful state, having lost their families in the massacres."[129] According to Dikran Yeretsian, at one point "there wasn't a single grain of wheat at the orphanage." Nora Altounyan appealed to Cemal's adjutant Nusret Bey, who provided large amounts of wheat to the orphanages from the military's storage facilities.[130] Rev. Shirajian, for his part, cultivated relations with Walter Rössler, whose support the institution enjoyed. In his memoir, survivor John Minassian credited the German consul with protecting the orphanage.[131] Rev. Shirajian remained the orphanage director throughout the war and continued to serve in that capacity long after the Ottoman defeat.

Many Armenians, mostly women, worked for the orphanage in return for a meager ration.[132] Dudu *mayrig* took care of children with injuries and those with lice. Takouhi Alexanian, a deportee from Adıyaman, was responsible for showering, cleaning, and changing the clothes of newly arrived orphans. Menend Mekhlian from Mancılık (near the Black Sea), Lucia Roubian Shirajian, and a woman by the name of Kimid shrouded the bodies of dead orphans secretly, with care so as not to upset the children. Roubian Shirajian came down with typhus in the line of duty and died.[133]

Initially, lessons were planned, but local officials advised against such a move, as Armenian schools were not allowed to operate.[134] However, the orphans did receive some schooling.[135] Caretakers bent the rules and engaged children with activities that did not leave a paper trail. They taught them songs, poems, prayers, and entertained them "with games to lessen the sad feelings and painful memories etched in their minds and, if possible, draw a smile from them," wrote Elmas Boyajian.[136]

Initially, Altounyan's hospital donated much-needed medication, while a few physicians donated their time.[137] They included Dr. Khachig Boghosian, "who in the eyes of deportees was the most popular and beloved physician," wrote Charek.[138] Dr. Boghosian was one of the Armenian doctors Cemal Pasha relied on to contain the spread of typhus. This was not a random decision. "Dr. Boghosian's reputation for treating this disease had spread beyond the confines of the Armenian community. We were treating people from all levels of Turkish and Arab society," wrote Elmasd Santoorian, the nurse who owed her own survival from typhus to Dr. Boghosian.[139] Years later, Dr. Boghosian wrote about the difficulties of the first few months of the orphanage's operation:

> The so-called orphanage was a hastily constructed shelter, with futons side by side filled with hay or sawdust, where more than one child slept. Their care was entrusted to a few dozen female adolescents and women. A large room was allocated to those who entered every day on the verge of death, and the majority died a few days later. The burying of the bodies was not an easy task. They were stuffed in bags and taken after dark to Sheikh Maksood, their final resting place.[140]

But eventually, the health conditions improved, and the death rate fell. Jackson noted in a March 1918 report how "disease was stamped out [in the orphanages] and the children were in a very thrifty condition."[141]

When the British occupied Aleppo in 1918, Shirajian's orphanage alone was sheltering 1,500 orphans. The tally was 2,016 a year later.[142] More than sixteen thousand children had received food and shelter at the orphanage, some six thousand for a long period. According to Shirajian, many children were half dead when they reached the orphanage, and 521 indeed died while at this institution, "but at least had the good fortune of dying in bed, instead of being dragged on the streets."[143] Yet central authorities frowned upon the support given to Armenian orphans by some Ottoman officials and considered the orphanages in Aleppo "totally unacceptable."[144]

Other orphanages also operated in the city. Swiss teacher Beatrice Rohner secured permission from Cemal Pasha and established an orphanage that took in more than one thousand children, with the financial support of the U.S. embassy in Istanbul and other donors.[145] A prominent German woman in Aleppo, Martha Koch, was instrumental in the effort—a fact left out of consul Jackson's reports. Naim Efendi reminisced:

> At that time there was a German woman, a humanitarian—I think her name was Hoch—who gathered herself and with the help of others one or two hundred innocent infants; she urged the government to care for these orphans, such compassion angered the provincial governor, and infuriated the Deportation Office. But nobody said anything publicly.[146]

The Ottoman authorities eventually succeeded in shutting down Rohner's orphanage in the early months of 1917 and transferring seventy boys to an institution in Antoura to be Turkified.[147] Elmas Boyajian mentioned the shutting down of this "fairly large orphanage whose food supply came from the local authorities, and thus was a thorn in the side of the government," noting that around the same time, authorities also demanded a list of children from Shirajian's orphanage, where Elmas worked, and sent eighty of them to Muslim institutions for Turkification.[148] A third orphanage, administered by Hovannes Juskalian (known as Hovhannes Efendi), quickly grew to shelter eighty orphans, many more than he was officially permitted to house.[149]

Assistance to the orphanages provided through the U.S. consulate was crucial. "The Consulate furnished most all [*sic*] of the funds required to keep up these establishments, the balance being provided by some native Aleppo people and some contributors," reported Jackson to the secretary of state.[150] A representative of ACASR reported in May 1916 to headquarters, via the State Department, that "relief work here [Aleppo] supports 1,350 orphans, who are only a portion of the destitute children now in the city."[151] The council also supported several of these orphanages, including institutions that did not operate under the Apostolic Church's umbrella. Its ledgers record significant sums transferred or loaned for food purchases beginning in August 1915.[152] In the meantime, Cemal Pasha continued to protect the children's homes. Şükrü Bey did not seem to be interested in causing trouble at this point either. In November 1915, he visited at least one such orphanage and recognized it as an established institution.[153] Ultimately, the Aleppo Armenian orphanages that survived the war stand as perhaps the most compelling case for the role personal connections with Ottoman and German officials played in saving lives during the Armenian genocide. None of these institutions would have remained open, let alone expand, without interventions on the local and regional level by well-connected German officers and diplomats and Ottoman officials.

Not all children were in orphanages. Hundreds roamed the streets fending for themselves—stealing, begging, and collecting food from garbage dumps. One such example was Nshan, an Armenian boy from Diyarbakir, barely twelve, who with a few other boys monopolized the dumpster of Hotel Baron, attacking anyone who dared approach it. Nshan, his gang, and a street dog that helped them guard the refuse huddled together in a corner of the city at night and lived off the dumpster during the day until the end of the war.[154] The voices of children like Nshan, to quote Holocaust scholar Debórah Dwork, are "conspicuously, glaringly, and screamingly silently absent" in our histories of genocide.[155] This absence is even more glaring in Ottoman historiography, where orphans and destitute children are "habitually ignored, and essentially invisible and voiceless actors."[156] The same can be said about Armenian genocide scholarship.

Cemal Pasha: A Reappraisal

"The Armenian world seemed to consider Cemal Pasha as a godsend," wrote Turkish nationalist and feminist Halide Edib in her memoir.[157] Indeed, many survivor accounts portray Cemal as more humane than, or even the antithesis of, his fellow triumvirs Talaat and Enver. The CUP leadership in Istanbul saw the concentration of Armenians along the railroad as a machination by Cemal or a favor to Armenians, argues resistance network member Charek. He notes that in the region under his control, Cemal had successfully aligned commanders and officers with his interests and, sometimes, in opposition to Istanbul. He had also galvanized "strong personalities who held important positions in the civilian administration, and who were dissatisfied with the Ittihad Party's [CUP] dominion." The very fact that this was a dominant impression among Armenian intellectuals and leaders who had close contacts and friendships with these officials points to success in Cemal's part in, to put it bluntly, playing both sides. Charek portrays Cemal as an unflinching resister of the CUP's eliminationist policies. "Thanks to this reality, the crimes against Armenians remained limited to the neutralization or deportation of important individuals, police brutality, and robberies."[158] But not all shared that opinion. An Armenian group that set out to avenge the genocide by killing its key perpetrators assassinated Cemal in 1922.[159]

The division among historians is also significant. Some historians suggest that Cemal resisted the genocide following an "at least partly independent strategy," while others argue that Cemal adhered to "a certain military rationale that consisted in profiting from the Armenian deportees' labor-power before liquidating them."[160] Scholars Raymond Kévorkian and Donald Bloxham attribute his treatment of the Armenians—less harsh than his colleagues'—to political ambitions in the region and a secret desire to establish a separate state in Syria under his leadership with the Allies' blessing.[161] Historian Fuat Dündar and sociologist Fatma Müge Göçek posit that he aimed to offset Arab influence in the region, the latter arguing that ten accounts she consulted portrayed Cemal as "a significant figure negotiating the safety of the Armenian deportees, most who survived ended up in his province."[162] Historian M. Talha Çiçek argued that Cemal's seemingly independent policies in the Fourth Army region must not be confused with readiness to revolt against his fellow leaders. He also dismissed the argument on counterbalancing Arabs, pointing to the relatively small number of Armenians settled in Syria.[163] On the other end of the spectrum, historian Ümit Kurt argues that "Cemal's perception of the Armenian 'Question' was not so very different from the general stance of the CUP, and thus that of Talaat and Enver."[164] Whatever Cemal's motives, his actions clearly set him apart from those of his fellow triumvirs and merit closer examination.

Rather than pegging Cemal as a perpetrator or a humanitarian, the social network analysis I offer allows for the possibility of both. Cemal had cultivated relationships with key Armenian community leaders and notables throughout his career, particularly while serving as governor of Adana for two years beginning in August 1909.[165] These relationships became stronger at least in part due to their expediency when Cemal assumed supreme civilian and military powers in Syria during World War I. As we saw, the commander of the Fourth Army needed the support and services of Armenian notables, particularly those of Dr. Altounyan and the Mazloumian bothers. Cemal was also an advocate of using Armenian deportee labor to advance the war effort, anchoring hundreds of Armenian women in Aleppo to work in military factories and recruiting thousands of men to labor along military supply lines and thus avoid the death fields.[166]

His pragmatism led him to be opposed, at least intellectually, to extermination, although he generally retreated when Talaat pushed back on policies regarding

Armenians. He was an advocate, instead, of killing the Armenian to save the man, to borrow the words Capt. Richard H. Pratt used for Native Americans.[167] He initiated and aggressively implemented policies designed to destroy the cultural fabric of Armenian communities by undermining the religious institutions, banning Armenian education, and encouraging Islamization, arguing that it allows Armenians to save their skin. When Bishop Kiud Mkhitarian, the representative of Catholicos Khabayan, met with Cemal in Damascus in October 1916 and complained about forced-Islamization policies being enacted upon the surviving fragments of the Armenian nation, Cemal fired back: "I look at this matter *philantropiquement.* To keep themselves alive until the end of the war, let this wretched people become Muslim if need be, become Jewish if need be, become *gyavoor* [infidel] if need be, even become monkeys if need be. . . . Do you understand? Now go tell this to your Catholicos!"[168]

While Cemal maintained good relations with key figures in the Aleppo Armenian community, his policies often proved detrimental to tens of thousands of deportees arriving in the city. The most deleterious were decisions made in meetings he presided over in October and November 1915, which received the central government's seal of approval.[169] These include Cemal's ten-point decree for disease control, the first point of which stipulated that all deportees staying in the city be deported within five days to regions designated for them. His handling of the situation in Damascus, however, was a different story. While the majority of deportees arriving in Ottoman Syria were concentrated in Aleppo Province and eventually along the lower Euphrates and in Ras ul-Ain, several thousand others were deported along the Damascus–Hauran route. Cemal Pasha formed a committee in March 1916 to assist in the settlement of Armenians in this area, comprised of Syrian dignitary Hüseyin Kazım Kadri Bey, military doctor Akif Şakir, a former governor, and according to the German consul in Damascus, the deputy governor of Damascus. The German consul reported in May 1916 that the head of the committee, Hüseyin Kazım, "who is generally held in high esteem," confided in him that he planned on resigning, "because he was no longer able to work. Not only were his measures not carried out, but the authorities were doing exactly the opposite." He believed that the authorities were not serious about assisting the deportees in Syria, "and was even afraid that they were to be systematically exterminated." Hüseyin Kazım indeed resigned. His replacement was no less helpless.[170]

As news of massacres of Armenians spread, German officials privately expressed concern to Ottoman officials about the detrimental effect of these reports on war propaganda,[171] and Cemal played a key role in covering up and denying these atrocities. He banned photographing deportees. Rössler reported to his superiors:

> Djemal Pasha issued a strict ban on photographing the exiles. In his report, a copy of which I obediently enclose and which he gave me to be used in strict confidence, he ordered that, to avoid punishment, all of the Baghdad Railway's engineers are to hand over the prints, plates, and films which they have. Photographing Armenians is to be considered the same as taking photographs of theatres of war without permission.[172]

When shoals of corpses began to drift down the Euphrates, eliciting concern among diplomats and horror among locals, Cemal Pasha sent a telegram to Diyarbakir governor Dr. Mehmed Reşid (14 July 1915) instructing "that the bodies carried downstream by the Euphrates should not be left exposed, but should be [pulled from the river and] buried in the districts in which they are found."[173] (Clearly, hygiene was not his only concern here.) Cemal also prepared and showcased collections of documents and decrees he had issued to safeguard Armenian deportees. "I was given the files containing the orders issued by Djemal Pasha himself regarding the treatment of the Armenians," wrote the head of the German Information Service for the Orient, Baron Max von Oppenheim, noting that he advised Cemal to publish these and other documents obtained from Istanbul "at an opportune moment so that Turkey can take timely steps against inevitable accusations."[174]

Conveniently, Cemal blamed Talaat for some decisions that were detrimental to deportees, while taking credit for others that portrayed him in a positive light, even when he was following orders from the center.[175] After giving an order to ban American and German aid to Armenian deportees in spring 1916, Cemal told German ambassador Paul Wolff Metternich "*in confidence* [emphasis added] that he personally would like to relieve the lot of the Armenians within the scope of his possibilities, but that he had received strict orders from Istanbul to prevent any German and American participation in assistance for the Armenians."[176] But Cemal's solutions were not always less radical than Talaat's. Aleppo governor Bekir Sami cabled Talaat in August 1915 asking for guidance, as Cemal had ordered the deportation of Armenians of all denominations without exception. Sami cited an earlier order from the Ministry of Interior about the exemption of Protestant Armenians from deportation.[177] Deportees, of course, knew nothing about these discussions.

In the words of one of his own top officers, Ali Fuad Erden, "Cemal Pasha loved being loved by the people. He loved popularity."[178] He thus cultivated an image of a humanitarian, which seemed credible for many deportees, who were led to believe Cemal was helping them despite Talaat's orders, even when that wasn't the case.[179] German officials did not conceal the fact that they saw through Cemal's strategy of denying the implementation of anti-Armenian policies when he could, blaming it on the center when he could not, and occasionally resorting to, in the words of the German consul in Damascus, Dr. Julius Loytved Hardegg, "a politically clever measure" to reinforce his image as a defender of Armenians.[180] Through his efforts to conceal the annihilation of Armenians by showcasing a good deed here and a good deed there, and by employing deportee labor to advance his military plans and packaging the policy as "helping Armenians," Cemal emerged as one of the first effective deniers of the Armenian genocide. "The deportees in the [fourth] army region were settled in cities, towns, and villages. No one was sent to the desert, and no one's nose bled," asserted Ali Fuad Erden.[181] Although this may be true to a certain extent in regions like Damascus and Hauran, for the majority of deportees caught in the triangle between Aleppo, Ras ul-Ain, and Der Zor, all under the jurisdiction of the Fourth Army, this statement is patently false. Yet to this day, Cemal is a favorite of scholars who deny the genocide. Indeed, in his 2009 book on Cemal, Turkish historian Hikmet Özdemir has argued that the effort of the Fourth Army is one of the first such humanitarian interventions of the twentieth century.[182]

Ultimately, although he disagreed with Talaat on a number of policies and approaches regarding Armenians, Cemal was far from waging "regional resistance," as Hilmar Kaiser puts it, against the center. The complexities and the inconsistencies in his treatment of the Armenians point to the importance of avoiding labels like *génocidaire* or a resister to genocide. Cemal distinguished individual Armenians with whom he had cultivated relationships from Armenians as a group. For the first group, his actions sometimes were inconsistent with those coming from the center, while for the second he was, by and large, a believer in and a willing executioner of Istanbul's policies—and a direct participant in the molding of those policies.

PART TWO

From the City to the Desert

CHAPTER THREE

Wartime Civilian Internment

Concentration Camps in Ottoman Syria

> Send us to hell. Send us to hell again.
> You made us know it, alas, all too well.
> Save paradise for Turks. Send us to hell.
>
> —Vahan Tekeyan, 1917, translated by
> Gerald Papasian and John Papasian

When Republican Senator Henry Cabot Lodge compared the fate of Cubans to those of Armenians during a debate in the U.S. Senate in February 1896, he was not referring to concentration camps Cuba's colonial governor Valeriano Weyler had just "invented."[1] The senator from Massachusetts was blasting British Prime Minister Lord Salisbury's response to the 1894–1896 massacres of Armenians in the Ottoman Empire, and demanding that the United States, in its own backyard, take "more positive action" against the Spanish Empire's excesses. Lodge drew a chilling parallel:

> There, in Cuba, is useless bloodshed, brutality, destruction of life and property, all the horrors that can accompany a savage war which is not submitted to the rules

of civilized warfare. Is our civilization to break down as the civilization of Western Europe has broken down before Armenia?[2]

The speech came as General Weyler had just announced his policy of "reconcentration." Almost two decades later, while the Armenians were being forced out of their ancestral towns and toward the Syrian desert, the concentration camp Weyler conceived arrived in the Ottoman Empire, after having made several stops around the globe.

"In a field that rain has turned into a pond, thousands of tents are set on the mud and waterholes. By the tents lie dead and dying people, so many that undertakers the authorities appointed from the camp population can hardly keep up," wrote Father Dajad Arslanian after the Great War, describing his arrival in the Bab concentration camp, northeast of Aleppo (modern-day Syria), in November 1915.[3] Father Arslanian was one of hundreds of thousands of Ottoman Armenians interned in concentration camps set up by the Young Turk leadership during World War I. Although he survived, most who went through the camp system died of starvation, disease, exposure, and violence. And while the Armenian genocide has received rigorous scholarly examination internationally over the past two decades, it has only recently been linked to the wartime internment of civilians. In this chapter, I address this lacuna in the historiography, situating the deportation and destruction of Armenians in Ottoman Syria within the global history of internment. Providing an overview of the structure, administration, and life in concentration camps based on Armenian accounts, Ottoman archives, and Western diplomatic records,[4] I argue that this glaring manifestation of total war—one directed toward the empire's very own Armenian subjects—constitutes an important moment of transition in the use of internment as a weapon of annihilation.

Genesis

The forcible concentration of civilians in camps or fortified zones was invented as a military practice in the late nineteenth century, becoming a feature of highly destructive and asymmetric colonial wars fought by the Spanish in Cuba, the British in South Africa, and the Americans in the Philippines.[5] These early cases exhibited a two-pronged counterinsurgency strategy: the removal of civilians from areas of conflict and their internment in camps and fortified zones; and the use of scorched-earth tactics, depriving fighters of their support base, shelter, and means of subsistence, and facilitating the brutal suppression of insurgencies. Scholars also emphasize that imitation was central to the global proliferation of concentration camps in this period.[6] As sociologist Jonathan Hyslop has argued: "The concentration camp arose as the response of new, professionalized military cultures to the challenge of guerilla warfare. The instrumental logic of violence led to the coercive and callous reorganization of civilians on a mass scale, as a means of containing and controlling subject populations."[7] Yet despite the heavy toll on civilians, the intention was not to destroy the interned population, but to suppress uprisings.[8] A further motive was collective punishment of the ethnic group or tribe to which the insurgents belonged.[9]

A threshold was crossed when the German army established concentration camps in German South-West Africa (GSWA, modern-day Namibia) during its genocidal campaigns against the Herero and Nama in 1904–1907. The purpose here was not to defeat tribal insurgencies, which had been quelled when these camps were established. Instead, the aim was control of "suspect" groups, exploitation of labor, and destruction of lives.[10] Thousands died of deprivation, disease, and deliberate acts of violence, or were worked to death in these camps.

Historian Benjamin Madley sees the Herero and Nama genocides as a "crucial precursor" to the Holocaust, and the concentration camps as a "rough template for the Nazi camps."[11] Other historians categorically oppose this notion. Thomas Kühne argues that "the idea of a special German genocidal path is flawed, to say the least. Anti-miscegenation laws, mass death in concentration camps and the annihilation of peoples did not define German peculiarities but commonalities of European colonialism."[12] In his comprehensive study of the Nazi camps, Nikolaus Wachsmann, too, is dismissive: "Any attempts to draw a direct line to Dachau or Auschwitz are unconvincing."[13] Indeed, the line is not direct, but a growing body of scholarship traces continuities. With the camps for the Herero and Nama in GSWA, a precedent had been set for the *Konzentrationslager* as a weapon of total war and genocide, one that was absent in earlier European cases.[14]

Just as concentration camps in GSWA differed from their colonial counterparts in Cuba, South Africa, and the Philippines, so did the Ottoman camps for Armenians from others that sprang up across the globe during the Great War. Internment camps incarcerating millions of POWs and hundreds of thousands of "enemy aliens" mushroomed in Europe and beyond when the war broke out. The growing literature on camps established in Great Britain, France, Russia, and

Germany, the United States, Canada, Australia, New Zealand, South Africa, and Japan stands testament to the globalization of the internment phenomenon.[15] "The implementation of those practices facilitated the shift to total war and also helped shape a new brutality displayed by European armies toward noncombatants during and after World War I," Klaus Mühlhahn argues.[16] And yet the most nefarious manifestation of this "new brutality" during the Great War, the one that most forcefully supports theories of war totalization, occurred in the Ottoman Empire and remains in the shadows.

True, the destruction of Ottoman Armenians now features in many studies of the Great War, yet concentration camps set up during this genocide are rarely explored in the literature.[17] Scholars of World War I and civilian internment are hardly to blame for this glaring oversight. Armenian genocide scholarship itself has only recently started exploring the network of concentration camps where deportees were interned. Indeed, apart from a survey of these camps by historian Raymond Kévorkian in his landmark history of the Armenian genocide, and a number of articles and encyclopedia entries by the present author, one is hard-pressed to find any scholarly work on the topic.[18]

While the concentration camps established during the Armenian genocide can be placed along a continuum of imperial military extremism and wartime totalization, they also drew much from a centuries-old Ottoman experience of demographic engineering. John Keegan, for example, argued that the genocide was a byproduct of Ottoman imperial policy more than a policy born out of the Great War. He writes,

> Above all, the war imposed on the civilian populations almost none of the deliberate disruption and atrocity that was to be a feature of the Second [World War]. Except in Serbia and, at the outset, in Belgium, communities were not forced to leave their homes, land and peaceful occupations; except in Turkish Armenia, no population was subjected to genocide; and, awful though the Ottoman government's treatment of its Armenian subjects was, the forced marches organized to do them to death belong more properly to the history of Ottoman imperial policy than to that of the war itself.[19]

It is indeed important to underline the centuries-old Ottoman policies of demographic engineering, but without divorcing the internment and destruction of Armenians from the influence of European military culture on the Ottoman Turkish leadership and the context of the First World War.

Ottoman Trajectories of Civilian Internment

As the Ottoman Empire expanded from the fourteenth to the sixteenth centuries, and the central authorities tried to consolidate their gains, control the newly acquired territories, and develop trade and agriculture, deportation and settlement became an important component of their policies.[20] Historian Nesim Şeker discerns three phases of demographic engineering by the Ottomans: the consolidation effort (of the sixteenth to the eighteenth century), the settlement policies targeting Muslim refugees from the Balkans and the Caucasus in the late nineteenth century, and the deportation and settlement policies enacted during World War I.[21] The latter two phases were intimately connected. As Erik-Jan Zürcher has observed, the Muslim refugees driven out of the border regions where southeastern Europe and Tsarist Russia met western Asia "strongly identified with the Islamic empire and this was to prove significant as their arrival in the empire also more or less coincided with the emergence of separatist nationalism among the Christian communities of the [Ottoman] empire." Here, Zürcher had in mind "the collision between the two types of community—Muslim refugees and Christian nationalists," for example in Bosnia-Herzegovina and Bulgaria.[22] Confronted with a great wave of refugees, the Ottoman authorities gained experience handling deportations, camps, epidemics, and settling refugees in new environments. Soon, World War I provided the cover that the leadership of the ruling Committee of Union and Progress (CUP) needed to expel the empire's Christian population, freeing up space to settle Muslim refugees in their villages and neighborhoods.[23] The systematic nature of the Ottoman Armenian deportations, often executed with "mathematical accuracy," points to the fulfillment of a broader CUP plan of social and economic Turkification, beyond purported measures to ensure military security in border regions.[24] In this context, camps that produced death, sexual slavery, and sometimes labor were subsumed as modern tools in the Ottoman tradition of demographic engineering.

The Armenian deportees who survived the terrible journey and massacres along the route arrived in Ottoman Syria from the north or northeast, passing through a series of hastily erected rest areas and transit camps, before being interned in concentration camps near Aleppo, in Ras ul-Ain, and along the lower Euphrates, from Meskeneh to Der Zor. Although exact figures are impossible to ascertain without access to official Ottoman documents,[25] around four hundred thousand Armenians were interned for months in one or more of these camps. Most perished from starvation and disease, or were later massacred in the desert of Der Zor in the summer of 1916.[26]

On Paper and in Practice

Ottoman officials charted the deportation to the regions of Urfa, Zor, and Aleppo in a guideline (*talimatname*),[27] which scrupulously laid out the administrative structure and command chain for the transit and settlement network. It also provided the rest and settlement sites with functionaries who were responsible for deportation, storage, and distribution of supplies; detailed salary ranges for officials; outlined the necessity and the modes of ensuring deportees' comfort and security, with particular attention to women, children, and the sick; and called for temporary shelter (tents), long-term housing, cultivable land, livestock, and assistance for the poor. In painstaking detail, the ordinance outlined procurement and distribution processes (from securing flour in each locale to "immediately" establishing bakeries and producing bread) in all the transit and settlement areas.

The ordinance was a far cry from what unfolded on the ground, where deprivation, exposure, abuse, and danger to life and limb were pervasive, and where settlement was a euphemism for incarcerating hundreds of thousands of Armenians in concentration camps in the desert with paltry, if any, food rations and no means of self-sustenance. Describing the camps he witnessed between Meskeneh and Der Zor, Auguste Bernau, a German employee who served as Aleppo agent of the American Vacuum Oil Company, wrote: "'Camp' is saying a lot, because the majority of this wretched people . . . are left in the open air like cattle, without shelter, almost without clothing, are barely supported by a completely insufficient diet."[28] Even when the authorities did distribute bread to deportees (mostly in cities like Aleppo and Rakka), a starvation ration was set, distribution was often discontinued for weeks or stopped outright, and the process was plagued by corruption. As Bernau observed: "The Administration which took on itself to lead them through the desert does not care about feeding them. It even seems that it may be a principle of [the] government to let them die of hunger. A massacre . . . would have been more humane."[29]

The American and German consuls in Aleppo forwarded Bernau's report to their superiors in September 1916. Passages from the report appeared in newspapers in Europe and the United States. The *New York Times* published segments of Bernau's report anonymously, noting that it is prepared by an "'eyewitness,' whose character and standing are vouched for by the eminent men of this country."[30] This was not, however, the first time the newspaper of record reported on "prison camps" for Armenian deportees in Ottoman Syria.[31]

Control of Movement

Concentration and transit camps were close enough to towns or outposts with telegraphs to ensure Ottoman administrative control. The Bab camp in Aleppo Province, for instance, was twenty minutes from the town of the same name, while the Meskeneh camp, situated at the great bend of the southern Euphrates, had a telegram center nearby.[32] Although most camps in Ottoman Syria were not surrounded by barbed wire or any other forms of physical confinement, a series of measures prevented escape. Roads and bridges nearby were guarded, and gendarmes and camp guards made sure deportees did not leave the premises. Most duties inside the camps were typically entrusted to Armenian *bekcis* (guards), while gendarmes guarded the perimeters. Like the kapos employed by the SS as "auxiliaries of terror" in Nazi camps, the *bekcis* were expected to control and intimidate the other prisoners in return for certain privileges.[33] Moreover, camps were often in desert areas, bandits roamed freely, and locals were instructed to turn in escaped deportees wandering into their towns and villages.[34] For a brief period in Bab, a permit and, inevitably, bribes were necessary to go to town to purchase food, visit the post office, or attend to bureaucratic matters. With the spread of typhus in the camp, the authorities blocked the deportees' access to the city in the autumn of 1915.

Still, some managed to exit camps secretly and return with supplies or abscond to Aleppo and disappear into the fabric of the metropolis. Gurji Ananian from Marash, for example, arrived in Meskeneh in the summer of 1915 and escaped from the camp twice, trying to return to Aleppo. His first attempt, with thirty-four other inmates, turned into a week-long ordeal during which they were robbed twice by Arabs in the desert, captured by gendarmes, and dragged back to Meskeneh. He succeeded in his second attempt and made it to Aleppo after being beaten, harassed, and nearly buried alive by villagers along the way.[35]

The camps were semiporous, with locals generally allowed to enter to sell products, purchase children, or steal and abduct prisoners during night raids, with gendarmes often passively observing or aiding and abetting the perpetrators in return for a share of the booty. Accounts describe, for instance, how butchers came to the Bab camp to sell meat, and sometimes distributed usually discarded offal to needy deportees, but after some time, they started selling that too.[36] Those who managed to make forays into the city contributed to a camp economy that was otherwise tightly controlled by the guards and the city's merchants who had full control over prices of goods.

Sexual Violence

Sexual violence and slavery were rampant. According to a German eyewitness account, in the Ras ul-Ain concentration camp, "the Circassians and Arabs from Ras ul-Ain took the prettiest girls home with them. . . . The policemen carried on a flourishing trade with the girls. Against payment of a few Medjidies, anyone could take a girl of his choice either for a short while or forever."[37] Not all perpetrators remained anonymous. For instance, Kör Hüseyin, a camp official, raped many women at the Karlık transit camp near Aleppo.[38] Survivor Setrag G. Matossian, who was in Karlık in late June/early July 1916, wrote a few weeks after the 1918 armistice about the horrors committed by Kör Hüseyin: "As 10 p.m. approached, deportation director [*sevkiyat muduru*] Hüseyin bey's and his assistant Zeynel Çavuş's men, lamps in hand, would walk toward the beautiful girls they had selected during the day as appropriate to satisfy the cruelties of the bey and his assistant, and wake them up one by one. They were forcibly dragged to the bey's tent and released after a few hours."[39]

More than thirty Armenian girls from Sivas were forcibly married to locals, according to survivor Yeranuhi Simonian.[40] Forced marriage was not the worst that could happen. In the cover of darkness, Bedouins attacked and raped with the tacit agreement of guards. "Every night there was yelling and screaming at the camp. . . . I saw with my own eyes the rape of little girls," Simonian noted in her memoir.[41] According to Walter Rössler, a woman was raped by a group of eight men. She tried to commit suicide by throwing herself on a railway line as a train approached. A German engineer saved her and brought her to Aleppo.[42] "The girls, often even the young girls . . . have been kidnapped all along the route of the deportations, sometimes violated and sold, if not killed by the gendarmes who drove the sad caravans," observed Auguste Bernau.[43]

Many children forcibly taken by locals or sold by destitute deportees trying to save their youngsters from death resisted their new "owners" in any way they could.[44] Stepan G. Aghazarian was in his teens when he was deported from his hometown Marash and abducted in Ras ul-Ain, "a hell-hole in the middle of the Syrian desert," and taken to a nearby village:

> I soon found that in that same Bedouin village there were about a dozen Armenian girls, ten to twelve years of age, who had been abducted by Arabs. The Arabs complained that these girls had refused to eat and would not talk to their "masters." My new "father" . . . asked me to talk to [the girls] and convince them to cooperate with the Arabs and give nobody any trouble. He said somberly that if they were obedient, they would more than likely not be killed. So I went to the sullen girls and, as I had been asked to do, sat down and talked to them. They finally gave me their word that they would cooperate.[45]

Sexual violence during the Armenian genocide has been the subject of increased scholarly attention in recent years, commensurate with growing historiography examining rape as a tool of genocide and a "life force atrocity."[46] In concentration camps and along deportation routes, the violation of women also served as a perverted manifestation of male bonding through control over the bodies of victims. It also took place within a broader context that encouraged sexual violence (and looting) to incentivize popular participation in the genocide.[47] Rapists like Kör Hüseyin and abductors of women like Zeynel Çavuş's thugs were part of an elaborate economy of sexual exploitation across the Ottoman Empire that was created in an environment of impunity and fueled by individual initiative, peer dynamics, and local power brokers.

Liquidation

The liquidation of camps occurred in two distinct phases. The camps around Aleppo were shut down beginning in the winter of 1915, and the deportees were driven either toward Ras ul-Ain or the lower Euphrates, while the camps in Ras ul-Ain and along the river were emptied starting in the spring of 1916, when the survivors were marched to Der Zor. The emptying of the Dipsi camp illustrates this process. In late April 1916, some twenty gendarmes were dispatched from Meskeneh to liquidate Dipsi. Considering the condition of most prisoners, emptying the camp and sending everyone downstream was not easy. The gendarmes set fire to tents and assaulted deportees to force them to move.

While in GSWA the shutting down of camps signaled an end of the genocidal violence against the Herero and Nama, the liquidation of the Ottoman camps was followed by further massacres. Most of the deportees who survived the camp system perished in two waves of violence in Ras ul-Ain (March 1916) and Der Zor (in the summer and fall of 1916). Estimates vary, but conservative figures indicate some thirty thousand were killed in the former, and up to two hundred thousand in the latter. Thousands of others survived primarily through the efforts of the humanitarian resistance network, while thousands more, mostly women and children, were saved from the carnage by tribesmen in the region who forced them to become their wives, workers, and sex slaves.

Many survivors wrote about their camp experience in newspaper articles and memoirs published in the years following the genocide, yet it took almost a century for the first scholarly examinations of their internment to appear. The massacres—and sporadic instances of armed resistance—overwhelmed the accounts, while scholarship focused on dispossession, deportation, death, and denial. As a result, periods between massacres were relegated to footnotes. In his *History of the Armenian Genocide*, Vahakn N. Dadrian, the pioneer of Armenian genocide studies, wrote that for survivors arriving in Syria the "authorities had created a string of waystations in the desert from which they were regularly dispatched to their ultimate death by a variety of methods."[48] A footnote then directed the reader to an article that, compelling as it is in other respects, says little about the camp system and what we refer to today as the second phase of the genocide.

Yet, as I demonstrate in this book, the camp system was an integral part of the genocidal process. While it is true that neither mass murder nor heroic acts of armed resistance occurred in these camps, deprivation and exposure that destroyed life constituted an extermination policy, and the humanitarian resistance of the Armenians was staged in reaction to it. The concentration camps in Ottoman Syria during World War I bridged colonial and modern histories of internment and comprised the deadliest pre-Holocaust loci for civilians imprisoned in wartime. The importance of addressing the Ottoman camp system, and the need for comparative research on the function and trajectory of internment in the late nineteenth and early twentieth centuries, cannot be overstated.

"One counts by the hundreds the anonymous burial mounds . . . [for] these victims of a barbarism without name," wrote Bernau on his journey through Meskeneh and Der Zor in 1916.[49] The annihilation of the European Jewry was ongoing when Raphael Lemkin coined the term genocide in 1943–1944, giving the barbarism Bernau refers to a name. But the Holocaust was not the first such crime, the KL system was not its first locus, and the line from GSWA to Auschwitz was not direct after all. It passed through Ottoman Turkey.

CHAPTER FOUR

Gateways to the Desert

The Sebil, Karlık, and Bab Camps

> Every morning, the ominous cries of gendarmes and guards were heard: "Kalkın, yıkın, cıkın!" (Get up! Tear down [the tents]! Get out!).
>
> —Yervant Odian

In their effort to round up deportees in Aleppo and send them away, the police and gendarmerie initially focused on people gathered in large groups at schools, churches, and *khans*. Afterwards, they mounted door-to-door search operations, often at night, to track down, arrest, and deport the thousands of people who were in hiding in the city. These arrests would occur "with the complicity of many Armenian spies, particularly three brothers from Hajin," explained chronicler Aram Andonian.[1] Deportee registration ledgers mandated by the authorities facilitated rounding up victims in private homes where they had found refuge.[2]

Some managed to make themselves useful to the Ottoman military, thereby securing permission to stay in the city or move to another. "One day I observed the police arresting and deporting to the desert any Armenian young man they could find in the city. I was terribly worried.... I heard that the Turks were in need of dentists. I went to the authorities and they immediately inducted me into the Turkish army," wrote survivor Nathan Koomrian years later. He was quickly deployed to Damascus as a dentist for the military.[3] But most Armenians were not able to anchor themselves in the city. Father Dajad Arslanian, who was in Aleppo at the time, described the environment of terror:

> Everyone would shudder upon hearing of *Sevkiyat* [dispatch, deportation], as it was the most horrific and destructive action [for the deportees]. Not being exempt from it in Aleppo either, everyone tried to hide in houses and even in cellars. That way, they remained free for some time.
>
> But the police did not remain idle. They went into the hiding places in homes, dragged them out, and took them to the police station, or a building called Karlik khan. Sometimes, they let them go after receiving huge bribes. Many paid weekly or monthly sums to the police station in their neighborhood and thus managed to remain in their hiding place for months.[4]

Survivor Kevork Soultanian corroborates Father Dajad's account. Deported from Eskişehir, the Soultanians arrived in Aleppo and were dispatched to Karlık. One of their companions, Nechan Kehyeyan, had a brother in Aleppo named Garabed, who intervened and brought them to the city. After spending a week in Garabed's house, the Soultanians rented an apartment from a Christian Arab and tried to stay out of sight but were found by the police and interrogated. With another intervention from Garabed, and another bribe, they were allowed to stay. But the police came back every week, and only left after picking up five to ten *mecidiye* on every occasion.[5] This seems to have been the going rate to remain in the city or secure entry into it. When Yeranuhi Simonian arrived in Aleppo in March 1916, her well-connected brother-in-law told her that deportees were not allowed in the city and were sent to Karlık. Once they had reached the camp, he promised to find ways of saving her. She had spent a week under tents in the rainy weather when her brother-in-law returned, accompanied by her sister, whom she had not seen for fifteen years:

> As my sister, with tears in her eyes, rushed towards me to embrace me, I pushed her away and withdrew. Countless fleas were swarming on my clothes. Deprived of water and soap for months, my body had become a nest for microbes. Finally, my brother-in-law counted ten gold coins into the hand of the officer, then they

took me directly to the bath and, throwing away my clothes and shoes, dressed me in new clothing.[6]

Caught in the maelstrom of Karlık, survivor Yeghishe Hazarabedian's family "decided that we would move out of our present quarters and lose ourselves in other sections of the city." They moved into a small house with the family of Hovsep Dishchekenian, who resided in a neighborhood where the district police chief, Ahmet Efendi, was also from Marash. Within weeks, however, an attempt to enlist Talaat Pasha's support to remain in Aleppo until the end of the war failed—thanks, in part, to Ahmet Efendi himself—and the two families "were taken by ox-cart, under heavy guard, to the nearby open field called Garluk. From there, we were sent by wagons, which we had to hire, to the town of Meskeneh."[7] Hazarabedian's account of the intervention is corroborated by central government telegrams and Ottoman official Naim Efendi's account. Hazarabedian explained: "The Ministry of the Interior wired the governor of Aleppo to the effect that the Hazarabedian and Dishchekenian families were to be allowed to remain in Aleppo until the war ended."[8] Naim Efendi, on the receiving end of the telegram, described how, despite the telegram from the Interior Ministry demanding that specific families remain in Aleppo, the authorities deported them.[9] In the corresponding Ottoman document, we come across the names mentioned in Naim's document, alongside additional ones (also mentioned in Hazarabedian's account): Melkon Hazarabedian, Levon Amiralian, Hovsep Dishchekenian, Nshan and Santoukhd Bourounsouzian, Gostan and Hovan(nes) Varjabedians (all from Marash), Hana[?] Kurekjian (Aintab), and Toros Chaghlasian (Kilis).[10] Hazarabedian explains the circumstances of the intervention with Talaat thus: Dishchekenian's relative, Hagop Agha Khrlakian, a member of the Ottoman parliament, "has been able to get permits from Talaat Pasha . . . for all his relatives to remain in Aleppo for the duration of the war." So they approached Khrlakian's son Hovsep, who was also in Aleppo, who contacted his father, who in turn requested the exemption letter from Talaat.[11] Here too, Ottoman documents corroborate Khrlakian's intervention.[12] Although many deportees managed to secure documents that anchored them in Aleppo, the experience of the aforementioned families demonstrates the futility of the process, even when Talaat, who was "more than a primus inter pares" in the triumvirate that ran the empire, was the one who issued the order.[13]

During periods when the police swept the city for deportees, desperation drove those who did not have bribe money, connections, or a hideout to hole up in institutions sheltering children, thinking these would not be raided. Elmas Boyajian remembered the mayhem at Shirajian's orphanage with grief:

> Many sought refuge in the orphanage to escape for a few days the wrath of the government. Hunger and misery brought ruin, disease, and death. On one such occasion, those who came to the orphanage carried measles, and my son died [from it]. The crowds would pile up, and there was not enough water in the wells to do the laundry.[14]

Payladzou Captanian and her newborn, Tsavag, too sought refuge at the orphanage when the police raids intensified. They remained there for eight days, during which Tsavag contracted an eye infection, but recovered.[15] Despite the grave risks, Shirajian could not bring himself to refuse shelter to deportees desperate to avoid the desert. But sooner or later, the police dragged most of them to Karlık and Sebil, two transit camps on the outskirts of the city.

Transit Camps

Karlık stood on a hill twenty minutes by foot north of Aleppo, while Sebil was "a large plain . . . about one hour's walk from the city."[16] The deportees were dispatched to their destination from these transit camps.[17] "The entire line extending from Karlık to Der Zor was a nest of misery, a graveyard," noted deportation official Naim Efendi.[18] Jesse B. Jackson, who visited these camps on a weekly basis, described the horrendous conditions:

> The arriving deportees were collected principally in Karlukh . . . or in an encampment established along the railway tracks on the Southwest side of the city. In the latter named place the authorities had provided tents for a part of the people, but as the number usually exceeded 2,000 or 3,000, and the tents would not cover more than 500, the great majority were obliged to remain in the burning sun, and later in the season were exposed to the rains and snows; at Karlukh there was practically no shelter whatever, so that in their weakened condition the victims were added to each day, hundreds dying from disease and exposure.[19]

The humanitarian support network did its best to provide the deportees with warm meals in these camps before they departed for the unknown. "The Aleppo Armenians did what they could to remedy the dire situation of the deportees who were brought to the city and its environs," Andonian remembered. Fundraisers, clothing drives, and volunteer work were the order of the day in the city. "Outside the city, in the garden of Sebil and the heights of Karlık, numerous cauldrons were placed on huge tripods to prepare food for the deportees. Many brought clothing, underwear, bedsheets, and other indispensable items to them."[20] Jackson was one of the many. As the American consul reported, he "invariably distributed funds or bread to those in need" during his routine visits.[21] But by the fall of 1915, the arrival of large numbers of deportees and the authorities' crackdown on relief efforts plunged the camp into utter misery. Captanian reached Sebil when the camp had already descended into desolation. There were no cauldrons. "Some women had copper plates, converted stones into stove tops and were cooking food. Others had run out of money and . . . only ate bread, watching the fortunate ones cooking."[22]

Families were broken apart—some managed to stay in Aleppo, while others were dragged to Karlık. Survivor Manuel Kasuni, a deportee from Aintab who had arrived in the city in late summer of 1915, found work with local Armenian bakers and stayed, while his brother became a teacher at the German school and was redeported a month later with his family to Karlık. Walter Rössler intervened on their behalf, and they were eventually sent to Hauran instead of Der Zor.[23]

Well-to-do deportees and those with connections stood a better chance of remaining in Aleppo. Survivor Hagop Seropian's family left the transit camp of Katma (north of Aleppo) and arrived in Sebil hoping to gain access to the city. They were intercepted by the police who insisted that entry to Aleppo was strictly prohibited and ordered them to leave for Karlık. "We had heard that the Karlık camp was the entry-point to hell," Seropian wrote years later. The family had a lengthy discussion at the police station and, by bribing the head of police with five liras, were able to avoid Karlık; they were sent to the camp in Jemileh instead.[24] Survivor Hayganush Khubeserian from Talas managed to sneak onto a train to Aleppo and arrange for her relative Jirair Basmajian, who was a translator on the Baghdad Railway, to meet her and her family there. Basmajian told her at the Aleppo station that deportees were not allowed to enter the city proper and needed to go to the Karlık camp. "We will find a way later to save you from there," he said. Basmajian bribed officials with ten gold liras and arranged her family's return to the city.[25] Local authorities tried to implement deportation orders without missing opportunities for self-enrichment. This balancing act was not always successful. Rössler observed in late July 1915 that "the deportations have stopped in Aleppo because it seems that a conflict has broken out between the higher authorities over the fact that richer Armenians have succeeded in gaining exemption, whereas the poorer of them have been handed over to the police."[26] Most deportees were part of the latter group. They were redeported from Sebil and Karlık to Bab and then beyond. Hundreds entered the transit camps every day, and hundreds departed.[27]

New arrivals who did not have tents were taken in by compatriots and sometimes by complete strangers. Captanian found hundreds, mostly women, gathered at the camp without shelter. Noticing that a few families had made makeshift tents with rugs, she approached one and was welcomed in.[28] When Father Dajad arrived in the camp in late November 1915 "it was raining non-stop. Not having a tent, I was kindly invited into the tent of Mikayel Beylerian of Ovacik."[29] Even those who enjoyed the luxury of tents were neither warm nor dry. Made of flimsy cloth, unstable, often riddled with holes, these tents were only a meager improvement from sleeping in the open. "Rickety tents made out of thin, torn canvas were not good enough to protect the people inside from the harsh weather conditions," recounted survivor Odian, who was at the camp in December 1915.[30] Captanian, too, describes the devastation caused by two heavy rain showers in the few days she spent at the camp.[31]

Disease was ubiquitous. Captanian describes deportees in Sebil picking lice from their underwear, and a barber at the camp shaving the heads of elderly women who could only pay back with blessings.[32] Dysentery "committed horrible massacres" at the camp, and the dead were piled on garbage carts and taken away, remembers Odian.[33] Father Arslanian survived Karlık; other priests did not. Naim Efendi reported:

> A priest from Ankara was taken from the place he was staying in Cedide at eight o'clock in the night by Bab-ul-Farac Police Superintendant Fevzi Efendi and brought to Karlık, where he was shot and killed. He was buried in the Muslim cemetery in the area near the barracks.[34]

Some Aleppo urbanites exploited the abject poverty and suffering of the deportees. Women came to the camp in their carts and offered to buy children. Some among the neediest and those who held little hope for survival sold their children for the price of a kilogram of bread.[35] "In Sebil, thousands of Armenian boys and girls were sold to Arabs, Turks, and Jews from Aleppo. Children aged 7 to 10, particularly girls, were in demand," explained Odian.[36]

Sexual abuse was common in Sebil and Karlık. Chief among the perpetrators was camp official Kör Hüseyin, who raped many women at Karlık.[37] Mgrdich Bozouklian from Nevşehir was the head of the guards at the camp and Kör Hüseyin's enforcer. Bozouklian kept his privileged position by acting mercilessly towards his fellow Armenians and by singing (partly because Kör Hüseyin loved his voice).[38] When Major Aziz Bey, an Ottoman officer, fancied a twelve-year-old Armenian girl, Bozouklian made every effort to make her consent.[39] Failing, he abducted her and brought her to the major, who kept her as his slave for a year, until he was dispatched to Damascus and let her go.[40] According to Andonian, Bozouklian helped deportation functionaries at Karlık violate several other girls and women. When the Allies entered Aleppo, he escaped to Aintab, where his family had lived during the war.[41]

Bozouklian's case highlights the issue of collaboration with the perpetrators, an important yet understudied subtheme in the history of concentration camps during the Armenian genocide. Deportees viewed the Armenian camp guards with a profound loathing that permeates accounts and memoirs. They were "people in whose veins blood had dried up," and "aborted persons who were devoid of human and national feelings," writes Seropian.[42] Once they lost their sources of power—and many did as soon as they were redeported to the next camp—these collaborators were shunned and abused by deportees. Chroniclers made sure to mention their names when they prepared lists of perpetrators. In his memoir, Seropian names ten of "the most evil" of such collaborators in the camps.[43] In a notebook Andonian prepared after the war recording the names and criminal deeds of perpetrators, names of Armenian collaborators appeared alongside those of Turkish, Kurdish, Chechen, Circassian, and Arab officials. These included Hayg Boyajian and Hrant Mamigonian, both from Aleppo, who worked for the authorities as agents and denouncers; Garabed Momjian who abused his position and stole deportee aid; Avedis Kaselian from Hajin, "a very influential man in Meskeneh"; and Rev. Artin Khachadurian, who was part of relief committees throughout the war and, according to Andonian, enriched himself by stealing deportee relief money.[44]

Armenians collaborating with gendarmes were often ruthless as they helped organize departure from the transit camps of Sebil and Karlık. Artin Ketabgian of Kayseri, a teenager when he arrived in Sebil via Katma in late summer 1915, experienced the violence that accompanied redeportation to Bab:

> They put our carriage behind the hundreds of other carriages and told us to follow them. There were a few gendarmes and there was one gendarme who was riding a horse. I approached this gendarme. I told him, "We want to go to Hama; we will pay you whatever you want." This man was holding a whip in his hand and with it he hit me hard in the neck and I thought that my head was cut off. I started crying.[45]

Andonian described the transitory nature of the camp in Sebil around the same time (September 1915) thus: "Thousands of Armenians were under tents near Aleppo, in the deserted field called Sebil, waiting to hit the road. Every morning, the ominous cries of gendarmes and guards were heard: 'Kalkın, yıkın, cıkın!' (Get up! Tear down [the tents]! Get out!)."[46] The gendarmes pushed these deportees "on towards the desert beyond the reach of help, going from Aleppo first to Meskene, then to Hamam, Rakka, Sebha, Abou Harari, and finally to Deir-er-Zor and the surrounding villages," explained Jackson.[47]

The Bab Camp

After a brief period in the transit camps of Sebil or Karlık, most deportees forced out of Aleppo City in large numbers in fall 1915 were transported to Bab, southeast of the metropolis.[48] Bab is of pivotal importance in the history of the Armenian genocide. The primary gateway for redeportation to the desert, it was one of the largest concentration camps. More than a hundred thousand people were interned there during its operation, and tens of thousands were interned by the time the authorities closed it down. Already oversaturated with deportees arriving from many parts of the empire, Bab was sliding into utter misery when new waves of Armenians arrived there from Sebil and Karlık. Here, we shall examine survival and death in Bab from its inception in May–June 1915 until it was emptied in early 1916.

Arrival

One of the first camps to be established in Aleppo Province, Bab served as a destination for deportees from Zeytun and Hasanbeyli in May 1915.[49] Armenians from Dörtyol, Ocaklı, Ozerli, and Hajin joined them the following month. By 21

July, there were 1,466 deportees interned in Bab.[50] In these early months, the camp, which lay some twenty minutes by foot from the town of Bab, functioned as a transit site, as local officials expected to settle arriving deportees in nearby villages. Some well-to-do families even managed to settle in the town itself, and those at the camp were allowed free access to the town to secure goods and services. By summer 1915, it was evident that the Interior Ministry had no serious plans to settle deportees. Yet deportation of Bab inmates to concentration camps along the Euphrates proceeded slowly, as many people bribed officials in order to remain, and there was a steady stream of new arrivals. Thus, Bab morphed from a transit camp into a de facto concentration camp. With government orders to stop the entry of convoys into Aleppo City in September, new deportees poured into the camp. Bab soon devolved into a cesspool of typhus perched on a clay field of mass graves.

A first task of Aleppo's Armenian Apostolic Church Council for Refugees was to prepare reports on the number and situation of deportees arriving in the different districts and counties of Aleppo Province, in order to best meet their needs.[51] To this end, the council commissioned members of the clergy to visit these areas. Father Khachadur Boghigian was dispatched to Bab and Mumbuj, while Father Hovhannes Etmekjian was sent to Idlib, Riha, and Maarra in May 1915.[52] They submitted their assessments of each town, along with a complete list of deportees, on 24 May.[53] A month later, Father Khachadur was now sent to Idlib, Riha, and Maarra, while Father Sahag, a priest from Kilis, and pharmacist Iskender Efendi were dispatched to Bab, Mumbuj, and Der Zor, providing supplies and medical care.[54] An account that very likely describes their visit to Mumbuj states:

> In Manbij (Membij), a local Armenian priest accompanied by two parish board members, visited the refugees. They had two sacs of money that they distributed to the hungry and penniless people. It was like a miracle. . . . The priest handed seven gouroush (cents) to each one.[55]

These delegations' reports, often very detailed, provided the council with the information it needed to decide what action to take. Other community leaders from Aleppo, including the Catholicos himself,[56] visited the camps as well to check on the situation of the deportees, assess their needs, and try to lift their spirits. The Aleppo Armenian community leaders' visits to the camps in the early months of their operation were sanctioned by the local and regional authorities as their stated purpose was usually to provide spiritual guidance, and not distribute aid.

We can reconstruct the conditions in Bab and other camps in Aleppo Province in the early months of their operation from the reports these emissaries submitted to the council. According to Father Khachadur, Bab deportees' morale was high considering the circumstances, "although financial need is palpable" even as early as May 1915.[57] It was clear that the long-term prospects for settling the deportees in the area were not very promising. In an assessment of the living conditions in Bab, Father Sahag informed the council that the city, four hours northeast of Aleppo, "cannot match the other *kazas* [Idlib, Maarra, Jisr Shoughour] in agriculture. . . . Almost no mountainous structures. The air and water [quality] are average. There's not much to report on the local population, but the district governor was very well-intentioned towards us; he is a philosopher of a man. Craftsmen and farmers can live here, but not like they would in the aforementioned *kazas*."[58]

Prepared at a time when the council believed the deportees would be settled in towns and villages in the province, these reports seem to have missed the hostility toward the Armenian deportees by the population of the Bab area. "The understanding shown by the district government is praiseworthy, but the funds provided by the provincial authorities are only considered sufficient for a week or two, unless assistance continues regularly," explained Father Khachadur, noting that the district governor of Bab had himself raised fifty liras and delivered the money personally to the deportees.[59] After consulting with the deportees in Bab, Father Khachadur tasked two men, Setrak Bozoghluyan and Kevork Setian, with overseeing the distribution of aid and coordinating relations with the local authorities and the council, "to preempt discrimination and maintain harmony."[60] This was standard practice in camps as deportees tried to organize their daily lives. Camps accommodated Armenians from different corners of the Ottoman Empire, and a system of representation emerged as a necessity in order to minimize favoritism and friction as scarce resources were distributed and utilized. During these visits to the camps, the priest was generally joined by a doctor or pharmacist, who attended to the infirm and the elderly, vaccinated children against communicable diseases, and provided hygiene education.[61]

The council sent funds whenever possible: In the early weeks of its operation, it sent 1,891 *kuruş* to deportees from Hasanbeyli stationed in the Bab camp (25 May), and another 600 *kuruş* to an additional three hundred needy deportees stationed there (early June).[62] A few weeks later, an additional sum of ten Ottoman liras was sent to Bab with Father Sahag.[63] Funds were also distributed to deportees who had arrived in Aleppo City only to be redeported to other camps. Among such cases, the council allocated a total of 1,198 *kuruş* to 102 deportees who were being redeported from the city to the camp in Bab on 15 June.[64] In general, the council made sure those exiled from Aleppo City received some money, realizing that the farther from the city the deportees were dispatched, the more difficult it became for the network to effectively provide assistance.

Funds, food, medicines, and other supplies were generally sent to camps outside Aleppo City through members of the Armenian clergy, or other trusted individuals making the journey. The council covered the transportation expenses of its emissaries and diligently recorded these expenses in ledgers: transportation fees, porter fees, bribes—designated as "gifts" to local officials and police. As the government cracked down on relief efforts outside the city and such trips became more perilous, the council entrusted the difficult task of secretly entering camps to the skills of a few Armenians who often made the stopover in the cloak of darkness or disguised as Muslim or Jewish merchants. In many cases, lump sums were allocated to "needy deportees in Bab" in general, or specific sums to deportees from a particular town or village: "deportees from Hasanbeyli in Bab." The distribution process varied. In some cases, the emissary distributed the funds personally, while in others he or she handed the sum or goods to individuals assigned by the council or the deportees themselves. Here too, compatriotic ties mattered: Armenians from different areas sometimes insisted on having their own representatives handle the relief earmarked for them.[65]

The Aleppo Armenian community leadership was very responsive to the spiritual needs of the Bab deportees as a group and individually, sending deported priests who arrived in Aleppo to camps where a large number of their flock was interned. When Father Vahan arrived in Aleppo from Hajin for instance, he was sent to Bab and received a one lira monthly salary from the council.[66] Within days of his arrival, he sent a letter to the council on 28 June in which he appealed for help in providing medical assistance to a deportee girl with an eye infection. The girl was sent to Aleppo where she was treated at the council's expense.[67] Other individuals received the council's attention as well. Days after the very first columns arrived in Bab, a deportee from Zeytun who had fallen ill was brought to Aleppo and received financial and other assistance from the council.[68] With the arrival in Bab of thousands of new deportees from the eastern provinces of the empire in summer 1915, however, providing care to every deportee became impossible.

Life in the Camp

People did their best to organize life in the camp and to adapt to precarious conditions. The caravans arriving in Bab in May and June suffered few losses of human life, and families were by and large intact. However, the demographic makeup shifted abruptly in July and August, with the arrival of "thousands of widows, without a single adult male; they came from the regions of Armenia by the Munbuc [Mumbuj] road, in an appalling state, half naked," in the words of survivor Hovhannes Khacherian from Bardizag (Bahçecik).[69]

Despite their best efforts, the interned Armenians could not control health and hygiene. "Lice was inseparable from the deportees. Because no matter how much they tried to be clean, still it was impossible. Because with every *sevk* [deportation], the destruction of their tents contributed to the uncleanliness. The *memur*, the police, and the Armenian guards tossed everything (blankets, beds, and clothing) in the mud, and under such circumstances, expecting cleanliness was impossible," wrote Khacherian, who had arrived in Bab on 31 December 1915 and stayed until the camp was shut down.[70]

The camp began to spiral into squalor with the first fall rains. Erected on a field of clay, Bab was transformed into a swampland; the ground could not absorb the rain. In his memoirs, Hagop Seropian, who passed through Bab briefly on his way to the village of Mesudiye, recalled,

> We were barely two hundred to three hundred meters from the *khan* where we had stayed when the Armenian deportee camp appeared in front of our eyes in an endless field. The situation was indescribable. It had rained at night, turning the camp into a lake, the water reaching the poor people's knees, all their belongings drenched in the pool, as they, with no energy left inside them, were rendered motionless in the filth, swamps, hunger, and disease. . . . Under the tents that had collapsed from the night's rain and storm, thousands were unable to move, lying on their rags, in endless agony. No Red Cross, no help, no hope.[71]

Khacherian remembered waking up to see the camp covered in a thin blanket of snow one morning in February 1916. "This was the last thing the starving, naked, and sick wanted."[72]

Although there were still some people with money who could afford a decent subsistence, an overwhelming number of deportees was penniless. Many resorted to begging. "But begging now was like extracting water from rocks. No one gave money, because they knew that sooner or later they would be reduced to the same situation."[73] Gone were the days when the deportees adhered to strict hygienic measures. As bandits and thieves swarmed in the vicinity, deportees dared not venture far from the camp. The stench of excrement was unbearable. So was the miasma of unburied corpses. "Soon after ten corpses were removed, twenty others would fall," wrote Andonian after the war.[74] Typhus claimed dozens every day. Those who contracted the disease fought it in their tents or at a makeshift hospital, which seemed useless in a camp where hundreds had fallen ill. Survivor Verzhin Tengerian remembered, "There was a tent in Bab that was converted to a hospital. I had no energy to walk, but I got there crawling. I stayed there for many days, I got better, and then I was redeported to Der Zor."[75]

Cracking down on the humanitarian efforts out of Aleppo City in fall 1915, the authorities essentially severed the supply lines from the metropolis. Food grew even scarcer, and desperation drove thousands to eat whatever they could, including dead animals. According to Andonian, inmates scratched meat from the animal bones with rusted metal, "many times they fought over the meat, and ate without cooking. Those who found they could make fire to heat or burn the rotten piece of meat were considered lucky."[76]

Interactions with the Outside World

Although most camps in Ottoman Syria were not surrounded by barbed wire or any other tools of physical confinement, a series of measures prevented escape. Gendarmes, as well as camp guards—often Armenian deportees favored by the camp authorities—made sure the deportees did not leave the perimeters. But this was not even necessary. Bandits roamed around camps, often attacking at night; villagers were instructed to kill stray Armenians; and deportees were trapped between the interminable desert and the inaccessible city. No one could move without a permit.

Deportee life was thus restricted to the camp itself. Special permission and, inevitably, bribes were necessary to go to town to purchase food, visit the post office, or attend to bureaucratic matters. Thereafter, with the spread of typhus in the camp, the authorities blocked the deportees' access to the city in fall 1915. The Armenians alone had to die. But "life was impossible without access to Bab."[77] Merchants took advantage of the situation, bringing their products to the camp and selling them for double or triple the price. Sometimes, through connections or bribes, deportees secured *vesikas* allowing them to enter the city. But even then, gendarmes did not allow them to stay for long.[78] There were always exceptions. Creativity went a long way. When Hagop Arsenian of Ovacık arrived in the camp on 8 December 1915, "entrance to the actual city of Bab was totally forbidden to us" although he managed to "sneak to town" twice.[79] Those who managed to make forays into the city contributed to a camp economy that was otherwise tightly controlled by the guards and the city's merchants who set the prices of goods.

The movement of inmates in and out of Nazi slave-labor camps—and the underground economy that developed, in part, as a result—has been examined closely in Holocaust historiography, while it is completely uncharted territory in Armenian genocide studies. Still, we observe similar dynamics in both cases. At the Starachovice slave-labor camp, for example, prisoners knew which Ukrainian guards to approach to be allowed to leave and reenter the camp, which guards were willing to even accompany them to the city or let goods into the camp in return for bribes.[80]

The deportees were not safe in Bab even in the early months, as the locals treated them with hostility. "It was impossible to go to the market without receiving a good beating," wrote one survivor.[81] Even Father Khachadur and pharmacist Dikran Efendi, the council's emissaries from Aleppo City, were subjected to abuse. According to a deportee from Bab the two wanted to meet with the district governor of Bab, so he and a priest led them to his office. Passing through the market in Bab, locals started hurling cucumbers at them. "A *çavuş* [guard] from the municipality happened to be passing by at that time, and he succeeded in calming down the crowd." The narrator, sympathetic to Arab nationalism, was perplexed by the hatred locals in Bab showed the Armenians, "especially since we knew that they too had national ideals."[82] A few months later (around 20 August 1915), a mob "pounced on about 30 Armenian families put up there [in Bab] in tents and wounded 12 people. Only the immediate intervention on the part of the *kaymakam* prevented further misfortune," reported the German consul.[83] The situation escalated with the spread of typhus, for which Armenian deportees were blamed. The spread of the disease put the deportees in constant danger of being assaulted by locals. In one case, Bab dignitaries headed by the former mufti agitated against the district governor to accelerate the redeportation process and even took matters into their own hands attacking the deportee camp, beating up hapless deportees, and burning their tents.[84] The simmering local resentment against the Armenians in the aftermath of the typhus outbreak clearly facilitated the authorities' efforts to redeport all non-native Armenians in the province of Aleppo to the interior.

Yet extortion and theft were more common than violence in Bab. Post office employees were one group among many who tried to take advantage of the Armenians. When deportees went to the post office to pick up money sent to them, they were told that it had not arrived yet or that the post office had no currency that day. Many would be redeported without obtaining their funds, which were pocketed by the post office employees.

Some Armenians also benefited from the exploitation of deportees. When entry to the city was banned, Jivan Kaltakjian,[85] a notorious and well-connected pharmacist from Kayseri, secured written authorization from deportees to go to the post office and claim their money. Instead, he split the funds with the police, while the victims of his schemes were redeported.[86] Even when deportees ended up receiving their money, it was only a fraction of the total; the middlemen claimed that they were forced to pay the rest in bribes to the post office director.[87] Jivan would enrich himself at the Bab camp and then leave in late spring 1916 for Der Zor, where he hoped he would live a comfortable life under the patronage of Zeki Bey, the newly appointed district governor, whom he considered a friend. However, he was killed by bandits upon arrival to the city. Andonian recalled that the deportees in Meskeneh cheered upon hearing the news of his death.[88] Hovhannes Khacherian was more restrained: "As if for the multiple evils he committed, [Jivan] eventually became one of the victims of the massacre. Yet neither I, nor many others will shed a tear for him."[89]

Meanwhile, bandits lurked on the thirty-minute road to the city, attacking the deportees, robbing them, and sometimes beating them up. The camp itself was also a target. Taking advantage of the semiporous nature of the camps—locals could enter under the pretext of doing business, with little supervision over their activities—thieves loitered in the camp during the day, scouring tents for items worth stealing. At night, they would stage their attack. Accounts of thefts in the night permeate survivor testimonies and memoirs. For example, thieves descended upon the tent of Peniamin Stamboulian of Konya one rainy night and tried to steal a bag of clothing and rugs. Stamboulian had tied the bag with a rope attached to his waist, so that he would wake up if anyone tried to take it. In the struggle, the tent collapsed, and the candle lighting the tent was extinguished. "The thieves were pulling from the outside, me and my wife from the inside. Yelling and screaming were in vain. I and my wife were pulled out of the tent with the bag. When the thieves noticed the bag was tied to my waist, they cut the rope with a knife, threw the bag on the back of their mule, and left." No one came to help.[90]

The gendarmes and the robbers fired in the air during bandit attacks. Deportees believed the guards were in league with the robbers and received a cut of the booty, as their intervention often came too late. The camp guards played both sides. After "repelling" a bandit attack, they demanded "gifts" from the deportees, who had to raise ten to fifteen liras amongst themselves to reward the guards.[91] Certain gendarmes received bribes from a cluster of tents and protected those faithfully, occasionally killing bandits in the process. In one such case, Bab authorities reprimanded the gendarme for his harshness toward bandits.[92]

The abduction of young girls from the camp posed a serious problem. "If anyone, from the dignitaries of the city to the lowest gendarmes, demanded a girl in the camp, it was impossible to say no. The person who said no would be punished by death, and the girl still was not saved. Who could one appeal to? The district governor? The head gendarme? They each kept five to ten girls, as 'servants.'"[93] Some Armenians gave away their children voluntarily, believing it was the only way to save them.[94] Verzhin Tengerian made this decision when she contracted typhus in Bab. "We were starving, thirsty, and naked, and on top of that came typhus. I too got sick, my daughter had no one to care for her. Thinking that death was inescapable for me, I voluntarily handed her to an Arab who approached me at that time," she related in her testimony.[95] Many of these girls were later sold by their owners or simply left to their fate on the streets.[96] Others were more "fortunate" and ended up marrying local Muslims, often under coercion, and staying in the city. Selling one's children or giving them away to save their lives constituted what scholar Lawrence Langer would call a "choiceless choice."[97] After the war, many girls who were sold or forcibly taken into Muslim homes, married their "owner," and had children were faced with an impossible choice of their own: to leave their new family behind and be reunited with their next of kin or to stay on. An effort to rescue these women and children and return them to their communities was partially successful. Stanley Kerr, who headed one such initiative, faced numerous challenges in Bab. "The children were being told that the Americans had come to steal them, and this represented a new disaster. They remembered the terror of separation from their mothers four years earlier," he explained. Still, many were rescued through such initiatives.[98]

Death and Burial

Father Dajad was taken to Bab from the Sebil transit camp in November. He and his companions, with their belongings loaded on donkeys, arrived to a chilling scene in the early morning:

> In a field that has become a lake from the rain, thousands of tents are set on the mud and waters. On the edge of the tents, a crowd of dead and dying people, so many that the buriers of the dead among the deportees, assigned by the government, could hardly keep up.[99]

Learning that all the priests in the camp were either sick or dead, Father Dajad took matters into his own hands, immediately appealing to the district governor for help in burying the 350 to 400 people dying every day of typhus, which had "encircled the camp like a fire." The official provided the camp with fifty *mezarcıs* (buriers) and a head burier to oversee the process, which Father Dajad described in detail. The buriers were divided into two groups. Every morning one group toured the five thousand tents with the priest, gathering the corpses placed outside,[100] while the other group dug graves in the cemetery outside the camp. In the afternoon, the corpses were transported to the cemetery and buried in the pits. "Between December 1915 and January–February 1916, some 36,000–40,000 people were buried [like this]," observed Father Dajad.[101]

According to information provided to Andonian by another eyewitness, "without exaggeration," five hundred deaths were registered in the camp every day in late 1915 and early 1916. On 11 and 12 January alone, 1,209 died in the camp, according to the *mezarcı-başı* (head burier) Hagop Efendi.[102] A permutation of this figure appears alongside key information in a report by Rössler:

> An Armenian who has the courage to go to Bab from time to time in disguise in order to bring the poverty stricken a support allowance (German Sisters have not been allowed any activity outside of Aleppo), reports that at the end of January during the 2 and a half days of his stay in Bab, 1,029 Armenians died.[103]

Many of these deaths were from typhus. Buriers dug mass graves four to five meters deep and filled them with corpses. "They used to drag the bodies from the arms or hair and throw them into the ditch, where other buriers would intelligently line up the corpses in a way that maximized the number of corpses that fit in the ditch (small corpses next to large ones, etc.). It took some 20 *mezarcıs* to perform this process."[104]

The buriers, who were all Armenians, were the last to be deported from Bab when the camp was liquidated. Receiving meager compensation from the authorities, these *mezarcıs* "searched the corpses in hopes of finding money on them. They also took the gold teeth, although those who were hungry generally pulled their own gold teeth and sold them for bread."[105]

While many who came down with typhus ended up in the hands of the *mezarcıs* straight away, a few received medical care and survived. Father Dajad wrote that Bab municipal doctor Vahan Efendi "worked in a humane fashion, but [his efforts] were still not enough for the enormous need."[106] Not all reviews of doctor Vahan are positive, however. In his account, Hovhannes Khacherian accused him of scorning deportee suffering and taking better care of those who had money.[107]

Although the majority of the deportees were interned at the camp, Bab City and the nearby village of Tetif (also Tefrije) hosted a small number of deportees. These comprised some families who had managed to bribe officials with hefty sums and move into apartments, and women and children who were abducted from Armenian deportee camps in the area and brought to Bab or Tetif, with some eventually marrying their kidnappers. The risk of redeportation loomed over the families who, like their fellow deportees in the city of Aleppo, had to continually bribe local officials to stay in town. Abducted women ran a lower risk of redeportation, especially if they had married their captors. Almost all families who had settled in Bab and Tetif were deported in early 1916, while most abducted Armenian women married to captors and children doing labor for families continued to live there.[108] Among those who spent the winter of 1915 in Tetif were the Kitabjians from Kayseri. "We realized that they were going to deport us from Bab as well. We decided to escape to a small village nearby. We arranged for an Arab to take us there. He came one night and took us to his village of Tetif. He rented a room from his house and we paid him rent," explained survivor Artin Kitabjian. Within months, the Kitabjians too found themselves in concentration camps along the Euphrates.[109]

The Decline of the Bab Camp

The Bab camp had shrunk in early 1916 from around five thousand tents to "a few thousand."[110] Deaths and the now regular *sevk* had done their work. Bab was conceived as a transit camp, and though the process was initially slow, it accelerated in January 1916, when the central authorities ordered the liquidation of camps in Aleppo Province, pushing the deportees out toward the Euphrates line.

The head guard (*bekcibaşı*) in Bab in early January was an Armenian from Çorum named Krikor Çavuş. He and his henchmen were particularly violent when redeporting families who refused or were unable to pay bribes.[111] They executed the final round of redeportation, while thrashing men, women, and children with sticks.[112] According to Khacherian, they yelled, "Haydi kalkın, çadırları yıkın, bir kimse kalmacak, haaa" (Get up! Bring down the tents! No one will remain here!). No Armenians were to be left in Bab and Tetif. Khacherian remembered that the *kaymakam* of Bab gathered the town leadership and told them: "Bilmiş olun ey arablar, ki bunların bir kişi bile kalsa, bizlerden intikam alacak. Olmayaki birkimseyi saklayasınız." (Know full well, oh Arabs, that even if one of these survive, he will avenge us. Don't even dare hide any one of them.)[113]

By early spring 1916, the Bab camp had shrunk to barely a hundred tents housing mainly the guards, buriers, cart drivers, and some of their family members. These people were the last to be deported when camps were shut down, as they were integral to its functioning and to the redeportation process. They were sent to Meskeneh soon thereafter, by order of a Committee of Union and Progress official who had arrived in Bab.[114] "Only six *mezarcıs* remained with their families to inter the unburied corpses," Khacherian recalled. "Then they were sent to the hospital in Tetif to bury the corpses of locals, and upon the completion of that task within a few days, these last remnants of the Bab camp were deported, alongside Armenians who had settled in Tetif."[115]

From Bab to Meskeneh

As thousands of wretched deportees poured out of the Bab camp heading to Meskeneh, starvation, disease, and exhaustion continued to claim lives. "The Bab–Meskeneh road is nothing but a cemetery," Khacherian observed.[116] Many deportees passed through a transit site near Mumbuj, three to four hours west of Bab.[117]

The trek was particularly treacherous because Arab villagers from nearby Sefire (As-Safira), four hours from Aleppo City, descended upon the deportees, abducted boys and girls, and stole whatever they could, as gendarmes looked the other way.[118] Several of the abducted children were then sold. "Apraham, Sarkis, and Khatun, the three children of Sholakian Apraham, were sold at this price [20 *kuruş*]. The last was 14, the first was 10," wrote Andonian. He then mentioned another person, Genjo, at whose house he stayed upon his escape from Meskeneh to Aleppo, and who had abducted several children. "Genjo's wife volunteered, without any emotion, that the two boys playing in front of the house were Armenian," Andonian recalled.[119] Although Andonian referred to the villagers of Sefire as thieves, he stressed the fact that they never killed, despite orders by local authorities to kill any escaped deportee they encountered. Many Armenians did manage to escape from the deportation convoys between Bab and Meskeneh, but their chance of survival was slim. They either returned to Bab or hid near Meskeneh, without entering the camp itself. Most were eventually denounced by local Arabs, captured by gendarmes, and sent to the camp, where they were beaten upon arrival.[120]

The redeportation from Bab continued throughout the winter and early spring of 1916. In April, an intermediary agent of Sister Beatrice Rohner witnessed the arrival of a convoy from Bab:

> As I was in Meskene, there came a caravan of sick women and children from Bab. They are in indescribable condition. They were thrown down from the wagons like dogs. They cried for water, they were given each a piece of dry bread, and were left there. No one gave them any water though they remained a whole day under the sun.[121]

Between January and April 1916, thousands of such deportees from Bab erected their tents in the Meskeneh concentration camp near the Euphrates River. Their suffering was nowhere near over.

Along the Euphrates

The Meskeneh Concentration Camp

> They arrived [in Meskeneh] by the thousands, but the majority left their bones there.
>
> —Auguste Bernau, German employee of American Vacuum Oil Company

Armenians destined to be "settled" along the Euphrates River were redeported from Aleppo Province in spring 1915 first to Meskeneh, and then farther downstream to Dipsi, Abuharar, Hamam, Rakka, Sebka, and Der Zor. Conceived as a transit camp, Meskeneh became the final resting place of tens of thousands of deportees who died from typhus, intestinal diseases, deprivation, and violence. In this chapter, we shall see how Ottoman officials organized and administered the site, and we will follow the interplay between the guidelines and orders received from the center and their implementation, as deportee agency influenced the behavior of administrators significantly. We will drill down on survival, collaboration, and humanitarian resistance at the camp from its inception in May 1915 until its closure in winter 1917, focusing on spring

1916, when camps in Aleppo Province were shut down and the deportees were evacuated to Meskeneh.

Corpses before Convoys

Corpses carried by the Euphrates River passed through Meskeneh days before the arrival of the first convoys. As he journeyed from Aleppo to Baghdad in May 1915, survivor Hayg Toroyan saw clusters of five to ten bodies whose feet and arms were bound together.[1] References to floating bodies near the riverbanks abound in eyewitness accounts. "For a whole month corpses were observed floating down the River Euphrates nearly every day, often in batches of from two to six corpses bound together. The male corpses are in many cases hideously mutilated (sexual organs cut off, and so on), the female corpses are ripped open," observed German missionary Laura Möhring.[2] German diplomatic records are replete with references to such sightings in the early months of the deportation. "Corpses, often bound together, drifted down the Euphrates river" in Jarabulus, several kilometers north of Meskeneh, the German ambassador noted on 9 July.[3] A week later, Walter Rössler wrote:

> In Djerablus, a corpse was washed ashore. When the military Kaymakam there was asked why he did not at least have the corpse buried, since the Koran stipulated burial, he replied that he could not determine whether it was a Muslim or a Christian. (The genitals had been cut off the corpse.) He would only allow a Muslim to be buried.[4]

A more detailed picture of the flood of corpses emerged in Rössler's reports in late July.

> It was observed in Rumkaleh, Biredjik and Djerablus that bodies had been floating past on the Euphrates for a total of 25 days. The corpses were all bound together in the same way, two by two, back to back. . . . The bodies had stopped floating past for an interval of several days and then began again in much larger numbers. This time they were mainly the bodies of women and children.[5]

The sight of corpses in the river remained etched in Ottoman Jewish officer Eitan Belkind's memory. "On the second day of our journey [to Der Zor] we saw a corpse floating in the Euphrates River. We were astounded but the soldiers who accompanied us assured us saying that it was only the corpse of an Armenian. . . . We continued on our way, and as we progressed we saw many corpses of Armenians floating on the water, food for the fish," he remembered.[6]

Initially, the bodies elicited speculation among Muslims in the area. Some discovered that these were murdered Armenians. Toroyan spotted a soldier on the banks stripping a corpse of its clothes and shoes. From the pockets the soldier pulled out a notebook, soaked and mostly illegible, which upon Toroyan's inspection turned out to be the diary of an Armenian grocer from the village of Samsat on the banks of the upper Euphrates.[7] Many locals, however, had no idea who the dead people might be. Rumors started to circulate that they were Turks and Kurds killed by Russians. To reassure the population, governors from the eastern provinces cabled authorities in Syria that the bodies were "external enemies," according to the Arab *mukhtar* (mayor) of Meskeneh.[8]

As convoys of deportees arrived in Meskeneh, bodies continued to pour downstream by the dozens. "The corpses stranded on the bank are devoured by dogs and vultures," recounted Mohring.[9] The deportees had little choice but to drink from the river, their only source of water. "Only extremely muddy water from the river Euphrates, polluted by corpses, manure and scraps, is to be had at the camps," wrote Dr. Schacht, a German visiting Der Zor, about the condition of the river months later.[10] Locals, however, started to complain about water contamination, which led to the spread of cholera. In an effort to remedy the situation, authorities ordered Armenian deportees to drag the corpses from the river and burn them.[11] But localized measures were not sufficient to address the panic and discontent. Cemal Pasha sent a telegram to Diyarbakir governor Dr. Reşid (14 July 1915) "that the bodies carried downstream by the Euphrates should not be left exposed, but should be [pulled from the river and] buried in the districts in which they are found."[12] Reşid responded that the river "has very little contact with our province. It is likely that the bodies being carried [downstream] are coming from Erzerum and Mamuretulaziz. The bodies of those killed during acts of rebellion are being dealt with either by casting them into abandoned and deep ravines or, as has been done in most cases, by burning, burial being the rare exception."[13]

Concerned by the outcry over river contamination and eager to silence rumors of massacre, authorities had the corpses removed and buried. Yet the occasional sighting of bodies, mainly those of Armenian women who had committed suicide to avoid what they perceived to be a more horrendous fate, continued, while children playing in the area—by now used to the sight—threw stones at them for amusement.[14]

Arrival

When Hagop Seropian's family arrived in Meskeneh after an arduous journey in fall 1915, they were ushered in by a group of Armenian camp guards headed by *bekcibaşı* (head guard) Yervant, from Izmit.[15] Seropian observed that the Armenian guards were the underlings of the local director of deportations, the Circassian Hüseyin Avni Bey. They abused their power and benefited from their position.[16] The Seropian family was allocated a spot a little farther away from the tent city. They soon encountered some compatriots from Konya, who pitched their tents next to theirs.[17] As we have seen, oftentimes deportees from the same village or town clustered together, creating an environment of familiarity and security in a precarious, hostile environment.

Meskeneh, situated at the great bend of the southern branch of the Euphrates, was a tiny village. Its population interacted closely with the concentration camp nearby, and its mayor was embroiled in a months' long investigation involving members of the military and deportees interned at the camp.[18] Around the camp, as one survivor recalled, there was "nothing more than a building, masquerading as an inn, a couple of miles from the course of Euphrates and hard against some bleak hills,"[19] and a telegram center near the inn on the western banks of the river.[20] "On the other side of a series of sand dunes a couple of miles from our camp there were the barracks housing those companies of gendarmes who were regulating the deportation columns," recalled survivor Loossin Chorbajian Majarian.[21] Construction of a military supply line in the area began in early May 1916.[22] That work was already underway when survivor Yeghishe Hazarabedian arrived at the camp in early spring 1916. "The whole thing was under the orders of a captain and his company who, when not working on the construction of the barracks, lived in the inn. Outside of the inn there were some fifty Armenian laborers who had volunteered to work on the project so that they would escape being driven farther down the river . . . to Deir ez-Zor," he explained.[23]

The camp itself was a ten-minute walk from the *khan* in the direction of the river.[24] In early 1916, as tens of thousands of deportees poured into Meskeneh, they pitched on a hilltop overlooking the khan, while authorities reserved the area near the river for those scheduled for imminent deportation.[25] Deportees who wanted to delay redeportation at any cost sought permission to move to the camp on the hills. Most camps in the region had a section at a distance from the main encampment reserved for administrators and their assistants. Some deportees managed to set their tents there, for a price. When Father Yetvart Tarpinian arrived in Meskeneh in March 1916, Avedis Kaselian, a physician from Hajin who enjoyed the privilege of living in a secluded area of the camp in the hills, moved the priest near his tent and made him responsible for health matters.[26] Loossin Chorbajian Majarian's family also benefitted from this prime desert real estate:

> One day, my father returned to our tent after a visit to the barracks city, and he bore some good news. He had bribed some of the gendarmes and they had issued orders that we were to strike our tent in the encampment and move to a place near the barracks. The gendarmes had told him that we would be spared further displacement.[27]

By the end of 1916, when the camp was nearly empty, camp director Hüseyin Avni moved the remaining deportees from the heights to the area near the Euphrates.[28]

Meskeneh had operated as a camp from the onset of the deportations, but its importance grew with the closure of camps around Aleppo City in January 1916. Prior to that, deportees had arrived at a slow but steady pace at Meskeneh. In early May 1915, the U.S. consul in Aleppo reported: "From Zeitun about 350 families, or about 2,000 persons have been sent to Marash and from there to Aintab, and are expected to arrive in Aleppo about May 15, to be sent to Meskeneh, while about 250 or more families are expected to follow before May 20 to report to the governor of Aleppo."[29] While many of these early arrivals were redeported to Der Zor, others were interned at the camp for longer periods. On his journey from Aleppo to Baghdad, Toroyan passed through Meskeneh (15 November 1915) where—on the right bank of the Euphrates—he saw an estimated 1,500 Armenians "sheltered under 10–15 umbrella-shaped tents."[30] The majority were women and children from Mersin, Harput, Adana, and Izmit; the few men among them were mostly from the western provinces.[31] Survivor Hagop Arsenian arrived from Bab with his family on 12 December, noting "the endless desert land devoid of grass and greenery."[32] In the three weeks Arsenian spent in this transit camp, he witnessed disease and hunger, and spent more than two weeks in bed after contracting gastrointestinal flu.[33]

With the arrival of deportees from Bab, Meskeneh metastasized from an encampment of a few hundred tents to several thousand. When German diplomat Wilhelm Litten passed through Meskeneh on 3 February 1916 he witnessed "a large campsite with over 2,000 tents. More than 10,000 people.... Apparently no latrines. All around the town and the campsite a broad belt of human excrement and refuse, through which my carriage also had to drive for a while."[34] Hazarabedian provided a similar estimate of two thousand tents. Upon his arrival in early spring 1916, he "found that the people here had been brought from Aleppo, Bab, Jerablus, and that this camp was only a temporary staging area from which one threw himself into the cauldron of Deir ez-Zor."[35] Toroyan too witnessed the arrival of deportees:

> In that period new deportees arrived from Aleppo. They were unable to even sit down; they threw themselves on the ground and slept, unconscious. . . . The Armenians who were there did not show any interest in the new arrivals—everyone was burdened with their own pain. Lines of people, fallen, sleeping, one weeping, another sobbing, and no one came to ask about their suffering.[36]

Life and Death in the Camp

From May 1915 to April 1916, 110,934 deportees passed through Meskeneh according to a handwritten document by camp director Hüseyin Avni. The redeported constituted 28,834 Armenians, which means that 80,000, or approximately 72 percent, died at the camp from various causes. Andonian pointed out that three hundred to five hundred people died in Meskeneh every day at one point.[37] Even the most conservative numbers are staggering: roughly one of ten deportees arriving in Syria-Mesopotamia died in Meskeneh.

Deportees did not wait idly to die. They organized life in the camp, set up an orphanage, tried to establish continuous lines of communication with other camps, and to protect themselves from looter and bandit attacks. Dozens managed to bribe their way back to Aleppo, while others escaped, sometimes more than once.

Here too, there was little to eat. The authorities have "no care about feeding them," observed Bernau. "Happy are those [who have] a little money which enables them to get flour, if they can get some, and at this time some watermelon from the neighboring villagers or some sick sheep for the price of gold from passing nomads."[38] Arab women came from nearby areas to sell food and other necessities to the deportees, at inflated prices. "Barely one *okha* (oka, 2.83 lb) of straw for burning was sold for 20 paras," noted Toroyan.[39] Even gendarmes arriving in the area brought bags of flour to sell to deportees at gouging sums.[40] While those who could afford the flour prepared bread dough and threw it on the fire, children nearby begged them—sometimes their own relatives—for a piece. "But people, in their extreme and superhuman suffering, had become unsympathetic and heartless, not even heeding to the pleas of starving children," Toroyan recalled.[41] And thus, those who could not afford anything, particularly the children, would "throw themselves voraciously on anything that falls into their hands: they eat grass, earth, and even their own excrement," described Bernau.[42] According to Hazarabedian, children were "reduced to urchins, to beggars—that is if they were strong enough to beg."[43]

The destitute condition of the children roaming the camp prompted a group of women to set up an orphanage on 11 March 1916. Three women from Niğde took on the responsibility of caring for the orphans, with support from priest Yetvart Tarpinian, who had arrived in Meskeneh only a week earlier.[44] As word spread, more and more orphans came to the tent. What started as a shelter for a few soon provided refuge to a hundred children. The women desperately tried to secure supplies for them: they pleaded with camp officials, asked deportees for donations, and solicited outside help. They were not always successful. One of the women, Rakel Kirazian, was beaten up on several occasions by *anbâr memuru* (warehouse official) Ali Riza for repeatedly requesting food for the starving children.

Those who got married at the camp—and there were indeed dozens who did so despite, or because of, the destitute conditions at the camp and the uncertain future—made donations to the orphanage to celebrate the occasion.[45] Numerous references to the role newfound love and marriage played in the lives of Armenians during the genocide, scattered throughout survivor memoirs and accounts, point to the importance of studying this phenomenon. When Ephraim K. Jernazian proposed to his future wife Marie in Urfa, she retorted, "How can an Armenian think about marriage in 1916?" To which Jernazian replied, "If we stay apart, we are in greater danger of dying. Together, we can help each other. If we die, let's die together."[46]

Some deportees at the camp gave from the little they had. The most significant assistance came from two Evangelical Armenian women who were referred to as "members of the *ruhci* sect." They offered to provide bread to the orphans regularly, and did so, with funds from a German woman missionary based in Aleppo.[47] After a confrontation with camp director Hüseyin, the two women and many of the orphans in the tent were deported to Der Zor.[48] Soon thereafter, in July, two officers opened another orphanage. According to one of the officers, Lt. Col. Galip, who served as logistics support commander in the region, the institution housed 164 children.[49] Tarpinian noted that the orphanage sheltered five hundred by the end of that month.[50] According to Ottoman documents, the logistics supply depot in Meskeneh provided very little food to the youngsters. "We used to give 50 kilos of pounded wheat, and 50 kiyyes (approximately 1.3 kilograms) of flour daily, and one or two lambs a week" from the depots, Galip Bey stated while he was being investigated for "misuse of authority" a few months later.[51] In late August, inspector of deportees Hakkı Bey sent 250 of these orphans to Der Zor. He promised he would take Father Tarpinian and the rest of the children next time and establish a hospital there headed by the priest. That plan never materialized. The deported orphans were killed during the Der Zor massacres.[52] The remaining children continued their destitute existence in the tent. Bernau described their condition:

> I have seen, under a tent of 5 to 6 square meters, around 450 orphans, crawling pell-mell in the dirt and the vermin. These poor small ones receive 150 grams of bread per day, sometimes even [less] and it is more often the case that they go two days without having anything to eat. Also death makes among them cruel devastations. This tent sheltered 450 victims during my stay. Eight days later, at the time of my return, intestinal diseases had taken 17 of them.[53]

Adults did not fare much better. Warehouse officials (*iâşe ve anbâr memûrları*) provided the bare minimum, and sometimes not even that. Often, deportees did not receive anything for weeks, and officials blamed the deprivation on lack of supplies. In fact, much of the supply was sold to deportees at exorbitant prices, leaving the majority of the camp to starve.

Bribes were the key to staying in Meskeneh or, in the case of a fortunate few, making it back to Aleppo. Most survivor accounts mention graft, and many credit it for their survival. "The poor people couldn't do anything. There was only one way to salvation: if they had the financial resources, they could satisfy the camp official, so that he would be lenient with them," explained Seropian.[54] The Seropians and five other families from Konya collected one hundred Ottoman liras and asked camp director Hüseyin Avni to be redeported last. He agreed and ordered them to set their tents far from the redeportation campground. Their reprieve had lasted no more than a month and a half when Hüseyin Avni's Armenian guards informed them that the *sevkiyat* was near complete. Their turn had come.[55] Arsenian, too, paid bribes simply to remain in the camp while he was sick. "As if we had rented the spot where we pitched our tents and every day, through Mr. Charkejian, we sent payments to the officials, so that during my illness they would not touch us and would not dismantle our tents."[56] When Odian arrived in Meskeneh toward the end of the redeportation process when barely 1,500 Armenians remained at the camp, deportees who were working on road construction told him that some Armenian bakers and grocers avoided redeportation through bribes.[57]

Deportees plotted a way out. Survivor Loossin Chorbajian Majarian too describes in her account how her aunt's husband Stepan Deirmenjian led five small groups of family members to Aleppo almost "without incident."[58] Others tried leveraging connections. Hagop Agha Khrlakian, a member of the Ottoman Parliament from Marash, pleaded with Talaat to order the return of a relative from Meskeneh to Marash. Despite the intervention, the relative was redeported to Der Zor, whereupon Talaat himself telegraphed the Aleppo governor demanding an explanation.[59] While in Aleppo, the Dishchekenian and Hazarabedian families also tried to leverage their kinship with Khrlakian to avoid redeportation "since he has been able to get permits from Talaat Pasha, Minister of the Interior, for all his relatives to remain in Aleppo for the duration of the war."[60] Their attempts did not yield results, however. The two families were sent to Karlık, then to Meskeneh and beyond.[61]

Dysentery, typhus, and typhoid fever wreaked havoc and death. "Sweeping dysentery has made many victims among them, especially among the children," lamented Bernau.[62] Many deportees waited for days for grave diggers to remove the bodies from their tent.[63] Buriers dug a huge pit, filled it with corpses, and then covered it with a mound of sand. Not all victims were buried, and those who were did not always remain interred. "Oftentimes, the corpses would be dragged out and eaten by dogs," with the stench from scattered limbs filling the air. The deportees, who walked to the Euphrates to get water, had to pass these horrors every day, and at some point, "our nose no longer picked up the smell."[64] But if illness did not kill an inmate, it could delay deportation. Articles 13 and 25 of the guideline for redeportation stipulated allowing the sick to rest and providing them with medication.[65] Pharmacist Kevork Kutnerian was among the few even vaguely qualified to help the sick, and he wrote reports to help secure exemption from immediate redeportation.[66]

Communication among Deportees

Deportees realized that sharing information between the two campsites at Meskeneh and among Meskeneh and other camps along the Euphrates was key to survival. They prepared handwritten flyers reporting developments and rumors. When a new convoy arrived, the "reporters" would approach the new arrivals and ask them for information about conditions in the towns and camps whence they were deported.[67] Andonian noted that he himself had prepared many such flyers. In general the newssheets did not carry dates, because the reporters rarely knew what day it was, he explained.[68] The flyers offer a window into daily life in the camp, and broaden our understanding of events.[69] One entry announced: "A new camp director has arrived in Meskeneh. He is a Circassian by the name of Hüseyin. On the day of his arrival there were 20,000 deportees in this accursed place. They were piled on one another, and in terrible condition. The director instituted some order and assigned a doctor and a pharmacist."[70] Flyers also informed deportees of outrages experienced by convoys, abuses by camp officials, the frequency of redeportation from Meskeneh, and other such warnings. One particularly chilling entry simply said: "Final news: Do NOT go down[stream]. Do NOT go down[stream]."[71] Few, however, had the means to heed these warnings.

There were also the messengers, orphans at Meskeneh who sneaked out of the camp and conveyed messages to other camps as far away as Der Zor. It took these children twelve days to get to Der Zor and return, as they had to make stops to beg for food. The deportees experimented with different ways of concealing messages that these boys were tasked with transporting. They tied pieces of paper to their testicles, or hid them in their mouths, or wrote the information on their backs, and then covered the writing with dirt.[72] The orphans who were referred to as "human newspapers" challenge tendencies in the historiography to view children as passive victims caught in the vortex of mass violence. Although studies have explored the destruction of Armenian children during the genocide, a history of children *as agents* is yet to be written.[73]

The "Good" Camp Director and His Deputies

Deportee perception of camp officials and employees, from the director to the camp physician to the buriers, was influenced by a combination of personal experiences, rumors, and prejudices. A pharmacist can be described as bad and corrupt by one person and as good and helpful by another. Taken together, these accounts allow us to learn a great deal about the modus operandi of certain camp officials. Hüseyin Avni, a Circassian from Mumbuj, is one example. Avni was the third and most important camp director in Meskeneh. It was during his tenure that the number of deportees spiked from twenty thousand to more than one hundred thousand in spring 1916.[74] He accepted exorbitant bribes to provide preferential treatment and better "real estate" at the camp or to delay redeportation, but unlike others, he was not brutal and murderous. And for deportees who were trying to eke out survival, a camp director who did not torture and murder could pass as "good," no matter how corrupt.

Deportees praised Avni for not mutilating and murdering people. Andonian, for example, noted that during the several months he spent at Meskeneh during Avni's tenure, he never saw him resort to violence. The one complaint Andonian had was that Avni never punished or tried to curb the abuses of *bekci*s and carriage drivers.[75] Survivor Karekin Yeghpayrian, who had good relations with Avni, spoke highly in particular of Avni's wife, noting that she cared for the deportees back in Mumbuj despite the risks, and Avni never prevented her from doing so.[76] Avni remained camp director until spring 1916, when the Directorate for the Settlement of Tribes and Emigrants (IAMM) replaced him with Kör Hüseyin.

When deportees were pushed toward the Euphrates line in the fall of 1915, the central authorities assigned deputies to Avni so that he could cope with the sudden influx of inmates.[77] The deputies were Ömer, a Circassian from Mumbuj; Sarıklı Hasan from Antakya who was dispatched from Aleppo; a man by the name of Ahmed who joined later and did not remain for long; and Naim Sefa Efendi.[78] A heavy drinker and gambler, Naim Sefa Efendi was generous with decisions easing the plight of deportees—as long as they paid up. Through him, many Armenians managed to save themselves by bribing their way back to Aleppo.[79] Naim Efendi was recalled to Aleppo after one of these Armenians was arrested and confessed. The latter, despite being imprisoned for many days, did not divulge the names of others who had escaped the Meskeneh camp and disappeared in the fabric of the metropolis.[80]

Redeportation and the State's Monopoly on Violence

Deportees spent anywhere from a few days to a few months in Meskeneh, depending on the redeportation schedules at the camp and the bribes they could pay. Redeportation from Meskeneh occurred both by land and, for a short period, in double-boats or barges called *shakhtoors* (*şahtur* in Turkish) by locals. In Meskeneh, camp officials discontinued the practice of redeporting Armenians by water after local bandits attacked, robbed, and overturned several barges, killing most people on board. Redeportation by land was no less dangerous. The deportees were attacked and robbed, often with the tacit approval of the accompanying gendarmes, who shared the booty and asked the deportees to pay for the bullets they fired to protect them.[81] Many others died of exhaustion. On his journey upstream from Der Zor to Meskeneh, German diplomat Litten kept a chronological record of every corpse he saw along the road. He concluded, "I have seen with my own eyes around 100 bodies and almost just as many fresh graves on the road from Der Zor to Meskeneh. I have not counted graves which in some town were combined to form cemeteries. I have seen around 20,000 Armenians. I have restricted all my estimations of numbers to those I have actually seen for myself."[82]

Survivor Karekin Hovannesian was deported from Sivrihisar in August 1915 and arrived in Meskeneh several weeks later. As the date they would be redeported approached, they tried in vain to convince the deportation official at the camp (*sevk memuru*) to send them by land.[83] In the end, the deportees from Sivrihisar rented two barges for the journey and left on 16 December 1915. They were attacked by looters who robbed them and overturned the boat, killing most of the 132 people on board. Only eleven people, including Hovannesian and his brother, managed to swim ashore and survive.[84] They continued on foot, only to be attacked and robbed again. "Totally naked, we were confused and did not know what to do. It was late and it got very cold. One of our friends, Bedros, who had managed to survive with his son, took his son on his lap and sat on the road. He was unable to continue on," he remembered.[85] The others pressed on to Abuharar. The next day, they heard that Bedros and his son had died. The second *shakhtoor* arrived intact in Abuharar shortly thereafter. The surviving deportees from Sivrihisar were redeported to Rakka, again on a *shakhtoor*. The *sevkiyat* with *shakhtoors* was discontinued after a series of attacks, the last one of which was on the Sivrihisar deportees.[86] A few days earlier, several other barges that had left Meskeneh had also been attacked. Arsenian recalled that on 13 December 1915,

> 6 to 7 large barges sailed on and were filled with all the Izmitsis, under the leadership of Onnig Khachadurian, to be moved unknowingly to the great and final slaughterhouse: Der Zor. They were happy that they had taken the shortest and easiest way. Later the news reached us that these boats were attacked, many of the people had been killed, and others drowned in the treacherous waters of the Euphrates.[87]

Andonian learned the history of these attacks immediately after the war from the Meskeneh camp director himself. They were plotted by Mahmud Nedim, the director of the Mumbuj municipality, who established the system of redeportation by *shakhtoors* and ordered the Arab bandits to attack them.[88] Mahmud Nedim, who was notorious at the Mumbuj camp for his brutality and corruption, ordered the abduction of women from caravans and gifted them to gendarmes and other officials.[89]

The decision to temporarily discontinue the transport of deportees by water after the bandit attacks on the barges raises an important question: If the state was hell-bent on the destruction of deportees, why did it take measures to protect them from attacks?[90] Sociologist Max Weber posits that "a state is a human community that (successfully) claims the monopoly of the legitimate use of physical force within a given territory. . . . The right to use physical force is ascribed to other institutions or to individuals only to the extent to which the state permits it. The state is considered the sole source of the 'right' to use violence."[91] For the Ottoman state, this monopoly of violence during the war was crucial, particularly in a region where tribes and bandits had a history of challenging the authority of the state.[92] Although the state itself did employ the services of outlaws in the region, and even relied heavily on them during the Ras ul-Ain and Der Zor massacres, it could not afford an anarchic situation where bandits defined the agenda and timetable of a state-organized process of deportation and destruction, and worsen an already existing security problem for the population in the region.[93]

The Liquidation of Meskeneh

When the decision to empty camps and push the deportees in the direction of Der Zor was rolled out in spring 1916, Meskeneh, like most camps farther downstream, was emptied and reduced to a tiny encampment where the remaining few hundred

Armenians languished. Kör Hüseyin, who replaced Hüseyin Avni after the latter's resignation in December 1916, came to Meskeneh with a clear assignment from IAMM: to liquidate what was left of the camp and shut it down as quickly as possible.[94] "Six black tents near the river banks, made of goat hair, sheltered 150–200 old women, mostly sick or dying, some not even capable to move. Many defecated in the tent itself. They had no one to help them. The stench was so strong at a few of those tents that it wasn't even possible to go near them," wrote Andonian.[95] Near the barracks stood the tents of the coachmen and handymen. Hüseyin isolated the two campgrounds from one another, and through a series of brutal measures liquidated the rest of the camp; most deportees died in Meskeneh, and the rest were dragged to Der Zor.[96]

PART THREE

Der Zor Bound

CHAPTER SIX

Death and Resilience

The Military Supply Line

[The Euphrates] had become the mute witness of Armenian suffering.

—Patriarch Zaven Der Yeghiayan

Armenians redeported from Meskeneh were later held for a few days to several months in other transit camps and settlement areas on the banks of the Euphrates before being driven to Der Zor. These sites along the Euphrates ranged from villages of a few dozen tents (Abuharar) to a city of about three thousand households (Rakka) and either took in deportees as settlers or hosted nearby transit camps. Although the sites stood a few hours' carriage ride apart, each maintained distinct characteristics. The interaction between central and local authorities, military and civilian leaders, and among officials of different sites ultimately determined the fate of hundreds of thousands of deportees along the lower Euphrates. Each camp, every deportee, was caught in a net of orders, counterorders, power struggles, corruption, and violence, in a desert corner of a warring empire. Still, deportee agency proved a factor. This chapter examines the complex dynamic between genocidal assault and humanitarian resistance in these sites from the fall of 1915 to the end of the war.

Dipsi

Deportees cast downstream from Meskeneh in carriages or on foot arrived in Dipsi some five hours later. The transit camp was situated in a hilly area in the desert, a half-hour walk from the river. The site accommodated a small gendarmerie adjoining a rock formation, with a nearby cave serving as prison. The tents were set on two barren hills separated by a valley where the winter rain coalesced and flowed to the river. The valley served as a natural barrier between the two parts of the camp. On the right side, approximately five hundred tents were erected for the well-to-do, guards, carriage owners, and some laborers who were tasked with keeping this privileged area clean. On the left side, thousands of inmates were encamped in an area referred to as *hastane* (hospital).[1] "All the impoverished [people] are brought from Meskeneh and left naked, hungry, and thirsty in this place called the hospital, until death arrives and reaps them," observed survivor Krikor Ankut, who was at the camp from March 1916, when the camp had already shrunk considerably, until it was shut down in late April.[2] Here too, the head of the camp guards was an Armenian, Artin Çavuş Nordigian. This strong-built young man from Adana took bribes to allow deportees in transit to stay overnight at the camp before marching onward.[3]

Established in late fall 1915, Dipsi had become "a huge encampment of thousands of deportees settled in the dirty and filthy land" by January.[4] A month later, German consular official Wilhelm Litten passed through and saw around six hundred tents; most likely he did not visit the other side of the valley to witness the *hastane*.[5] Arriving in March, Ankut estimated two thousand tents in total.

During the six months Dipsi was in operation, deportees who were well enough to move on spent a few hours to several weeks at the camp. The Seropians were among thirty-eight families who could afford to rent carriages in Meskeneh and, accompanied by three gendarmes, arrived in Dipsi only to stay there for a few hours. Seeing the horrid condition of the deportees at the camp, the group secured permission from the deportation official on duty to go to the next camp, and paid the carriage drivers an additional sum to take them there.[6] The Arsenians, by contrast, bribed camp officials to stay for a few days. "On the fifth day, a monstrous one-eyed gendarme, carrying an axe in his hand, began tearing down the tents and beating up the sick." At that point, carts were not available even for those who could afford them. The Arsenians carried their possessions on their backs to the next camp.[7]

Dipsi also had a "permanent" population. These were the thousands interned at the *hastane* who were in no condition to move. All they could find to eat was *ebegömeci* (*Malva sylvestris*, deportees also called it *ebemgömeci*), a plant that grew on the banks of the Euphrates in the spring. With most people sick and dying, the *hastane* was drenched in filth: corpses rotting, feces and garbage everywhere. Realizing the inevitability of death, many traded or simply gave away their children to Arabs who entered the camp to sell goods. One father sold his daughter for half a *batman* (about 7.5 kilograms) of wheat flour.[8]

A few Armenians managed to make their way back to Aleppo after some time in Dipsi. Takouhi Seraydarian from the village of Kurdbelen was among them. She was at the camp in spring 1916 when it had shrunk and only the sick were left there. Her son was ill, so she stayed. Every so often she went to the Bedouins in the village, to repair clothes they had stolen from deportees; her labor earned her bread and dates.[9] Seraydarian had kept letters she had received from her husband's relatives who were serving in the Ottoman army in Shkodra, Albania. She showed these letters to Turkish officers and told them they were from her sons "fighting for the state, while you send their parents to exile." The officers gave her a letter of exemption from deportation.[10] "This document saved me from the Der Zor massacre," she revealed years later. Seraydarian and her son, together with a few others, found their way back to Aleppo following the telegraph lines. They walked at night and hid during the day to avoid being spotted by bandits.[11]

Those who had nowhere to go were not safe either. Local Arab herdsmen killed dozens of women at the camp for gathering *ebemgömeci*, which also served as food for their livestock. And then there were the executions inside the camp for those who were accused of breaking the law. "Those who were sentenced to death were killed there [at Dipsi] and dumped into the river," recounted deportation official Naim Efendi.[12]

In late April 1916, approximately twenty gendarmes were dispatched from Meskeneh to liquidate Dipsi. Considering the condition of most deportees in the *hastane*, this was tantamount to a death sentence. The gendarmes set fire to tents and assaulted deportees who could barely move. "The wealthy and the poor had to be re-deported. . . . Within half an hour, the convoy was on its way to Abuharar. Horrible crimes were committed that day at the *hastane*: many died of beatings and other were burned alive," recounted Ankut.[13] A "cemeterial silence" reigned in Dipsi on 7 June 1916 when Ankut passed through on his way from Abuharar back to Meskeneh. By then only the gendarme station stood there, amid a sea of scattered objects.[14] Shortly thereafter, Hazarabedian also journeyed through Dipsi and observed a "place that had once been a staging area for deportees but now stood abandoned," with only a few orphans left behind, begging for food from travelers and deportees.[15]

Abuharar

Abuharar (Ebuhureyre in Ottoman documents), listed as a transit camp in the September 1915 redeportation guideline, was one of the larger camps along the Euphrates, at one point accommodating more than forty thousand deportees.[16] A police station and a *khan* stood nearby.[17] Thirty kilometers from Dipsi,[18] Abuharar lay in a desert stretch sandwiched between the river and the road to Der Zor. Deportees walked for seven to eight minutes to get to the water.[19] The camp was so vast, Seropian explained, that deportees who went to the outskirts to relieve themselves had difficulty finding their tent on the way back. "But several times a day one had to come out of the circle, get away from the tents, to relieve oneself," he remembered.[20] Deportees took measures to preserve cleanliness in most camps. Accounts emphasize the importance of leaving the camp to attend to bodily functions, or when burying the dead. Yet there were instances when deportees did not adhere to these rules, be they self-imposed or enforced by fellow inmates or camp officials, particularly when disease and malnourishment had worn people down, or when bandit attacks were frequent. Arsenian, a pharmacist whose tenure at Abuharar partially overlapped with Seropian's, explained that a few months after his arrival he was "elected supervisor of cleanliness and hygiene of the tents."[21] His account is yet another indication of deportee agency under the harshest conditions.

Survivor accounts provide sufficient information about camp officials and guards to offer a general idea about the camp administration. Rahmeddin Onbaşı (corporal), who served as camp director for many months, had a reputation for beating and killing deportees. In the words of Artin Kitabjian, who stayed in Abuharar for a few months in 1916, Rahmeddin "made all Armenians suffer a great deal. He was a beast who had no pity."[22] Rahmeddin forbade those who could not afford bribes to stay at the camp for more than a few days, while rich deportees remained for long periods. Some of those who stayed for long periods secured their livelihood by engaging in small-scale trade, while most others simply used up whatever money they had brought with them.[23] Andonian remembered that

Rahmeddin was recalled to Aleppo at some point for his excessive violence, but returned soon thereafter. On his way back to Abuharar, while passing through the Meskeneh camp, he brandished his revolver and fired several rounds in the air yelling, "You complained. What happened? I am back at my post." Andonian remarks that upon his return, he was even more brutal than before.[24] Indeed, few Ottoman officials were held accountable for their behavior in camps in Ottoman Syria, and those who were typically faced trial for misappropriation of supplies.

Deportation director Mohammed Onbaşı, equally notorious for brutality, often relied on his Armenian guards to do his dirty work.[25] His right-hand man, the head of the guard, was an Armenian from Izmit named Hagop(os) Agha Ghazarian. Seropian described with passion the pain and suffering Ghazarian caused his fellow Armenians. "My God, with his orders and denunciations he caused death and ruination to so many Armenian young men, so many Armenian families, so many honorable Armenian mothers, so many three-, twelve-, fourteen-year-old helpless orphans, who were the future light of Armenians."[26] Andonian, too, noted that inmates despised Ghazarian. When Abuharar was shut down after the last convoy left that camp (early June 1916), Ghazarian was deported to Hamam. No longer a guard, he was abused by the deportees there for all the suffering he had caused. He was eventually deported to Der Zor.[27] However, some in Abuharar had benefitted from ties to Ghazarian. Arsenian, for instance, boasted in his memoir that he "succeeded in making our friend Hagop Agha Ghazarian the *bekchibashi* of the guards of our camp."[28] He said nothing about Ghazarian's reputation. What probably mattered for Arsenian was the advantage he secured through his friend in the daily struggle for survival.

Armenian carriage drivers could also be brutal. Survivor Shmavon Der Stepanian noted: "from Meskeneh to Der Zor every refugee camp had its *mekkarecibaşı* and *mekkareci* [head of carriage drivers and carriage drivers]," and, "if I say that those who are being dragged, and those who are doing the dragging are Armenians, I wouldn't be mistaken." He complained that carriage drivers "tortured and looted their own brothers more than the gendarmes," remembering how as they were being redeported from Abuharar to Hamam, one carriage driver pushed a child off the cart to his death.[29]

In late May 1916, Euphrates supply line commander Lt. Col. Galip Bey visited Abuharar and recruited laborers and craftsmen to work at *menzil*s (points along the supply line) in Meskeneh and Hamam. Hundreds of people along the Euphrates line paid large sums to be designated as laborers and avoid Der Zor or even return to Aleppo. Those who were not registered as workers were redeported.[30] Walter Rössler reported, "Under the silent toleration of the local military kaymakam, about 250 Armenians from Meskeneh have succeeded in walking back to Aleppo, where they arrived in a pitiful condition. As a result of this, the vali gave orders to the villages not to let any Armenians return to Aleppo."[31] This phenomenon was brought to the attention of the Directorate of Deportations in Aleppo following the arrest in Karlık of thirty deportees from Meskeneh. According to a telegram from Meskeneh, "When asked where they came from, they said the Logistics Support Commander [Galip] gave them two days' supply of food and sent them to work at the women's factory in Aleppo."[32] The central authorities dispatched deputy director of deportations Hakkı Bey to Meskeneh to "do whatever is necessary."[33] A several months' long investigation of Galip and his associates followed.[34] During the inquiry, Meskeneh deportations director Hüseyin testified that Galip sent back several thousand deportees to his camp as "cart drivers and artisans," including many from Abuharar and Hamam. He added that some deportees managed to escape to Jerablus and other towns in the process.[35]

The standard practice was followed here too: The undertakers, the cart drivers, and the guards were redeported last.[36] Bodies had to be buried, those who could afford to pay had to be transported by carriage, and the sick and intractable had to be forced to march. Deportees leveraged connections and paid bribes to be assigned to posts that delayed redeportation. But there was a limit to these deferments, and even the privileged faced deportation in early June 1916. Hazarabedian was among them. He recounted his interaction with Rahmeddin:

> About two months after our arrival [in Abuharar], one of the guards, Rahm ed-Din, whom we had dubbed Kara Onbashuh, that is "Black Corporal," for obvious reasons, . . . said he was under orders to close down the place and evacuate it soon but, he added, "I'll make every effort to keep you and your families to the last." We thanked "Black Corporal" for his solicitude, but suggested that all of us be taken to Hamam, a rather nearby Syrian desert town, and see if we could get permission to stay there.[37]

The trek from Abuharar to the "rather nearby" Hamam was a grueling nine-hour journey with no transit camp in between. This meant that convoys that departed from Abuharar in the afternoon had to sleep in open air at whatever stretch of the desert they had reached by nightfall.[38] Within weeks, Abuharar was completely emptied.

Hamam

Erected on a stretch of desert on the western banks of the Euphrates, the transit camp of Hamam was the next stop for deportees.[39] The nearby village of Hamam (a small Arab tent-village of ten to fifteen families administratively connected to Rakka) had a telegram office and a police station—key components of communication and control needed to run camps—as well as two khans for travelers, used primarily by officials and officers.[40] Much of the new construction in the area, including at least one of the khans, was done by Armenian deportees.[41] At the height of its operation, several thousand tents stood at Hamam.[42] Around five thousand deportees were interned there when Litten passed through in February 1916.[43] He described a transit camp run by amateurs and neglected by authorities:

> Two war volunteers who had been here for 15 days had taken over command of the gendarme station in Hamam. They complained about the bad conditions they were having to face helplessly. Every day new Armenians would arrive whom they had to order to move on. But there was nothing to eat. Therefore there was nothing to do other than to send the starving on as soon as possible, so that the bodies would at least not be lying in the village.[44]

By June 1916, however, military preparations in Mesopotamia brought this backwater village into prominence, turning it into a hub along the Ottoman military supply line on the river. Constructing a robust supply route along the river stretching from Birecik/Jarablus all the way to Der Zor and Hit required thousands of laborers.[45] Storage facilities and armories needed to be built, roads repaired, supplies transported and stored, and livestock cultivated.[46] The need for deportee labor was pressing, and the survival of thousands of Armenians grew inextricably connected to the Ottoman army in the region. The camp at Hamam was divided into two. One part accommodated deportees who worked in the labor battalions, while the second was a transit area where deportees spent a day or two before being pushed farther downstream.[47] Thus, those with useful expertise or money for bribes avoided immediate transport to Der Zor.[48] Hazarabedian explained how three families managed to remain at the labor camp:

> Because Khoren, the son of Gosdan Effendi Varjabedian, was by profession a graduate surveyor who had taken his degree at the governmental School of

> Surveying in Constantinople, he was appointed a foreman of the project while Hagop Dishchekenian's son was accepted as a carpenter. As for us, the Hazarabedians, we remained with the "temporarily detained" group through the intervention of my brother's brother-in-law Nushan Arukian, who served as a security guard. We moved in with him in his tent.[49]

Supply and communication lines along the Tigris and Euphrates for troops and goods were key for battalions on the Mesopotamia front. Supply lines had proven crucial in the British victory in Basra (November 1914), their subsequent withdrawal from Ctesiphon (November 1915), and their ultimate defeat in Kut al Amara (April 1916) after a five-month siege.[50] The history of supply lines on the eastern front during the Great War remains understudied. Yet documents and memoirs point to the fact that the Ottomans—and, of course, the British—exerted much effort to maintain a robust line of communication and supply in Mesopotamia. Galip Bey supervised the work along the nodes on the Euphrates line from Meskeneh to Der Zor.[51] Hamam's sudden rise to prominence as one of the nodes (*menzil noktası*) along the supply line ushered in more Inspectorate for Troop Movements (*menzil müfettişliği*[52]) officials, and more demands for bribes. Officials knew that most deportees were willing to sacrifice a great deal to be selected for labor. The situation was ripe for exploitation, and the rank and file of camp officials and guards sought to profit from it.

Noticing the exorbitant sums of money pocketed by the line and point commanders, Ishak Çavuş, the Circassian head of the military station in Hamam and deportation director of the camp, told deportees that he did not recognize the selection made by others and would redeport everyone to Der Zor. His bluff worked, and those selected for labor bribed him as well.[53] The push by the point commanders to increase the number of Armenian laborers in a bid to secure more bribes, and the insistence of deportation officials (*sevk memuru*) on redeporting Armenians to Der Zor caused conflict.[54] But the majority did not have money to buy into this economy. In a letter (28 June) from Hamam to Beatrice Rohner, Preacher Vartan Geranian reported:

> There are many hundreds of poor deserted children, women and men here, weakened by hunger and sick, absolutely wretched figures, wandering aimlessly amongst the tents. At every meal at least 20–30 come to beg for a bit of bread. Many families have not eaten for days and do not have the courage to go begging.[55]

It was in this condition that the deportees were forced to march on. By September 1916, only 1,600 deportees were still at Hamam.[56] Bernau observed a "picture of hunger and horror. The men had been requisitioned for maneuvers, navvies or road-menders, as wages they receive an indigestible and insufficient piece of bread to give them the strength necessary for their exhausting work."[57] In other words, slave labor with a starvation ration was the alternative to death in Der Zor.

While deportee labor was readily available, the camp administration often found itself too understaffed to fulfill its responsibilities.[58] One official who volunteered his services at the camp in summer 1916 was a young, cross-eyed man, nicknamed Kör Fatih (Fatih the blind). The *müdür* (director) of Ayn Issa north of Rakka, he sometimes came to Hamam to run the redeportation process. He raped many women at the camp and had a reputation for taking bribes to allow deportees to remain at Hamam, and then redeporting them anyway.[59] Accounts from this period are full of references to camp officials and officers raping or selling women and children.[60] Resul, an Arab who served as a deportation official (*sevk memuru*) in Hamam, distributed women to gendarmes. Among the outrages he committed was the rape of Yester Koustikian, a fourteen-year-old girl from Bardizag.[61] Rapists and suppliers of women were part of an elaborate economy of sexual violence that was created in an environment of impunity, but regulated by individual initiative and peer dynamics, and not the central authorities.

Although several thousand Armenians avoided redeportation temporarily by being drafted into labor battalions along the river, the construction of the supply line was part of a broader military effort that viewed the Armenian presence along the Euphrates as dangerous. The decision to empty the camps from Meskeneh all the way to Der Zor was, in part, a consequence of the army's activity in the region, and concerns about Armenians posing a danger, whether through disease and contamination or sabotage. "Forbidding harmful Armenian people from congregating along military routes and the immediate deportation of the latter to the interior are appropriate," ordered Talaat by telegram on 19 July 1916.[62] Ten days later, he spoke of "steps that are required for the distribution and settlement to suitable places of the Armenians whose congregation in the river basin of the Euphrates and the military route is going to be dangerous for military transport" (29 July 1916).[63] Between Aleppo and military supply lines and fronts, there were no "suitable places" to dispatch Armenians, save under the sand.

Rakka

For the most part, Rakka stood as the antithesis of death by starvation, disease, and massacre that plagued the Euphrates line during the Armenian genocide. One of the largest and most important towns in the area, it hosted thousands of deportees, a significant number of whom settled in the town and escaped redeportation to Der Zor thanks to a combination of factors, not least of which was local authorities' and the Arab population's recognition of the skills and economic value of the incoming Armenians. Bernau knew he was witness to a unique phenomenon when he passed through the town on his journey from Aleppo to Der Zor in September 1916. "One must recognize merit wherever one meets it," he wrote, speaking of the goodwill of the district governor. "And what would be only strict duty in normal times on the part of an Ottoman civil servant towards Ottoman subjects, can pass for generosity and even heroism in the current circumstances."[64] And while sympathetic governors were a thing of the past from Aleppo to Der Zor, replaced by officials who were ready and willing to execute the Ministry of the Interior's plans, Rakka's consecutive district governors maintained a policy of laxness, if not outright humanitarianism, even at a time when Armenians were being butchered by the tens of thousands less than ninety miles down the river.

A town of up to three thousand households in 1915, Rakka is situated on a vast highland on the northern banks of the Euphrates, some thirty to forty-five minutes from the river.[65] Entering the town from the south, one encountered its market with dozens of shops and a few khans. Near the center of the market, behind the municipal building, stood the town square with the mosque and residential streets branching off in all directions. The Circassian neighborhood (*Çerkez mahallesi*), where Circassians were resettled some two decades earlier, occupied the western part of the town.[66] That the town was envisioned as a settlement area in Muftizâde Şükrü Kaya Bey's September 1915 directive on deportations and settlement does not explain the survival of several hundred Armenians there for the entire duration of the war.[67] After all, deportees were removed from most "settlement areas" in the region and massacred in summer 1916. In Rakka, only a small proportion of deportees, left homeless on the streets, faced a similar fate. The fact that the Armenians settled in Rakka were not redeported for the duration of the war was never a forgone conclusion, yet time and again, local dynamics prevented such action.

Some of the first deportees to be settled in Rakka arrived the very same month Şükrü Kaya's guideline was issued.[68] They were around 120 people from Zara (east of

Sivas) and the surrounding villages, mostly women and a few teenagers who came via Urfa. They were followed by several dozen women from Kangal, Yenikhan, and other villages of Sivas. These early arrivals received aid from the local authorities.[69] Kapigian noted that there were orders to settle twenty thousand people in Rakka temporarily. The local authorities, chiefly the young *kaymakam*, an Aleppian named Fehmi, and the *sevk memuru* Abid Agha benefitted from this settlement policy "as if it were a goldmine."[70] Kapigian described the process of entry into the city:

> Deportees arrived in Shamiye [across the river from Rakka] and stayed at a transit camp there for a few days. The *kaymakam* and Abid Agha cross the river every day and select among those who pay five to ten liras and bring them to Rakka, redeporting the rest to Der Zor. . . . They did the same to our caravan: They took the deportees from Erzerum in for five hundred liras and other gifts. And when we entered Rakka, there were already fifteen thousand deportees there.[71]

Others corroborated Kapigian's assertions about settlement in Rakka. Hratch A. Tarbassian was in the same convoy as Kapigian, arriving in Rakka on 5 January 1916.

> After walking several days under the burning desert sun, we reached Rakka, where we again bribed government officials to allow us to remain in that town. The Armenians from Khodortjur, Garmrug, and other places were driven toward Der el-Zor. We succeeded in keeping with us only one Armenian family and Mr. Garabed Kapigian, a teacher and writer, from Sepasdia. In Rakka, families from Garin [Erzerum] rented rooms in Arab houses, where they stayed for several months. One day the Kaymakam called Gariners to his office and, after giving *vesikas* (travel permits) to each of them, advised them to stay out of sight.[72]

Tarbassian and Kapigian agree about the circumstances of entry. Tarbassian even mentions Kapigian as someone who was not from Erzerum but managed to remain in the town. Yet he is silent about an issue that was of paramount importance—and a source of profound anger—for Kapigian, so much so that the latter allocated several pages to it in which he excoriates the people of Erzerum.[73] Apparently, the Armenian dignitaries from Erzerum went into Rakka and cut a secret deal with *kaymakam* Fehmi Bey, paying him five hundred liras to grant all Erzerum deportees entry into the city. "An official came to the camp and selected those [in our convoy who were] from Erzerum, separating them from those from

Pokr Hayk [Lesser Armenia] and Suruj," Kapigian wrote. "Many of us, posing as *Erzerumtsis*, had passed to the other side. The dignitaries of Erzerum one by one pointed us out, and had us removed from the group . . . [by force]."[74] The ties that bound deportees from the same city or village together during the deportations proved decisive here. In this particular case, those in the convoy who hailed from Erzerum were settled in Rakka and were likely to survive the war, while the rest were sent to the abattoirs of Der Zor.

Rakka's influx of deportees stopped soon after the entry of the *Erzerumtsis*. Kapigian recounted that Fehmi and the commander of the gendarmes in Rakka were removed from their positions after an officer from Urfa arrived to conduct a corruption investigation and found large caches of money including "the five hundred liras of the *Erzerumtsis*, mixed with Russian rubles." The *kaymakam* was sent to Aleppo for court-martialing, and deportees were no longer admitted into the city.[75] Deputy *kaymakam* Fahri Efendi, nicknamed Fahri the madman (*deli*), took charge for a brief period. He treated the town's Armenian population well.[76] He even secured entry into Rakka of several Armenian clergy and community leaders who were among deportees encamped on the other side of the river.[77]

Contemporaneous reports and accounts provide evidence on the number of Armenians settled in Rakka at different periods during the war. A month after the *Erzerumtsis* arrived, some one thousand deportees lived in the city and its surroundings according to Jesse B. Jackson.[78] In early September 1916, Bernau passed through and estimated "5 to 6,000 Armenians, especially women and children . . . dispersed in the various districts in the city, and living in groups of 50–60 in the houses which the leniency of the governor procured for the poorest."[79] The discrepancy in these figures can be explained by the fact that some Armenians were not in Rakka proper, but in nearby villages, and that hundreds of others had signed up in the summer of 1916 to work for the military on the construction of the supply line on the Euphrates.[80] Another estimate comes from a census of deportees in the region upon a request from Urfa.[81] Launched during Fahri Bey's tenure as *kaymakam*, the survey was completed during his successor's time and tallied somewhere between eight thousand and nine thousand Armenians in Rakka.[82]

In an eerie foreshadowing of Hugo Bettauer's fantasy novel *The City without Jews* that, in turn, foreshadowed the Holocaust, approximately seven hundred to eight hundred Rakka Armenian deportees were sent to Urfa in early 1917.[83] This development, which is striking because the Armenian population of Urfa had been massacred less than two years earlier, came as the city's need for laborers and experts in various fields grew desperate. Many Armenians sent to Urfa, to which Rakka was administratively connected, were forced to convert to Islam, while others were pushed on to nearby Karaköprü to work on road construction.[84] "The Turks had forcefully Islamized a number of Armenians whose services they needed desperately. Among them I met Dr. Abuhayatian, who had become Dr. Arif Kadri. There were also a pharmacist and dentist whose names I can't recall," survivor Hovhannes Toros Doumanian wrote.[85] Jackson, too, discussed the episode of Armenians returning to Urfa in an extensive report he prepared in 1918:

> It was in December, 1916, that the people of Ourfa, finding themselves without pharmacists, millers, bakers, tanners, shoemakers, dyers, weavers, tailors, or other artisans and tradesmen, presented a petition to the authorities to secure permission for the removal to Ourfa of a number of the Armenian tradesmen then located in Rakka, about three days distant from Ourfa. The petition was sent to Djemal Pasha who ordered 2,500 of such persons, including their families, to go to Ourfa, and before May, 1917, over 6,000 deported Armenians from the surrounding towns and villages had been collected there.[86]

As waves of people from Rakka and surrounding villages were forced to depart to Urfa, the number of Armenians in the *kaza* (district) of Rakka had shrunk to 4,521 by May 1917, according to official figures.[87] Thus, at the end of the war, there were two hundred Armenian households in Rakka, "in addition to those who lived in Arab tents."[88]

Deportees in Rakka had to live inconspicuously to avoid redeportation, but they also had to secure their livelihood. There were several hundred well-to-do deportees, some with families, who lived comfortably. They rented apartments and stores for one to three liras a month, considerably higher than the usual rate; they were the prime consumers in the city; they provided a fillip to crafts and trade at a time of war; and many sold their valuables for a fraction of the price in the markets.[89] Local officials and the Arab elite of the town realized the importance of these Armenians for the local economy, resisting efforts to deport them. "[They] did not spare efforts to courageously defend the Armenians even in the more dire and dangerous times . . . [so that among the deportees sent to the desert] those who survived in large numbers were the Armenian deportees of Rakka," argued Kapigian. He added that the reason for this was financial gain more than humanitarianism.[90]

Armenian deportees settled in Rakka had several possible sources of income.

Those with entrepreneurial skills and craftsmen fared well on their own. Many received funds from relatives and friends overseas.[91] But relief efforts were the only means to keep hundreds of others alive. Initially, local authorities distributed bread to four hundred to five hundred people, mostly women, but allocations were meager, the process was irregular, and the officials were corrupt. Later, bread distribution was discontinued and the poor were handed ninety *kuruş* a month, barely enough to purchase bread for a few days, but up to 2,500 Armenians received the allocated funds.[92] "Every deportee had a *cüzdan* [booklet-shaped official document], certified and sealed by the government and the *muhtar*s, and the allocated amount was registered there. The distribution of funds was quite regular," explained Kapigian, until it was discontinued at the end of 1917. The funds were sent from Urfa, the district governorate (*mutasarrıflık*).[93] Aid also came from the U.S. consulate in Aleppo, missionaries, and the Aleppo Armenian community.[94] On Easter Day 1916, two hundred Turkish liras that the Armenian Prelacy of Aleppo had sent to the camp were distributed to the needy.[95] Kapigian pointed out that after the crackdown of the authorities in the fall of 1915, and particularly with the arrest of Father Harutiun Yesayan, who chaired the Prelacy's committee for deportees, and one hundred others in Aleppo, the Armenian community was no longer in a position to send much.[96]

The greatest threat to deportees settled in Rakka came in the summer of 1916, when the provincial district governor of the Zor district telegrammed the *kaymakam* of Rakka, Fahri Bey, asking him to dispatch his Armenians to Der Zor. Fahri rejected the request, arguing that he got his orders from the Urfa district governorate to which Rakka was administratively connected. He further noted that his town was a settlement area for deportees based on an *irade* (decree from the Sultan), and only another *irade* could reverse the decision.[97] The *mutasarrıf* of Urfa responded similarly. Thus, the Armenians of Rakka were by and large spared deportation to the slaughterhouses of Der Zor.[98]

Yet those in Rakka who could not afford a place to stay and were not contributing to the economy were redeported. Kapigian speaks of several hundred starving deportees who had no means of fending for themselves, let alone renting a house and remaining out of sight. These less fortunate individuals were gathered and sent to Der Zor. The redeportations occurred several times in spring and fall 1916. In another case, a group of people who were settled in nearby Arab villages were removed by the locals from their tents and brought to town in April 1916. "They remained [in Rakka] for a week, those who had money rented homes and were protected. And one day, they collected the rest, crossed them to the other side, and sent them to Der Zor."[99]

Kapigian's hypothesis as to why the Armenians of Rakka escaped deportation is helpful but incomplete. He had been in Rakka for more than half a year by the summer of 1916. His account of the events in town indicates that he was well informed and well connected, but he had no way of knowing the dynamics at the center. The most he could possibly know would have been what the highest authorities at Rakka had confided in him or others. That the local authorities and elites resisted instructions to deport Armenians who had become key to the town's economy is clear. But local officials are ultimately in the service of the state, and the most they can do is make their case and resist. The center can push back. Other governors and district governors in the region were removed from their posts for not fully cooperating with the center. However, as we saw in the cases of Aleppo and Smyrna, the center also relented sometimes. Whatever the reasons behind Talaat's decision to not push harder in this case, one thing is clear: the Armenians in Rakka by and large escaped massacre.[100]

Scholars studying the economics of the Armenian genocide have focused primarily on the confiscation of property. Several other economic dimensions, chief among them the impact of local and deportee Armenians on the economies of cities like Aleppo, Smyrna, Istanbul, and the much smaller Rakka, await historical examination. Economics explains, at least in part, why Armenians in these cities were not deported (or in the case of Rakka, redeported) during the genocide.[101] Furthermore, the exploitation of Armenian capital (and labor, particularly in Aleppo, Urfa, and along the lower Euphrates) has implications on key issues in genocide studies: the agency of state functionaries and local leaders, their connections with Armenians, the survival strategies of victims, and the long-term impact of genocide on societies. Economics was not the primary reason for the destruction of Armenians in the Ottoman Empire—in fact, it sometimes proved a reason not to destroy them.

CHAPTER SEVEN

Zor

That Immense Graveyard of Our Martyrs

> Your inhabitants,
> Slaughterhouse Zor,
> Will forever chew on Armenian corpses,
> And always drink blood.
>
> —Sahag-Mesrob

No place is more intimately associated with the Armenian genocide than the Zor district, the "settlement area" where up to two hundred thousand Armenians were massacred between March and October 1916. In this chapter, we examine genocide and humanitarian resistance in the region. We piece together the history of Zor from May 1915, when the first deportees arrived in the area, to the spring of 1916, documenting how a partial settlement policy for the remnants of the Armenian nation transformed into a second wave of genocidal killings in the spring and summer of 1916, and how Armenians resisted annihilation.

The District and the City

With a population of 66,294 (of which only 525 were non-Muslims) occupying an area slightly larger than Vermont, New Hampshire, and Massachusetts combined, the administrative district (*mutasarrıflık*) of Zor was one of the most sparsely populated regions of the entire empire, and for good reason: the scarcity of cultivable land; the scorching heat during the day, the biting cold at night; and the authorities' inability to exert control, root out banditry, and settle the area's nomadic tribes created a hostile environment.[1] As historian Fuat Dündar has argued, Talaat was fully aware of these challenges. He had stated during a parliamentary debate less than a year before the genocide that sending refugees to the area without major financial investments meant "all of them would [die] of hunger over there."[2] That less than a year later, while world war was raging, he deported Armenians to this region without making necessary provisions demonstrates that his intent was not mere relocation. Still, as historian Samuel Dolbee has shown, Der Zor was not a strictly barren and hostile environment, and although "sending Armenians to remote, inaccessible, hard-to-manage areas killed many, . . . it also allowed some people, mainly children, to slip away."[3]

Der Zor, the administrative center of the district, was the largest city in this desert region, with a population of fourteen thousand prior to the arrival of deportees.[4] Situated three hundred kilometers southeast of Aleppo (a six-day journey), it served as "an informal capital" and center for trade in Syria-Mesopotamia.[5] Standing on the banks of the Euphrates, it was surrounded by trees and gardens that "from a distance, gave us a good impression," observed author and survivor Yervant Odian upon arrival.[6] Dr. Schacht, a German captain in the medical corps, referred to it as "not an ugly city, with lovely, wide streets," as he passed through.[7] At its core, Der Zor consisted of a broad avenue and two parallel streets where administrative offices, the mosque, hospital, pharmacy, khans, and the market were concentrated.[8] Although predominantly Muslim, the city was home to a Christian community, with three churches serving the local Assyrian, Chaldean, and Armenian Catholic congregations. The latter comprised 120–150 families (215 people in total in 1914), mostly Arabic speaking, that had emigrated from Mardin in recent decades.[9]

The First Convoys

The first convoys arrived in Der Zor in May and June 1915.[10] The Council for Refugees established by the Armenian Prelacy in Aleppo dispatched immediate assistance to these deportees, most of whom had traveled from Zeytun.[11] In its 27 May meeting, the council resolved to send forty liras to support these deportees through the Catholic Prelacy in Aleppo.[12] When chronicler Mihran Aghazarian arrived in Der Zor on 24 June after forty-seven days on the road, he observed a camp of approximately 150 tents spread across the outskirts of the city, sheltering three thousand Zeytun Armenians.[13] These so-called tents were pieces of blankets and covers extended over four wooden pillars to shelter the deportees from the blazing sun. In the city, "the large khan [was] completely overcrowded. All of the available rooms, roofs and verandas had been taken over. Mainly women and children, but also a number of men were sitting on their blankets wherever they could find a bit of shade," wrote Sister Laura Möhring who visited the city in July.[14] By the time survivor Dikran Jebejian arrived in Der Zor in late summer, there were many vacant rooms, since Zeytun Armenians had been redeported in the direction of Mosul.[15]

A local committee in conjunction with the *mutasarrıf* ran the settlement process, which was grueling, inefficient, and corrupt.[16] When a convoy arrived, Armenians employed by the city authorities prepared a list of deportees.[17] In the meantime, the new arrivals had to wait in tents or in khans for weeks to find out whether they were to be admitted to Der Zor—typically after paying "administrative fees" and bribes—or sent away to a nearby area to live under tents "temporarily."[18] They had little, if anything, to eat. Carrion was an important source of nourishment for many. In the summer, they consumed desert locusts after grilling them on an open fire.[19] This form of nourishment in Syria was not limited to Armenians. The locust infestation of Syria—one of the worst the region had witnessed for decades—"exerted a massive blow in a short period of time, wiping out at least 536,000 tons of food (the actual amount must be vastly higher) over the course of six–seven months (from primarily April 1915 to October 1915)," writes historian Zachary J. Foster, leading to tens of thousands of starvation-related deaths in the year that followed.[20] The irony of starving people eating the very locusts that helped precipitate starvation was not lost on the press. "Noting how so many villagers were hungry that they were actually eating the locusts, the newspaper [*Al-Qabas*] described how 'the situation had reversed.' If once Syrians had fearfully shouted, 'The locust has arrived!' the popularity of eating locusts had made the insects justified in meeting the arrival of people with a similarly fearful shout of 'The Syrians have arrived!'" writes Samuel Dolbee.[21]

The Aleppo Armenian community sent help to Der Zor as early as May 1915, despite the obstacles they faced. Catholicos Sahag Khabayan, having secured permission from Cemal Pasha in July 1915 to dispatch priests to attend to deportee "spiritual needs" in camps, sent Father Sahag, a priest from Kilis, and pharmacist Iskender Efendi (Sarkis) to the district of Zor. He provided the delegates with a check for sixty liras to be cashed upon arrival. This was a risk, as it blatantly went beyond addressing "spiritual needs." And indeed, the Ministry of the Interior sent a telegram to the Aleppo governorate notifying them that Father Sahag and pharmacist Iskender Efendi, who carried documents from Aleppo authorizing them to visit Der Zor, were illegally distributing money to the deportees there.[22] This was followed by a telegram to Der Zor asking the authorities to send the two back to Aleppo immediately.[23] Despite its brevity, this trip was not only useful in terms of providing assistance, but it supplied the Catholicos with firsthand information on the number and condition of deportees in Der Zor, which he communicated to the consuls in Aleppo. On 31 July, Walter Rössler filed a report mentioning the visit and the intelligence it furnished: "Those arriving in Der Zor come from Zeytun, Yarpuz, Alabash, Albistan. There were 15,328 of them, of which 10,000 were put up in the town, the rest in the surrounding area."[24] Father Sahag likely secured these numbers from Armenian employees of the local government tasked with conducting censuses and providing statistics pertaining to arriving convoys. Der Zor district governor Ali Suat Bey was in Aleppo around the same time, having accompanied Father Sahag and pharmacist Iskender Efendi from Ras ul-Ain to Aleppo to guarantee their safety, and corroborated these numbers.[25]

Summer of 1915

The first convoys were fortunate compared to those that arrived in the summer of 1915: only four hundred lives were lost on the trek.[26] As convoys continued pouring in, the Interior Ministry instructed various regions to stop sending deportees to Der Zor, as the number of Armenians in the district had exceeded 10 percent of the local population by early July.[27] However, one that had departed before the injunction was issued arrived in August. They comprised only of a fraction of their number at departure. Remnants of a convoy of 1,730 women from Kharpert (Harput)[28] reached the campsite across the river on 14 August and were left to their fate. The next day, Aghazarian, a Turkish scribe, a policeman, and a local Assyrian by the name of George Soukkar crossed the bridge to prepare a list of the deportees and begin settlement proceedings. Soukkar is remembered warmly in Armenian sources as a person who worked hard to settle deportees in the city. "He spent so much time with the deportees that he too eventually contracted typhus and died [in early 1916]," observed Andonian.[29] The Kharpert convoy was in harrowing condition. Aghazarian describes the scene:

> Not a single peep or movement: All of them had turned into corpses on the burning sand field. Prodding them gently with our feet we tried to tell the living from the dead. Those who were alive asked for water. . . . They had nothing. They were bare naked. . . . I learned that they were mostly from Kharpert Mezre, and had been on the road for three months. George Soukkar covered them with pieces of cloth, while we registered 542 living, and 23 dead. Only that many had arrived in Der Zor.[30]

In August, numerous convoys arrived from Armenian-inhabited provinces, predominantly comprising emaciated women, who passed through the main avenue en route to Salihiyye, fifteen minutes west of the city, to settle among the walls of historic ruins there.[31]

Mutasarrıf Ali Suat Bey facilitated the settlement of deportees. Commending him on his efforts to alleviate the suffering of Armenians, his Western interlocutors described him as "a high class gentleman," "a humane person," and "a man of courage" for whom deportees "had only praise."[32] Armenians shared the sentiment: "We ought to mention Ali Suat Bey's name with great respect," writes Aghazarian.[33] Moreover, as historian Hilmar Kaiser argues, Ali Suat Bey disputed with central authorities when gendarmes and bandits, upon the instigation of Diyarbakir governor Reşid Bey, attacked deportees in Diyarbakir, Ras ul-Ain, and elsewhere in the region. Ali Suat's efforts, however, had limited success, as Talaat turned a blind eye to his complaints and even rewarded the perpetrators.[34]

Ali Suat Bey's humanitarianism was an exception among the city's officials, many of whom abused and tortured deportees. The members of the committee dealing with the arriving convoys had little interest in settling them. "When the first convoys arrived from Zeytun, in the absence of Ali Suat Bey, and with no specific orders from the center, the committee decided to redeport them to Mount Abdulaziz and scatter the rest among Arabs. . . . I could now feel the shiver of death," observed Aghazarian.[35] The redeportation plan was eventually scrapped. Ali Suat Bey's presence helped the condition of deportees, but every time the *mutasarrıf* left town, "the committee resumed its [dirty] work."[36]

By late September, the number of deportees in Der Zor had risen to 23,300, two thirds of whom were in dire condition.[37] The guideline on the deportation and settlement of Armenians sent to provinces and districts including Der Zor strengthened Ali Suat Bey's hand, reinforcing the message of earlier telegrams designating Zor as a settlement area. He insisted that he was acting "according to orders."[38] Yet he continued exercising caution to calm mounting discontent among other officials and locals, while working "diligently in scattering the Armenians on farm lands, building homes for them, providing food, clothing and medical attendance, and [treating them] with great consideration."[39] Levon Shashian, an exiled Armenian intellectual from Istanbul, was Ali Suat Bey's partner and confidant during the settlement process. Shashian, "a kind-hearted, young gentleman . . . with a keen eye on political developments" had been deported from Istanbul to Der Zor on the accusation of being an arms dealer for Armenian rebels, but had soon become a friend of the district governor, as well as the de facto leader of the Armenian deportees in Der Zor. He was well-off and had rented the municipal garden "for special considerations," noted Aghazarian.[40] Shashian established an agency there purchasing assets from deportees at fair prices, sparing them the ordeal of selling their possessions for close to nothing in the town market, and storing them there, in order to resell to locals.[41]

Harsh Climate

Convoys continued arriving in the fall and early winter of 1915 in numbers that the city was unable to accommodate.[42] Thousands were shoved into camps in the biting cold across the river from the city. Dr. Schacht observed "a large camp above and below the town [Der Zor]. On the left bank of the river next to the pontoon bridge masses of dying people have been camped in huts made of foliage typical for this area. These are the forgotten whose only liberator is death."[43] The environment in the city itself was turning increasingly hostile toward deportees, as locals' resentment festered. "Insult and disdain had become a general phenomenon in the city: A trip to the marketplace for Armenians inevitably meant being beaten, spat on, and insulted."[44] Dr. Schacht witnessed how "the Armenians are stoned by the Arabs, beaten, jeered and laughed at."[45] The hostility of the locals in the city of Der Zor was reminiscent of the situation in Aleppo and Bab. Armenians were blamed for the ills that had befallen the region: disease, economic stagnation, and starvation. Indeed, typhus (particularly during winter) and malaria (during summer) was sometimes carried by arriving deportees and caused the death of thousands. Deportees were of course not afforded the delousing machines or the medical care German soldiers enjoyed. Without care, about half of those who came down with typhus died.[46] Survivor Makroohie Koomrian, who took refuge in her town's (Marash) American Central Turkey College for Girls while her family was deported and ultimately perished in Der Zor, remembered:

> In all the days of the deportation, I had received just one letter from my family, a note from my father asking that I send them some quinine because, he said, a disease called malaria had broken out among the deportees and quinine was the most effective medicine. I had been able to purchase a large quantity of quinine and immediately mailed it off to them, but I never learned if they received it . . . because I never received another letter.[47]

For the locals, it mattered little that Armenians were brought to this condition through government policies of deportation and massacre. All they could see was Armenians contaminating their region, and their resentment manifested itself in attacks on deportees and protests demanding that the local authorities expel the Armenians. This growing agitation was particularly palpable in Der Zor, where thousands of Armenians were settled and tens of thousands of others were huddled across the river, awaiting permission to enter. It is for this reason that for long periods in the fall and winter of 1915, the city was declared off-limits to new deportees.[48]

The establishment of an orphanage was perhaps the most notable good news for Armenians in and around the city in the biting winter of 1915.[49] It is noteworthy that Aghazarian attributed the establishment of the orphanage to the district governor's benevolence, while we now know that the latter was acting upon the orders of the central authorities.[50] Ali Suat Bey provided the Çelebi Khan near the municipality building for this purpose. Aghazarian was entrusted with the establishment and administering of the orphanage. On 14 November, the very first day, 470 orphans, aged two to twelve, were registered. Within a few days, the number rose to 1,700.[51] Aghazarian describes in some length the shortages and the difficulties he faced when running the orphanage:

> The earmarked assistance was altogether insufficient for so many [orphans]. At best, each received some lentil or bulgur soup and two hundred grams of bread every day. And there was nothing to cover them up with at night. . . . A few children lost their mind and some twenty died daily. I reported to Ali Suat Bey on a daily basis. He visited the orphanage a few times and made certain arrangements. Dr. Hagop Hagopian was assigned as health examiner, and our joint appeals resulted in the purchase of mats to cover the room floors. A month later, in February 1916, the orphans were partly clothed [while many had no clothing before]; and one of the local baths was allocated to our orphans. The number of deaths started to go down.[52]

Ali Suat Bey soon found himself in a bind. A number of Turkish officials complained to the Interior Ministry about what they described as the deportees' good living conditions (citing the example of the orphanage, among others), and pointing to risks of an Arab-Armenian collaboration in the region (28 February).[53] Conspiracy theories of such collusion continued to be stoked by local officials and gained greater traction after Sharif Husayn declared the Arab Revolt (5 June). These accusations may very well have helped precipitate the decision for massacres in the district.

Ali Suat Bey was asked to report to Aleppo by early March, but declined citing health problems.[54] Within weeks, three Committee of Union and Progress officials appeared in Der Zor. They "were known to the people as '*uzun cizmeliler*' (the ones with the tall boots). The operatives visited the orphanage at the first opportunity. Cautioned by Levon Shashian, I responded to all their questions with 'I don't know.' They left the city soon," recalled Aghazarian.[55] The appearance of these operatives in Der Zor in March 1916 coincided with the appearance of officials in Rakka.[56] The very same month, a series of measures were taken, including a strict ban on aid distribution to deportees,[57] and the removal of Ali Suat Bey from his position. (He was appointed deputy governor of Baghdad.)[58] In late March, Ali Suat Bey left Der Zor. These developments, coupled with the beginning of the massacres of close to thirty thousand Armenians in Ras ul-Ain, made March 1916 an ominous time for the deportees in the entire region, who had by that point come to believe that the worst was over and that there would be no more persecutions.

The weeks separating the massacres in Ras ul-Ain from the destruction of the Armenians in Der Zor constituted a preparatory period during which authorities poured as many deportees as possible into Der Zor and organized a practicable method of killing them. The wheels of a second phase of mass murder were set in motion.

While the authorities were planning the destruction of the Armenians in Ras ul-Ain and Der Zor, the resistance network continued working to save lives. Armenian couriers clandestinely brought supplies, often purchased with funds furnished by Western diplomats and missionaries, and distributed them in the camps. Lawyer Sami as-Solh, a Sunni Muslim politician who would later become a five-time prime minister of Lebanon, wrote about U.S. Consul Jesse B. Jackson's role in this effort in a letter penned in the immediate aftermath of the Great War:

> After having hid myself for some time in a house which he [Jackson] had indicated to me, I managed to flee from Aleppo, and sought refuge with the Anezi tribe near Der-el-zor. The deportation "en masse" of the Armenians to those regions had already started, and I had occasion to witness the humanitarian work which Mr Jackson performed with such admirable zeal. He used to send out men with food and clothing for distribution among the poor Armenians, and exercised, at the same time, unremitting efforts towards the welfare of the British prisoners and other foreigners in trouble. As the needs exceeded any singlehanded effort he secured the cooperation of some notables and officials who could loyally respond to so noble a call, and this he did with commendable discretion and tact so as to avoid any retaliation on the part of the Turks.[59]

Informative as it is, the article elides the fact that most of the couriers who delivered the assistance were Armenian members of the resistance network, who risked their lives and, more often than not, perished in the line of duty. Rev. Father Pierre Merjimekian, an Armenian Catholic Priest who was deported from Angora, described how Jackson relied on

> courageous distributors of relief, furnished by him and carrying large sums, [who] ran in all sympathy, like lightning as consoling angels, and wherever they encountered exiles they served out—to outstretched hands. Hama, Idlib, Damascus, Meskeneh, Rakka, Der el-Zor, Djerablous, Ras-el-Ain, Souroudj, Bedejik, Ourfa, Bab, Islahia, Katma, in fact all the localities in the vicinity of Aleppo received the visit of his distributors who, at the risk of their lives and the cost of a thousand sacrifices have helped and relieved thousands of exiles, starving in the deserts.[60]

In a book she published after the war, Sister Beatrice Rohner dedicates a chapter to a pious Armenian man by the name of Garabed, who went all the way to Der Zor on several trips, spreading the word of God and distributing Rohner's funds—gold coins sewn into his clothes and belt—to deportees in need, until one day he went to the desert and never returned.[61]

The Dress Rehearsal: Ras ul-Ain

Ras ul-Ain, with a predominantly Circassian and Chechen population, was a subdistrict of Der Zor that gained prominence during the Baghdad Railway construction.[62] According to the U.S. consul in Baghdad Charles F. Brissel, "The last station on the railroad from Aleppo toward Mosul, [Ras ul-Ain] is nothing more than some mud huts with scant means of accommodation."[63] Deportees arriving by road (via Urfa in the northwest or via Mardin in the northeast) or train (via Aleppo) passed through Ras ul-Ain on their way to Der Zor beginning in May 1915. Within weeks, convoys of women and children, many of whom were traumatized by violent robbery and the murder of their male relatives, conglomerated in the village. Their number soon exceeded ten thousand.[64] Listed as a transit camp (*merkez-i tevakkuf*) in the 8 October deportation guideline,[65] Ras ul-Ain had grown to a concentration camp of several thousand tents by fall 1915. By February 1916, it quartered twenty thousand deportees.[66]

For a few months, the Ras ul-Ain authorities and the Aleppo Armenian community provided assistance to the deportees.[67] The Armenian humanitarian resistance network even tried to bring as many people as possible from Ras ul-Ain to relative safety in Aleppo. Survivor Maritza Kejejian and a few others in her group were rescued by Aleppian Arakel Karajian with the help of his Circassian accomplice Arslan Bey, a government official, and transported to Aleppo.[68] Arslan Bey helped save forty Armenians by temporarily sheltering them in his house at great risk.[69] His collaboration with Karajian illustrates the importance of Muslim actors in the humanitarian and rescue efforts Aleppo Armenians waged during the genocide.[70]

Deportees dealt with shortages creatively and adhered to cleanliness measures. "We did not have soap, and did not even have money to buy some. We went to the water [there was a pond nearby] and used the sand as soap for washing clothes and bathing. We didn't have spare clothes, so we used to divide up into two groups. Some of us would go into the water until their clothes were dried, and then the others entered while we dried their clothes," explained survivor Yeranuhi Simonian.[71] In instances where local authorities provided bread, deportees selected representatives from each town to distribute it to their fellow townspeople. Survivor Haroutiun Mertchian refers to this process and proceeds to describe how within days, the distribution was halted, leading to mayhem. The gendarmes threw pieces of bread at crowds of deportees and were entertained by the ensuing stampedes, which killed many.[72]

As deportees tried to survive, availing themselves of outside help when possible, attacks, abductions, and looting continued to pose a serious threat. Deportees complained to Zor district governor Ali Suat Bey who was visiting town. According to Shukru Aghazarian, a deportee at the camp, Suat Bey returned with a security contingent, interrogated locals, and ordered the execution of four Bedouins responsible for robberies and the murder of an Armenian from Hajin.[73] This served as deterrent, but only briefly. Until its liquidation in the summer of 1916, the inmates continued to suffer from Circassian, Chechen, and Bedouin bandit attacks.

Women and young girls were the main targets. "The Circassians and Arabs from Ras ul-Ain took the prettiest girls home with them. . . . The policemen carried on a flourishing trade with the girls against payment of a few Medjidies, anyone could take a girl of his choice either for a short while or forever," according to a witness named Bastendorff.[74] There were more than thirty Armenian girls from Sivas married to locals, according to Simonian.[75] Forced marriage was not the worst that could happen. In the cover of darkness, Bedouins attacked and raped deportees with the tacit agreement of guards. "Every night there was yelling and screaming at the camp. . . . I saw with my own eyes the rape of little girls," she added.[76] According to Rössler, a woman was raped by a group of eight men. She tried to commit suicide by throwing herself on a railway line as a train approached. A German engineer saved her and brought her to Aleppo.[77]

Many children forcibly taken by locals or sold by destitute deportees trying to save their youngsters from death,[78] resisted their new "owners" in any way they could. Survivor Stepan Aghazarian, who himself was kidnapped, met about a dozen preteen girls whose abductors "complained that these girls had refused to eat and would not talk to their 'masters'" in the same Bedouin village where he was taken.[79]

Deportees were pressured to convert to Islam. Survivor Shukru Aghazarian did so upon the advice of the police chief in order to be able to stay in Ras ul-Ain and avoid being killed during redeportation to Mosul. He described the process years later:

> We deputized a group of elderly deportees to go to the Governor and tell him that we wished to convert to Islam. The official wired the Central Government in Constantinople to that effect. A few weeks later, a message came from the capital city approving our "conversion," and a Moslem clergyman came to us, taught us how to pray, Moslem-style, five times a day and changed our name to Moslem types.[80]

Many refused to convert. "The Circassians (or Tchetchens) endeavored to force us to become Moslems, but we answered them, 'We will throw ourselves into the water and die, but we will not become Moslems.'"[81]

In March 1916, authorities accelerated redeportation from the Ras ul-Ain camp. Armenians who had sought refuge in the houses of local Circassians were not spared either, according to Kejejian.[82] Convoys were marched in two directions: toward Der Zor and Mosul. Orders from the center stipulated that redeportation to Mosul avoid the main road, under the pretext that this "most important" military supply line needed to remain free from typhus and other epidemics.[83] By then, the Interior Ministry had sent a telegram to a number of provinces and provincial districts in the region, including Der Zor, prohibiting the entry of foreign nationals or non-Muslim merchants into areas of deportation and settlement of Armenians.[84] The Armenians could now be killed out of sight. Still, there were those who survived the mass murder and told what they witnessed. Yeghia Paraghamian of Tomarza was one of them. After surviving seven months in Ras ul-Ain they were given some dry *kahke* (breadsticks) and told they were being redeported toward Mosul. On the way, gendarmes left the convoy. As the deportees carried on, Bedouin and Chechen bandits descended upon them, killing men, abducting women and children, and looting.[85] Mihran Zekiyan's convoy "walked over corpses from Ras ul-Ain to Meyadin for a week." One morning, they woke up to find themselves surrounded by Kurds and Chechens who started slaughtering them indiscriminately. "I stayed among the dead for three days. I had no wounds, but was afraid to get out. During the day, I used to watch the thousands of crows flying over the corpses," he remembered.[86]

"It was common occurrence," Jackson recalled, to hear in Aleppo news of massacres in Ras ul-Ain.[87] German diplomats, too, were well aware of them. "A first transport has been attacked and smashed to pieces while walking towards Der Zor," reported the German ambassador to his superiors.[88] "The largest part of the [Ras ul-Ain] concentration camp, consisting of 14,000 people, had been destroyed" and "400 families had been led out of the camp and murdered en route," reported Rössler. He explained the annihilation process based on "reliable enquiries of a

German" who had returned on 22 April. "For a period of one whole month, 300 to 500 of them have been led out of the camp daily . . . and massacred about 10 km away from Ras-ul-Ain. . . . A Turkish officer who, because of these occurrences, was taking the kaymakam of Ras ul-Ain to task, received the calm answer that he was acting on orders," he reported.[89] Thus, within a month, the concentration camp in Ras ul-Ain had shrunk to two thousand deportees. Most of the former inmates were massacred on the roads to Der Zor and Mosul.

Annihilation

In the few months separating Der Zor district governor Ali Suat Bey's removal and newly appointed Salih Zeki Bey's arrival, the district was governed by the *muhasebeci* (bookkeeper), who was "incapable of doing evil" but also lacked authority, allowing others to exploit the deportees.[90] Salih Zeki Bey arrived in Der Zor via Aleppo and Ras ul-Ain. In Aleppo in early June 1916, Zeki was hosted by Armenag Mazloumian, the youngest of the brothers running the celebrated Hotel Baron, who did his utmost to predispose the new district governor of Zor positively toward Armenians.[91] As we shall see, Mazloumian's efforts were futile. Zeki Bey was on a mission. "I have it on the most reliable authority that [Zeki Bey] stated before his departure from Istanbul that there was no use in asking him to grant any favors to Armenians, not for permission for their departure from Deir, nor for any other consideration whatever to be shown to any of them," Jackson reported.[92] Zeki Bey was in Ras ul-Ain for several days around 18 June and visited Suvar, Sheddadiya, and Hasirca, all Chechen villages near the Khabur area.[93] He also visited camps along the Euphrates line and met with their directors.[94] During these visits, which continued in the weeks that followed, Zeki sought to accomplish two things: the redeportation of as many Armenians as possible to Der Zor, and the recruitment of Circassian bands, some of which had participated in the Ras ul-Ain massacres, to assist him in his annihilation plans. Zeki also hosted in his house three Chechens from Sheddadiya and Hasirca. "Their appearance in Der Zor was interesting. They stayed at the district governor's house that night and had a meeting until morning with him," noted Aghazarian.[95] For people aware of Zeki's activities, the writing was on the wall. Rössler commented that Bernau, who visited the region and prepared a report, was "convinced that as long as Zeki Bey, the present mutasarrıf, remains in Der-el-Zor, all the Armenians who enter his territory are doomed."[96]

Soon after his arrival in Der Zor, Zeki toured the city and was outraged that several dozen well-to-do Armenians who had settled in the city had all but taken over the market there during the commercial lull of the previous six months, "turning it into a veritable Armenia," according to one account.[97] Indeed, during Ali Suat Bey's tenure, the condition of many Armenians who had secured entry into the city had, in the words of Bernau, improved to the extent that "a certain number of them had even begun a small trade and would have been happy to remain in this town."[98] Survivor Dikran Jebejian remembered how deportees who had arrived from Smyrna, Tekirdağ, Bursa, and Istanbul took over the Der Zor market, renting the best stores at high prices in the town center.[99] Joseph Tawtal (Taoutel), a Maronite from Aleppo who worked in Der Zor at the time for the Germans and the Fourth Army, estimated that there were 126,000 Armenians in the area upon Zeki's arrival.[100]

The situation deteriorated within days of Zeki's assumption of his responsibilities as district governor. Three Armenians (Setrag Kasabian, Harutiun Satjian, and a man named Garabed, all from Zeytun) who prepared lists of deportees for the local authorities were exiled to Kevkeb (Kawkab, north of Hama) and two others (Harutiun Vosgerichian and Khosrov Shirikjian), who had close ties with the former district governor, to Sheddadiya under accusations of stealing from deportees and corresponding with the British army, respectively.[101] While the second accusation was dubious, the first may have had a kernel of truth in it and provided Zeki with an excuse for collective punishment. Rössler reports:

> An Armenian in Der-el-Zor, who believed that he was discriminated against during the distribution of financial aid, or attempted to procure an unfair advantage for himself, demanded a certain sum from one of his countrymen who was distributing the money, or he would notify the government of the secretly run relief action. He actually did this when his demand was refused, whereupon the mutesarrif stated, "If money has been distributed, it must have been for the purpose of purchasing weapons (although this was completely out of the question). Thus the Armenians are revolutionaries and must be destroyed." Even though the mutesarrif would have continued these atrocious acts without resorting to this welcome excuse, it was necessary to mention this move because a report that ignored it would not have been complete.[102]

A few days later, Zeki ordered those Armenians who were unable to provide for themselves to leave the city within three days and cross to the Jezire side of the river (the eastern bank), promising them food and shelter.[103] The deportees knew the conditions on the other side and did not heed Zeki's call. Within a week, he issued another order asking all deportees in the two neighborhoods where the bulk of the Armenians had settled to leave the city within three days, as "the houses in those two neighborhoods will be taken over by the military authorities." While some Armenians followed the order this time, most simply escaped to other neighborhoods and sought refuge in the homes of Armenians there. This was followed by a third announcement, asking *all* Armenians in town to cross to the other side, where they would be "settled in villages and receive land and planting seeds. Those who violate this order will be severely punished." Again, few came forth. Finally, the town crier announced the decisive order on 21 July: "All Armenians in the city, without exception, must exit the city and cross to Jezire within twenty-four hours. Thereafter, Armenians spotted in the city will be shot by the police. Arabs who keep Armenians in their homes will pay a fifty lira fine."[104] Survivor Armen Anush, hiding in a caravansary room in the city, later recalled:

> No Armenian businessman was left in the market. All the shopkeepers and workers were arrested in their stores. . . .
>
> The women or boys who worked for this or that master could no longer go out on the street, as leaving their workplaces meant being arrested and driven to the bridge and beyond, where the deportees were taken away caravan by caravan, to places like Sheddadeh and Khabur, to be burned alive or murdered with hatchets.[105]

Concomitantly, Zeki arrested thirty prominent Armenians in the city, including Shashian, Levon Sahagian (a wealthy Armenian from Aintab) and two priests.[106] In a letter (17 July) to Sister Beatrice Rohner, Araxia Jebejian reported, "Today they arrested all clergymen and male leaders. Some of the people have left, others will be going soon, and the order has been given out by the crier that they must all leave by the end of the week."[107] Shashian and some fifteen others from the group were taken away by armed Chechens and gendarmes, who tortured them to death.[108] The others, "teachers, lawyers, and clergymen are said to have been . . . imprisoned," reported German chargé d'affairs in Aleppo Hermann Hoffmann.[109] They, too, were tortured and killed, except three.[110] Similar arrests took place elsewhere in the region. In Marat, for example, more than a hundred men were thrown into prison, according to Dikran Jambazian from Tarsus, who survived the Der Zor massacre and escaped to Aleppo.[111] The same policy of decapitating the community before deportations—as was the case in Istanbul and other cities empire-wide on 24 April 1915 and the weeks that followed and in Aleppo in fall 1915—was thus put in motion in the Der Zor region.

With the Armenian community leadership exiled or killed, Zeki moved confidently and hurriedly with his annihilation plan. The first convoy of deportees, which included the families of the arrested community leaders, left in mid-July from the Jezire side of the Der Zor bridge. Twenty other convoys, large and small, followed in the next several months. As the first Armenian deportees were marched out of the city, Zeki telegrammed Sebka, Meyadin, and Ane (all within his jurisdiction) one more time, asking the authorities there to send him their deportees.[112] Armenians were also being pushed to Der Zor from as far away as Aleppo. "The embassy ought to know that the A's are being harassed to death. . . . There are about 8,000 in this neighborhood (Aleppo) and 200 were sent on the 12th [of August], 150 last night, and the collection goes on daily wherever they can be dragged from their hiding places. It is a complete extermination," an alarmed Jackson alerted his superiors.[113]

Diplomatic records support Armenian accounts on the emptying of Der Zor city and the massacres that ensued. Jackson notes how deportees "from certain regions such as Aintab, Marash, Angora, etc., [were] cited to leave on stipulated days. They were told that they would be conducted to certain villages on the Khabur river . . . and were sent off under strong escort of gendarmes. Some arrived at small villages on the Khabur, but the greater part were taken only a few hours from Deir-el-Zor, where . . . the most horrible butcheries imaginable occurred."[114] Hoffmann sought to corroborate a report he received on the massacres of deportees in Der Zor from a German officer visiting the region who "has just returned from there and is very familiar with the conditions . . . from earlier journeys."[115] He found that the officer's account is "confirmed to me to a considerable extent by other trustworthy sources."[116]

The massacres of the convoys followed a similar pattern. Leaders were arrested, thrown into prison, and most were eventually killed. Following the arrests, officials told deportees, mostly women and children,[117] that they were to be redeported to a settlement area and were marched to the desert. Other convoys joined them along the journey. Typically, gendarmes and a larger number of Chechen armed bandits accompanied the groups. They shackled and took away the men in groups of a few dozen.[118] Some men dressed up in women's clothing to avoid arrest, but few escaped detection.[119] The guards then broke down the convoys into smaller groups under different pretexts, marched them to isolated areas, and massacred them. Only women and children taken, abducted, or purchased by villagers and the occasional escapees had a chance to survive.[120]

In the immediate aftermath of the war, Hripsimeh Dadourian from Malgara (Thrace) who survived the Der Zor massacres in 1916 recounted her ordeal. Accompanied by "a significant number of gendarmes," her convoy was marched to an area near Marat in early August. A group of seven thousand joined them there. The second convoy had been told that they were going to be settled in Mosul, yet they had circled back. They were on the road for three days. Later, several smaller convoys from nearby areas also converged near Marat. The gendarmes were reinforced by fifty armed Chechens, and "from then on they were giving the orders." The Chechens conducted a census of the deportees. Their total number stood around twenty-two thousand, she remembered. After a few days in the area, the Chechens herded the group to Sheddadiya, where the deportees were taken away in small groups and massacred. Some escaped the massacre and came back, only to be ushered to their deaths in the days that followed.[121]

But even during the massacres in Der Zor, Armenians resisted. In Sheddadiya, realizing their fate, a group of deportees attacked with tent poles Chechen horsemen leading the convoy. Their rebellion was suppressed, and they were all killed. One survivor lists the names of four people who managed to escape the carnage that followed the Sheddadiya resistance and recount what transpired.[122] Many others escaped alone or in small groups, surviving the carnage. We owe the firsthand accounts of the massacres in remote areas of the Syrian desert to them.

By the end of August, "the road from Aleppo to Der Zor . . . has become relatively quiet," observed Hoffmann. "Away from Meskene, the camps have significantly been reduced. . . . Der-el-Zor only has a few craftsmen left who were working for the troops, whereas at the latter place only 8 weeks ago many thousands (estimated by another side as being 20,000) were still in the camp." According to him, all others interned in camps or settled in houses in the region "had disappeared."[123] Armenians who sent letters and postcards from Der Zor to missionaries also went quiet, "which confirmed the rumors we heard about the massacre that had taken place there," wrote U.S. consul in Harput Leslie A. Davis.[124]

Yet targeted destruction continued well into fall 2016. Graphic details emerged particularly of the destruction of children in the area. Kévorkian explains, "Investigations conducted after the Moudros armistice [on 30 October 1918] revealed that it was the police chief, Mustafa Sidki, who supervised the slaughter of these children from the orphanage in Zor on 9 October 1916, followed on 24 October by that of some 2,000 more orphans, whom Hakkı had rounded up in the camps to the north. Here they had been tied together in pairs and thrown into the Euphrates."[125]By fall 1916, relative calm reigned in the triangle formed by Aleppo, Ras ul-Ain, and Der Zor. Most camps were entirely emptied, and the Armenian deportees had by and large "disappeared." When British forces entered Syria in late 1918, there were, in all, 980 Armenians living in Der Zor.[126] Tens of thousands still survived, albeit in pitiable condition, in camps and villages along the Damascus–Hama line or in coastal areas. But they constituted an insignificant proportion of the population and were allowed to survive physically—but not as communities—if they could. When in early 1917, Talaat received a telegram from the governor of Aleppo about the anxieties of Armenians there regarding being deported, he asked the latter to reassure them that they were not going to be deported. After waves of persecution, the Armenian question had been resolved in the eyes of Talaat.

CHAPTER EIGHT

Surviving Talaat

The Network's Legacy

> You do not know me . . .
> I am that child, raised with love,
> Who, exhausted and half-nude,
> Fell asleep in the desert of Der Zor
> To never wake up.
> . . . I do not want adornments
> nor any warm, woolen clothes;
> Skeletons are always nude.
> But when you get warm bread from the baker,
> Make sure to remember me.
>
> —"Remember Me," Mushegh Ishkhan

Survivors struggled to find words for the horrors that transpired in Der Zor. "Death was for the fortunate," wrote Mihran Aghazarian.[1] "How we envied those who were already dead," echoed Aram Andonian.[2] In the summer and fall of 1916, a town on the fringes of a crumbling empire became a synonym for the deportation, dispossession, and destruction of the Armenians. Away from the eyes of the world, the sands of Der Zor crystallized the affliction of a nation, and generations of Armenians adopted the town as a synonym for the indescribable.[3]

For over a century, scholars, too, seem to have largely avoided retracing the path to Der Zor. Until recently one would have been hard-pressed to find scholarly work attempting to make sense of the complex history of the extirpation of the Armenians in the deserts of Syria and Mesopotamia. To this day, the destruction of the Armenian deportees who had arrived in Ottoman Syria, though central to the history of the genocide, and omnipresent in survivor accounts and writings of generations of Armenian intellectuals, remains understudied. With few exceptions, sourced in this book, all we had were snippets, overviews, and summaries of what transpired in the triangle formed by Aleppo, Ras ul-Ain, and Der Zor.

This void in Armenian genocide historiography was due to a combination of methodological challenges, political realities, and the inaccessibility of crucial primary sources. Much of what transpired in Ottoman Syria from the arrival of the first deportees in May 1915 until the massacres in Der Zor in summer 1916 did not fit the theoretical model developed by pioneering historians of the genocide. Their framework largely mirrored a Holocaust model based on extreme intentionalism. The plan for annihilating the victim group progressed systematically, unrelentingly, and according to an inflexible blueprint. Adherence to such a model made it difficult to explain, for example, how in 1915 Ottoman authorities were massacring Armenians in Diyarbakir, all the while providing bread and shelter to some deportees in Aleppo; or how in 1916 they were settling a few hundred deportees in Rakka, while massacring tens of thousands only eighty miles down the Euphrates River in Der Zor.

The Turkish state's denial of the Armenian genocide was also a major hurdle. Scholars invested significant effort into debunking arguments set forth by Turkish political elites and a handful of scholars who trivialized or denied the destruction of the Armenians. In this environment, where pioneers of Armenian genocide scholarship confronted the Turkish state's denialist propaganda machine, comparability with the fate of European Jewry during World War II became a key issue, and the stakes of adhering to a model closely imitating the best-known case of genocide remained high. After all, in the words of historian Taner Akçam, the Holocaust had become "the yardstick against which an event might or might not measure up as genocide."[4]

Lack of access to key Ottoman and Armenian sources as a result of restrictions on Ottoman archives, as well as language barriers, further complicated matters. Sometimes, even when language was not an obstacle, scholars focused on Ottoman and Western sources, avoiding Armenian documents and accounts so as not to be accused of using "tainted" or "biased," material. Often, this measure of prudence was declared outright. Discussing the Ottoman government's policy of relocation, Dadrian argued, "Even if one were to discount the vast corpus of data obtained from Armenian survivors, the aggregate testimony supplied on this issue by German, American, and Turkish officials . . . expose the falsehood of the claim of relocation."[5] Genocide denial, therefore, interfered in the advancement of scholarship on the destruction of the Ottoman Armenians.

From Demographic Engineering to Annihilation

What often seemed to be aimless marches for Armenians on the ground were an attempt at demographic engineering through annihilation.[6] Unbeknownst to the deportees, authorities were playing a game of statistics, setting limits for the percentage of Armenians in settlement areas. Yet, beginning in summer 1915, the influx of deportees arriving in Ottoman Syria, and the central authorities' insistence on capping the percentage of Armenians in the designated settlement areas at 10 percent, created a predicament with which central, regional, and local authorities grappled, and that caused deportees deep suffering as they were continually redeported because their presence exceeded the threshold.[7] Ultimately, the region became saturated, and Armenians had nowhere to go, as they were boxed between supply lines and areas crucial for the war effort. There was no way to settle hundreds of thousands of Armenians in a sparsely populated area and still keep their proportion below 10 percent—unless, of course, the surplus population was killed off.

The massacres in Ras ul-Ain and Der Zor in March and August–October 1916—a second wave of genocide after the near elimination of the entire Armenian population of the Ottoman Empire in 1915—defy attempts at scholarly interpretation. Some scholars have avoided addressing them altogether, relegating the "disappearance" of tens of thousands of people in the desert to footnotes or ignoring it entirely, while addressing the Ottoman policies of demographic engineering in a more sanitized manner. Historian Fuat Dündar, for example, expresses surprise that the Ministry of Interior ordered the transfer of deportees to Der Zor in summer 1916, contradicting its earlier injunctions against it because the area was already saturated with tens of thousands of deportees, far exceeding the 10 percent threshold. Yet Dündar does not entertain the possibility that the authorities were executing a radical policy of annihilating the "surplus population" in the Syrian desert, creating room for more who would share a similar fate. On the other hand, historians Raymond Kévorkian and Taner Akçam have argued that a second decision was made in early 1916 to eliminate the Armenian deportees in the region, with the massacres of Ras ul-Ain in March serving as a harbinger for what was to come later that year. Still, a detailed picture of the process that led to the Der Zor massacres has remained elusive.

As we have seen, when the first deportees arrived in Ottoman Syria, their destruction through massacres a year later was far from a forgone conclusion. The local authorities adopted ad hoc policies of dealing with the deportee influx until the center focused its attention on Ottoman Syria in fall 1915, and IAMM took control of the process of redeportation and settlement. It is in this period that a clear policy of preventing the surviving deportees from reconstituting viable communities was implemented. For the central authorities, it was imperative that the Armenians did not spread epidemics and that they died alone in camps. Yet, by early 1916, Talaat and his tight circle of Ittihadist leaders saw that demographic engineering could not be left to the forces of nature alone. Too many Armenians had survived and were scattered in a sparsely populated region, where they surpassed the 10 percent threshold. They were sandwiched between important military supply lines and urban areas, making their further redistribution in the region unrealistic. As Hilmar Kaiser has demonstrated, Reşid Bey received cover to pursue the destruction of the Armenian population and was not held accountable even when he went beyond his jurisdiction, persecuting deportees in Ras ul-Ain, bordering Diyarbakir. Ali Suat Bey's persistent attempts to prevent mass violence from spilling into the Zor Province did not bear fruit, as Talaat replaced him with Zeki Bey to carry out the final solution for the "demographic problem" in the region.[8]

Revival

A great irony of the Armenian genocide is that the bloodiest episode of destruction and brightest loci of revival for its survivors lay in the same region: Syria. Immediately after the war, as the bones of Armenian deportees lay unburied across its wastelands, Syria now boasted oases of revival. New committees were formed to tackle the challenges facing the Armenian community, often involving many who had been part of underground networks that had waged unarmed, humanitarian resistance during the genocide. The period between 1918 and 1920 is crucial, yet understudied,[9] in this regard, as it represents a collective shift from surviving genocidal policies to establishing normalcy. Although Ottoman Turkey's defeat in the war and withdrawal from Syria is generally treated as a clear demarcation line between these two periods, the circumstances on the ground were less clear cut: the massacres of Armenians had largely stopped in the region by the end of 1916, months before the Ottoman retreat (although forced assimilation and death by disease and starvation continued), and after the Armistice of Mudros signed on 30 October 1918, it took months for the Armenian community and its institutions to move from resisting annihilation to engaging in rebuilding.

Chaos reigned in urban and rural areas in the days between Ottoman withdrawal and the arrival of the British. Rev. Harootune Maljian, an Armenian Catholic priest imprisoned in Aleppo by the Ottoman Turkish authorities, related his ordeal in a chaotic environment:

> On October 12, 1918, a couple of Allied planes bombed Aleppo. At the same time, we heard that local Turkish government officials had all fled to an unknown destination.
>
> Allied planes reappeared over the city on the 22nd, 23rd and 24th of October. The air raid of the 24th was especially intense. From Friday morning to Saturday evening [25 and 26 October], Aleppo was without government. Things were in a state of chaos, developing into plain lawlessness. Finally, the Bedouins, the Arabs, after having looted the town, broke down the gates of the prison. Most of the prisoners escaped but those unfortunate enough to be caught back in the prison were mercilessly robbed and stabbed to death by the marauders.[10]

Damascus and Aleppo fell to advancing British and Arab troops in quick succession, on 1 and 25 October respectively, and within days, Ottoman Turkey was forced to sign the armistice, ending the war in the Middle East and surrendering the region to the French and British. The latter supported the government of Emir Faisal, who eventually ascended the tenuous throne of the Kingdom of Syria, which lasted mere months. Syria was forced into a French Mandate in July 1920. It is during this "very sensitive" period when Syria was a "rudimentary Arab state" that "enjoyed little domestic legitimacy" and loose British support that Armenians in Syria actively engaged in rebuilding in what was still a shaky foundation.[11]

With the Ottoman defeat, scores of Armenian survivors scattered across towns, villages, and encampments in Syria and headed to Aleppo, from where they hoped to return home. Hagop Der Garabedian, born in Marash in 1881, was among those who made it to the Syrian metropolis. He later wrote, "Twenty-five days after leaving Mosul we arrived in Aleppo. They put all the refugees in a transition camp in an old Ottoman military castle. I found folks there who were also heading to Marash, and kept their company. The only topic of conversation was whom and what we would find when we returned."[12] The Armenian deportees were, in fact, housed in two locations, the expansive military barracks (*zoranots* in Armenian) on the outskirts of the city and an inn, Kubbe Khan.[13] Der Garabedian painted a bright picture for refugees in the city:

> I stayed in the castle in the company of my compatriots from Marash. People from neighboring towns and villages were grouped together. This made it possible for newcomers to be easily united with folks from their hometowns. Food and water was plentiful and spirits were bulging with anticipation and excitement.
>
> During the day we had permission to go into the town of Aleppo and explore the sites. Almost everyone took advantage of the chance to see a big city and experience its sights, sounds, and smells. On Sundays everyone was free to attend whatever church they wanted.[14]

Deportees converging in Aleppo did receive significant support from the British (food) and American (clothing, bedding, medication) officials and relief groups. Armenian groups also provided robust financial and moral support. But the buoyant mood and "bulging" spirits in Aleppo had more to do with the promise of return to a free—and soon, many believed, independent—homeland on Ottoman territory following the defeat of the Central powers.

Other accounts paint a similar mood of enthusiasm among Armenians who lived in Aleppo before 1914. "We Armenians get excited too soon. . . . We were intoxicated with the illusion of a United Armenia," lamented Kapigian many years later, noting that performances, plays, and parties organized by Armenian groups became weekly fixtures.[15] However, this joyous mood in the city also fostered resentments. Antirefugee sentiment and perceptions of Armenians as collaborators with the British and French, whose designs in the region were viewed with suspicion, provided fertile ground for conspiracy and incitement, allowing local elites to mobilize dozens of Muslims against them. On 28 February 1919, the city of Aleppo, which had not witnessed a single massacre of Armenians during the entire period of World War I, became the stage for Armenian bloodshed. Mobs descended on unsuspecting Armenians in the city's Friday Market and attacked Armenian neighborhoods, killing several dozen and injuring many more. The victims were both refugees and long-established locals. Armenian bakers from Sasun who had made Aleppo home decades earlier and had famously taken over the breadmaking business in the city were killed in their bakeries. The British authorities managed to restore calm, arresting the rioters and those who had incited them (several were sentenced to death by hanging), and offering the Armenian community compensation for the damages.[16] Those arrested were soon discharged, however. In his memoirs, the newly appointed military governor of Aleppo Province, Ja'far Pasha Al-'Askari, explained the rationale behind their release:

> There were about eighteen people under arrest. We [a British general and Al-'Askari] decided that the best course would be to release them and hush things up, to prevent a cycle of similar outrages being set in train. I accompanied Gen. Hodgson to the place of confinement and delivered a stern admonition to the detainees, warning them never again to stir the populace, otherwise I would hold them personally responsible for any future public disorder.[17]

In the decades that followed, as Armenians in Syria strove to integrate into Syrian society, the memory of the Aleppo massacre was suppressed. Today, one would be hard-pressed to find Armenians who have heard about this pogrom.

As the last Ottoman Turkish soldiers pulled out of Syria in 1918, Armenians tried to reconnect with loved ones and their hometowns. From cities like Aleppo, Damascus, Rakka, Der Zor, and vast rural areas, many returned to their ancestral towns in parts of the former empire now occupied by Allied soldiers. Historian Keith Watenpaugh summarizes this period thus:

> At the armistice in 1918, approximately one hundred thousand Armenian Genocide survivors were living in and around the cities of Aleppo, Damascus, and Beirut. The southern tier of Anatolia, occupied by Great Britain and then France after the war, was chosen to serve as an area for their resettlement. Armenians had constituted much of the prewar population of the region and were found in both cities and the countryside, and thus, for many in the informal settlements, this meant a return home. By 1920, three-quarters of the displaced refugees in Syria had moved to this part of Anatolia.[18]

Although most survivors headed to these settlement areas in Asia Minor (only to be forced out by a resurgent, nationalist Turkey born out of the defeated empire's ashes about three years later),[19] thousands of others stayed behind and endeavored to remake their lives in Syria. These deportees joined those who already called Syria home even before 1914 to help rebuild community life.

Committees running the affairs of the Armenian community in Aleppo were largely in disarray or inactive by the end of the war. To remedy the situation and reboot communal life, the city's Armenian Prelacy invited fifty-one prominent community members (thirty-one of whom attended) to a meeting on 17 November 1919, to elect a provisional governing body, the Provisional National Administrative Assembly (PNAA).[20] From its inception, the efforts of this assembly focused on the youth. Deliberations on reopening the Aleppo Armenian Prelacy's schools took up the bulk of the PNAA's time. The school buildings had served as shelters for refugees during the war, and efforts to find the funds required for their cleaning, restoration, and operation expenses dragged on for months. The PNAA eventually decided in June to unequivocally commit to a 1 September 1919 opening.[21] The assembly also decided to assist homeless children and those who were in orphanages.[22] The largest of these was Shirajian's orphanage,[23] which had opened on 31 July 1915, at the height of deportee influx. After the armistice, the British authorities in Aleppo covered the orphanage's operating costs for a year and paid off its wartime debt,[24] freeing the Armenian administration to focus on improving education, training in trades and crafts, and public health and hygiene. In subsequent years, the French and the Americans paid for the expenses of the orphanage, which continued receiving children from Turkey and the Syrian desert. In the spring and summer of 1922 alone, more than two hundred children had found refuge at the institution.[25]

Returning the thousands of Armenian women and children held in Muslim households into the community fold was also a priority.[26] The PNAA discussed this matter on several occasions, and also raised the issue with the Armenian National Union, Arab and British authorities, and the American Red Cross,[27] all entities involved in the postwar relief efforts. The collaboration, imperfect as it was, between international organizations, regional and local authorities, and the Armenians—who were both victims and agents—led to the reclamation of thousands of women and children in the 1920s. It also underscores that a better understanding of the process of recovery and rebuilding hinges upon an appreciation of the role victim groups and their organizations—here, the PNAA, the Armenian General

Benevolent Union, and others—played, without which a critical approach to the history of humanitarianism is not possible.

Speaking mainly of Beirut and Aleppo, political scientist Nicola Migliorino observes, "The place where the reconstruction of the Armenian world began was the refugee camp.... It was in the late 1920s and in the early 1930s when the refugees could gradually start to move from these initial shelters and install themselves in new purpose-built popular Armenian quarters."[28] For Armenians in Syria, locals and deportees alike, reconstruction was a process that began in an environment of great danger and uncertainty between 1917 and the early 1920s. It is in this period that the Armenians tried to establish their safety after the genocide, commemorate the victims, and restore some semblance of normalcy. They received ample assistance and support from the Arab, British, and French authorities and Western humanitarians. Yet, they were at the core of the efforts to survive the trauma and revive community life, just as their efforts were at the core of the resistance to genocide.

Appreciation

Armenians expressed deep appreciation for the diplomats and missionaries who were part of the resistance network, even while the Great War was still raging. Just as Consul Jesse B. Jackson prepared to leave his post in May 1917, he received the following letter, signed by Armenian community leaders and from the committee of relief distribution operating in the city at the time, the administrative council of the factories and workshops operating with Armenian deportee labor, the Armenian Apostolic Church, the Armenian Catholic Archbishopric, the management of the Shirajian orphanage, and the Armenian community hospital:

> Aleppo, May 5, 1917
>
> Mr. Consul General:
>
> Since circumstances have made necessary your departure, we do not wish to permit you to leave without trying to inform you just to what point your charity has come to the aid of many miseries and sufferings, has moved our hearts and rooted within us a deep and eternal gratitude.
>
> When private charity could no longer succor all the multitude of the exiles dying of hunger and cold in the streets of the city, you have with a zeal never denied, aided, in a great measure these unfortunate beings.

> Through feeble words that can but imperfectly express the outburst of an ardent appreciation, listen to the voice of all those who perhaps owe you more than life, rise you in benediction and regret.
>
> To present to you, Mr. Consul General, the assurance of our highest consideration.[29]

Since then, hundreds of accounts, memoirs, monographs, and scholarly articles and books dedicated to Western humanitarians serving in the Ottoman Empire have been published in many languages. Numerous events organized by survivors, their children, and grandchildren around the world have honored these humanitarians, their children, and grandchildren. But the couriers—mostly Armenians, but also other Christians, Muslims, and Jewish people of the Ottoman Empire—who "at the risk of their lives and the cost of a thousand sacrifices have helped and relieved thousands of exiles, starving in the deserts," have received little attention.[30] This book connects them all.

I invite the reader to imagine a day in March 1919 at the Armenian cemetery in Aleppo. Having returned to the city after the war, Sister Beatrice Rohner has joined Rev. Eskijian's wife Gulenia, survivor John Minassian, and a few others for a visit to Rev. Eskijian's grave. After Eskijian saved his life, Minassian had become his courier, bringing packages of money from Consul Jackson for the resistance network. The others kneel and pray. Gulenia is crying. Now in his early twenties, Minassian is somber, reflective: "My heart bled once again as I stood silently by [Eskijian's] grave and, without tears, remembered his smile and his oft-repeated, 'Some day you will be able to pay back, my son.'"[31]

A short time later, Minassian visited Dr. Altounyan for a medical checkup, said his goodbyes to friends, and left for America. No matter where they ended up, many of those saved by the resistance network paid it forward by embarking on the next difficult task: rebuilding the nation.

Notes

INTRODUCTION

1. Letter from Gulenia Danielian Eskijian to Esther Barsumian, 13 February 1919, Eskijian Family Private Archives.
2. The phrase "civilian resistance" is employed by French historian Jacques Semelin. See *Unarmed against Hitler: Civilian Resistance in Europe, 1939–1943* (Westport, CT: Praeger, 1993).
3. Judith Tydor Baumel, "Women's Agency and Survival Strategies during the Holocaust," *Women's Studies International Forum* 22, no. 3 (1999): 329.
4. Robert Rozett, "Jewish Resistance," in *The Historiography of the Holocaust*, ed. Dan Stone (New York: Palgrave Macmillan, 2004), 341.
5. Vesna Drapac, "Women, Resistance and the Politics of Daily Life in Hitler's Europe: The Case of Yugoslavia in a Comparative Perspective," *Aspasia* 3 (2009): 55.
6. Anna Bravo, "Armed and Unarmed: Struggles without Weapons in Europe and in Italy," *Journal of Modern Italian Studies* 10, no. 4 (2005): 472–473. Nathan Stoltzfus's *Resistance of the Heart: Intermarriage and the Rosenstrasse Protest in Nazi Germany* (New Brunswick: Rutgers University Press, 2001) stands as one such "rare exception."
7. Paul Bartrop, *Resisting the Holocaust: Upstanders, Partisans, and Survivors* (Santa Barbara: ABC-CLIO, 2016), xxii.

8. That a term corresponding to the Jewish *Amidah* (translated from Hebrew as "stand"), which comprises a broad understanding of resistance, is nonexistent in the public and scholarly discourse on the destruction of the Armenians is telling. Moreover, even the scholarship on violent resistance remains thin. For a treatment of the Urfa defense, see Carlos Bedrossian, "Urfa's Last Stand," in *Armenian Tigrankert/Diarbekir and Edessa/Urfa*, ed. Richard Hovannisian (Santa Ana, CA: Mazda, 2000), 467–507. For the Shabin Karahisar uprising, see Simon Payaslian, "The Armenian Resistance in Shabin Karahisar, 1915," in *Sebastia/Sivas and Lesser Armenia*, ed. Richard Hovannisian (Santa Ana, CA: Mazda, 2000), 399–426. For Van, see Anahide Ter Minassian, "Van 1915," in *Armenian Van/Vaspurakan*, ed. Richard Hovannisian (Santa Ana, CA: Mazda, 2000), 209–244. For Musa Dagh, see Andrekos Varnava and Trevor Harris, "'It Is Quite Impossible to Receive Them': Saving the Musa Dagh Refugees and the Imperialism of European Humanitarianism," *Journal of Modern History* 90, no. 4 (2018): 834–862.
9. Donald E. Miller and Lorna Touryan Miller, *Survivors: An Oral History of the Armenian Genocide* (Berkeley: University of California Press, 1993), 72. The "engrained passiveness developed over centuries" argument echoes Holocaust scholar Raul Hilberg, who, even in the 1980s, insisted on "almost complete lack of resistance" by the Jews. The "2,000-year-old lesson could not be unlearned; the Jews could not make the switch. They were helpless . . . caught in the straitjacket of their history," he argued. See David S. Wyman, "Managing the Death Machine," *New York Times Book Review*, 11 August 1985, p. 3. For more on Hilberg's position on resistance, see his *The Destruction of the European Jews* (Chicago: Quadrangle Books, 1961). Although Hilberg revised his authoritative study in subsequent years, his position on Jewish resistance has largely remained the same.
10. Ronald Grigor Suny, *"They Can Live in the Desert but Nowhere Else": A History of the Armenian Genocide* (Princeton, NJ: Princeton University Press, 2015), 332.
11. Notable exceptions to a narrow definition of resistance include Raymond Kévorkian's *The Armenian Genocide: A Complete History* (London: I. B. Tauris, 2011) and Hilmar Kaiser's *At the Crossroad of Der Zor: Death, Survival, and Humanitarian Resistance in Aleppo, 1915–1917* (London: Gomidas Institute, 2002).
12. Established in Tiflis (Tbilisi, Georgia, today) in 1890, the ARF espoused reform and self-rule in Armenian-populated provinces of the Ottoman Empire. Its leaders were arrested beginning in April 1915. Misakian headed a three-member cell that also included Krikor Merjanian (Merjanoff) and Samuel Tarpinian that coordinated the work of a network of informants. See Yervant Pamboukian, ed., *Medz Yegherni Arachin Vaverakroghe' Shavarsh Misakian* [The First Chronicler of the Great Crime: Shavarsh Misakian] (Antelias, Lebanon: Catholicosate of Cilicia, 2017).

13. Kévorkian, *The Armenian Genocide*, 538–540.
14. Ghazar Charek, *Marzbede (Haji Hiuseyin)*, vol. 1 (Beirut: Azad Printing House, 1945), b.
15. John M. Cox, "Jewish Resistance against Nazism," in *The Routledge History of the Holocaust*, ed. Johnathan C. Friedman (London: Routledge, 2011), 329.
16. In the words of historian Hans-Lukas Kieser, "Talaat concentrated on cases of individual enrichment detrimental to the state—not on the basic crimes of murder and spoliation of the main Christian victims." Hans-Lukas Kieser, *Talaat Pasha: Father of Modern Turkey, Architect of Genocide* (Princeton, NJ: Princeton University Press, 2018), 241. For investigations of local officials who protected Armenians, see, for example, BOA DH.ŞFR 54/65, coded telegram 19 June 1915 from Interior Ministry to Zor; for the circumstances of Nesimi's murder, see Ugur Ümit Üngör, *The Making of Modern Turkey: Nation and State in Eastern Anatolia, 1913–1950* (Oxford: Oxford University Press, 2011), 78–79, and Burçin Gerçek, "Turkish Rescuers," The International Raoul Wallenberg Foundation, available online at http://www.raoulwallenberg.net/wp-content/files_mf/1435335304ReportTurkishrescuerscomplete.pdf, 23–25.
17. Nechama Tec, *Resistance: Jews and Christians Who Defied the Nazi Terror* (Oxford: Oxford University Press, 2013), 4.
18. Bob Moore, ed., *Resistance in Western Europe* (Oxford: Berg Publishers, 2000), 2.
19. Yehuda Bauer, *Rethinking the Holocaust* (New Haven: Yale University Press, 2000), 119.
20. Daniel Jonah Goldhagen, *Worse Than War: Genocide, Eliminationism, and the Ongoing Assault on Humanity* (New York: PublicAffairs, 2009). In the first chapter, Goldhagen identifies five modes of elimination, ranging from transformation, which he defines as "the destruction of a group's essential and defining political, social, or cultural identities," to extermination. I am not the first to employ the phrase "humanitarian resistance" in the context of the Armenian genocide. Historian Hilmar Kaiser has also referred to actions of Rev. Eskijian and others in Ottoman Syria between 1915 and 1917 as "humanitarian resistance." See Kaiser, *At the Crossroad of Der Zor*.
21. Yaron Ayalon, *Natural Disasters in the Ottoman Empire: Plague, Famine, and Other Misfortunes* (Cambridge: Cambridge University Press, 2015), 110.
22. The first deportees arrived within a month of the beginning of the arrests, deportations, and massacres. According to lists in the Aleppo Armenian Prelacy Archives, 322 deportees from Zeytun reached Bab, northeast of the metropolis, as early as 18 May 1915. See Armenian National Council, Records of the Council for Refugees, folder 41, 14–15. For a detailed examination of the chain of events that culminated in the deportation of the Armenians of Zeytun, see Aram Arkun, "Zeytun and the Commencement of the Armenian Genocide," in *A Question of Genocide: Armenians and Turks at the End of the*

Ottoman Empire, ed. Ronald Grigor Suny, Fatma Müge Göçek, and Norman M. Naimark (Oxford: Oxford University Press, 2011), 221–243.

23. Armenian National Council, Council Records for Refugees, folder 38, minutes of session 1.
24. For humanitarian efforts in Beirut and Mount Lebanon, for example, see Melanie S. Tanielian, *The Charity of War: Famine, Humanitarian Aid, and World War I in the Middle East* (Stanford: Stanford University Press, 2017).
25. Ayalon, *Natural Disasters in the Ottoman Empire*, 119.
26. See Taner Akçam, *The Young Turks' Crime against Humanity: The Armenian Genocide and Ethnic Cleansing in the Ottoman Empire* (Princeton, NJ: Princeton University Press, 2012), 259–261.
27. Keith David Watenpaugh, *Bread from Stones: The Middle East and the Making of Modern Humanitarianism* (Oakland: University of California Press, 2015), 4.
28. Ibid., 2.
29. Ibid., 23–24.
30. Talaat's brother-in-law and governor of Bitlis, Mustafa Abdülhalik, became Aleppo governor on 4 October 1915. He had burnished his anti-Armenian credentials in earlier months during his tenure as governor of Bitlis. Abdülhalik was intimately involved in the decision-making process in Bitlis. He had arrested Armenian dignitaries and leaders and recruited Kurdish bandits to buttress the Special Organization that committed the massacres. For an overview of Abdülhalik's role in the Bitlis region, see Mehmet Polatel, "The State, Local Actors, and Mass Violence in the Bitlis Province," in *End of the Ottomans: The Genocide of 1915 and the Politics of Turkish Nationalism*, ed. Hans-Lukas Kieser, Margaret Lavinia Anderson, Seyhan Bayraktar, and Thomas Schmutz (London: I. B. Tauris, 2019), 119–140; and Kévorkian, *The Armenian Genocide*, 337–353. Abdülhalik's appointment constitutes an important tactical move in what Armenian genocide scholars refer to as the "dual-track" mechanism: an official track employed government communication to convey (re)deportation orders, resettlement, and the liquidation of Armenian property, while an unofficial track ordered "extralegal acts of violence, such as forced evacuations, killings, and massacres" privately, through trusted party functionaries. Historian Vahakn N. Dadrian was the first to examine this process during the Armenian genocide. See, for example, Vahakn N. Dadrian, *The History of the Armenian Genocide: Ethnic Conflict from the Balkans to Anatolia to the Caucasus* (Oxford: Berghahn, 1995), 384. For a recent discussion on this mechanism, see Akçam, *The Young Turks' Crime against Humanity*, xxiv–xxv.
31. A telegram issued by the Ministry of the Interior on 18 October 1915 indicated that there

were thirty thousand deportees in Aleppo City alone awaiting redeportation. See BOA DH.EUM) 2 Şb. 68/80. By then, tens of thousands had already been deported to Bab, Mumbuj, and Maarra, or farther to Urfa, Zor, and Mosul. BOA DH.EUM 2 Şb. 68/76, telegram from Governor Bekir Sami to Interior Ministry on 5 September 1915.

32. Historian Raymond Kévorkian allocates a section, titled "The Official and Underground Armenian Information and Relief Networks Operating in Aleppo and the Surrounding Region," to humanitarian networks in the region in his monumental work on the history of the genocide. See Kévorkian, *The Armenian Genocide*, 641–644.
33. Khabayan was a religious leader of the Armenian Apostolic Church, heading the Catholicosate of Cilicia, which was headquartered in Sis (modern-day Kozan, Turkey). For more on the history and administrative structure of the Armenian Apostolic Church of Aleppo, see Avedis K. Sanjian, *The Armenian Communities in Syria under Ottoman Dominion* (Cambridge, MA: Harvard University Press, 1965), 261–273. For a biography of Khabayan, see, for example, Arshag Alboyajian, "Shnorhazart Der Sahag II Gatoghigos Dann Giligio," *Datev* 4 (1928): 254–293.
34. For a typology of actions taken by Muslims to assist deportees, see George N. Shirinian, "Turks Who Saved Armenians: Righteous Muslims during the Armenian Genocide," *Genocide Studies International* 9, no. 2 (2015): 208–227. For an exploration of rescuers' motivations, see Richard G. Hovannisian, "Intervention and Shades of Altruism during the Armenian Genocide," in *The Armenian Genocide: History, Politics, Ethics*, ed. Richard G. Hovannisian (New York: St. Martin's, 1992), 173–207.
35. For wartime Ottoman surveillance of diplomats, particularly the U.S. Consul Jesse B. Jackson, see Taner Akçam, *Killing Orders: Talaat Pasha's Telegrams and the Armenian Genocide* (Cham, Switzerland: Palgrave Macmillan, 2018), 153–157.
36. Hans-Lukas Kieser, "Beatrice Rohner's Work in the Death Camps of Armenians in 1916," in *Resisting Genocide: The Multiple Forms of Rescue*, ed. Jacques Sémelin, Claire Andrieu, and Sarah Gensburger (New York: Columbia University Press, 2011), 376–378.
37. Ibid., 377.
38. Alexandra Marin and Barry Wellman, "Social Network Analysis: An Introduction," in *The SAGE Handbook of Social Network Analysis*, ed. John Scott and Peter J. Carrington (London: SAGE Publications, 2011), 13.
39. Rev. Eskijian, too, had been affected by the Hamidian massacres: his father had been killed in front of his mother's eyes. See "A Short Biography of Rev. Ohannes S. Eskijian," Eskijian Family Private Archives.
40. Nelida Fuccaro, "Urban Life and Questions of Violence," in *Violence and the City in the Modern Middle East: Changing Cityscapes in the Transformation from Empire to Nation*

State, Nelida Fuccaro (Stanford: Stanford University Press, 2016), 10.

41. See, for example, Wendy Pullan and Britt Baillie, eds., *Locating Urban Conflicts: Ethnicity, Nationalism and the Everyday* (Basingstoke: Palgrave Macmillan, 2013), and Fuccaro, ed., *Violence and the City*.
42. Fuccaro, "Urban Life and Questions of Violence," 10.
43. Charek, *Marzbede*, 1:13–16.
44. Consul Jackson himself acknowledges the role of "friendly Bedouin Arabs adjacent to the city" in getting many Armenians out of harm's way. NA/RG59/867.4016/373, detailed report on "Armenian Atrocities" by Jackson sent to the secretary of state on 4 March 1918, in Ara Sarafian, ed., *United States Official Records on the Armenian Genocide* (London: Gomidas Institute, 2004), 597.

CHAPTER ONE. Before the Storm: Deportation and Humanitarian Relief

1. For a brief scholarly examination focusing on Aleppo's role as a hub during the Armenian genocide, see historian Raymond Kévorkian's "Alep, Centre du dispositif génocidaire et des operations de secours aux déportés," in Vartan Derounian, *Mémoire arménienne: Photographies du camp de réfugiés d'Alep, 1922–1936*, ed. Lévon Nordiguian (Beirut: Presse de l'Université Saint Joseph, 2010), 15–23.
2. Armenian National Council, List of Armenians around Aleppo, folder 41, 14–15. This first convoy came from Zeytun. For an overview of the minutes and reports of the Armenian National Council and the Council for Refugees, housed in the Aleppo Armenian Prelacy Archives, see Vahram L. Shemmassian, "Humanitarian Intervention by the Armenian Prelacy of Aleppo during the First Months of the Genocide," *Journal of the Society for Armenian Studies* 22 (2013): 127–152.
3. NA/RG59/867.4016/77, Consular agent Greg Young to Morgenthau on 5 June 1918, in Ara Sarafian, ed., *United States Official Records on the Armenian Genocide* (London: Gomidas Institute, 2004), 57.
4. Krikor Tatoulian, *Anteghowadz Kaghdnikner* [Buried Secrets] (Beirut: Atlas Publishing, 1967), 90. For the full text of a letter detailing the deportation from Shar to Aleppo, written down on 19 June 1915 by Father Vrtanes Karadaghian, and addressed to the Catholicos, see Antranig Dakessian, "Shari deghahanutiune" [The Deportation of Shar], *Haigazian Armenological Review* 33 (2015), 645–654.
5. BOA DH.ŞFR 54/122, cipher telegram from IAMM to the province of Mosul and district of Zor on 23 June 1915. For a comprehensive treatment of the assimilation policy of the Ottoman authorities, see Taner Akçam, *The Young Turks' Crime against Humanity:*

The Armenian Genocide and Ethnic Cleansing in the Ottoman Empire (Princeton, NJ: Princeton University Press, 2012), 287–339. For the Ottoman practice of measuring "distances between places by the hours that a horse can traverse at a good pace," see Ariel Salzmann, *Tocqueville in the Ottoman Empire: Rival Paths to the Modern State* (Leiden: Brill, 2004), 48n53.

6. For more on the history of the community, see Avedis K. Sanjian, *The Armenian Communities in Syria under Ottoman Dominion* (Cambridge, MA: Harvard University Press, 1965). The Armenians in the city of Aleppo on the eve of World War I constituted a prosperous community of around ten thousand, according to Armenian sources. Ottoman records provide a slightly lower figure. According to scholar Kemal Karpat, there were a total of 7,555 Armenians (3,603 Apostolic and 3,952 Catholic) in the Aleppo region in 1914. Karpat also lists 385 Protestants, most of whom were Armenian. See Kemal H. Karpat, *Ottoman Population, 1830–1914: Demographic and Social Characteristics* (Madison: University of Wisconsin Press, 1985), 176.
7. Beginning in May 1915, and for the duration of World War I, the Prelacy of the Armenian Apostolic Church in Aleppo maintained detailed records of its operations. See Armenian National Council, Council Records for Refugees, folder 22, 3.
8. Armenian National Council, Council Records for Refugees, folder 38, minutes of session 1.
9. Tavit Jidejian, Dikran Pironian, and Sarkis Jiyerjian respectively served as the chair, secretary, and treasurer of the council. Until his arrest, the Prelacy's vicar, Father Yesayan served as council president, serving as the liaison between the council and the Catholicos, as well as the local and regional authorities. Jiyerjian was deported to Der Zor, but an Arab camel driver helped him safely return to Aleppo in 1918. See Yervant Odian, *Accursed Years: My Exile and Return from Der Zor, 1914–1919*, trans. Ara Stepan Melkonian (London: Gomidas Institute, 2009), 215. The available records do not indicate the existence of bylaws. However, bylaws were indeed drafted in the postwar period as the council continued to provide relief to survivors.
10. The humanitarian resistance and relief efforts by Reverend Hovhannes Eskijian, pastor of the Emmanuel Evangelical Church in the city, is the focus of Hilmar Kaiser's *At the Crossroad of Der Zor: Death, Survival, and Humanitarian Resistance in Aleppo, 1915–1917* (London: Gomidas Institute, 2002). The Armenian Protestant Church also provided financial support to the council. On 24 June, for example, the council received a donation of eighty liras from the Protestant community in the city; see Council Records, folder 38, session 22.
11. For example, Eskijian contributed to the council's fundraising efforts in May 1915. Council

Records, folder 22, 1. The council also sent money to Bab and other camps around Aleppo with Rev. Eskijian on several occasions in 1915. Council Records, folder 22.

12. See NA/RG59/867.4016/219, enclosure No. 4 with dispatch No. 382 to embassy, Istanbul, Jackson to Morgenthau on 29 September 1918, in Sarafian, *United States Official Records*, 314.
13. NA/RG59/867.4016/77, Jackson to Morgenthau on 5 June 1915, and NA/RG59/867.4016/219 Jackson to Morgenthau on 29 September 1918, in Sarafian, *United States Official Records*, 57 and 308. Several small communities in Syria, Mesopotamia, and Palestine that were spared wholesale deportation during the war (Haifa and Jerusalem, for example) formed relief committees of their own, caring for arriving deportees. See Vahram L. Shemmassian, "Armenian Genocide Survivors in the Holy Land at the End of World War I," *Journal of the Society for Armenian Studies* 21 (2012): 227–247.
14. The bulk of the thirty-five thousand soldiers were from Aleppo, Beirut, Damascus, Jerusalem, and Mount Lebanon. See Eugene Rogan, *The Fall of the Ottomans: The Great War in the Middle East* (New York: Basic Books, 2015), 107.
15. Council Records, folder 38, session 2.
16. Council Records, folder 38, session 12.
17. Council Records, folder 38, session 2. Later, more employees would be hired. On 20 June, for example, the council hired an Armenian from Van, Nazaret Aghapegian, for ten *mecidiye* a month, to run errands and facilitate relief work around the city. See Council Records, folder 38, session 21. On 2 July, the council decided to pay a teacher from Zeytun, a certain Mr. Mahdesian, five *mecidiye* per month upon receiving a request from the latter to be compensated for the work he had been doing. Earlier, Mr. Mahdesian had been compiling lists of deportees and doing other clerical work without pay; see Council Records, folder 38, session 24.
18. Council Records, folder 38, session 3.
19. Council Records, folder 38, session 3. At its fifth session, the council decided to only distribute bread allocated by the municipality, but reconfirmed the four *metalik*s per person allocation.
20. Council Records, folder 38, session 4.
21. Council Records, folder 38, session 6. It is unclear whether the money was ever sent. The Patriarchate in Constantinople, under the leadership of Patriarch Zaven Der Yeghiayan, was itself involved in extensive relief efforts. In his memoirs, Der Yeghiayan details the humanitarian resistance and relief efforts mounted by the Patriarchate. See Zaven Der Yeghiayan, *My Patriarchal Memoirs* (Barrington, RI: Mayreni Publishing, 2002), 109–124.
22. Council Records, folder 22, 4.

23. Council Records, folder 38, session 8.
24. Council Records, folder 38, session 4.
25. Council Records, folder 38, session 4.
26. Council Records, folder 38, session 5.
27. Council Records, folder 38, session 10.
28. Council Records, folder 38, session 15. From the minutes of the same session, we also learn that the Armenian deportees from Dörtyol had a similar subcommittee assessing their needs.
29. Council Records, folder 38, session 28.
30. The same convoy carried Rev. Aharon Shirajian, an Armenian Evangelical community leader who would become the director of the largest orphanage for Armenian children in Aleppo during the war and its aftermath.
31. Paren Kazanjian, ed., *The Cilician Armenian Ordeal* (Boston: Hye Intentions, 1989), 290.
32. Yeranuhi Simonian, *Im Koghkotas* [My Golgotha] (Antelias: Armenian Catholicosate, 1960), 12. Simonian's family stayed only briefly at this house in June or July 1915. The landlord, worried about trouble with the authorities, threatened to report them. "Money, begging, and promises were to no avail," so her family was forced to leave the cousins' house and rent a room elsewhere. Fear of being caught forced the family to move several times within a month, until the authorities discovered their hiding place and deported them to Ras ul-Ain.
33. John Minassian, *Many Hills Yet to Climb* (Santa Barbara, CA: Jim Cook, 1986), 85.
34. Ghazar Charek, *Marzbede* (*Haji Hiuseyin*), 2 vols. (Beirut: Azad Printing House, 1945), 1:2.
35. NA/RG59/867.4016/373, Jackson to the secretary of state on 4 March 1918, in Sarafian, *United States Official Records*, 593.
36. Zabel Yesayan and Hayg Toroyan, "Zhoghovurti me hokevarke (Aksoreal hayere michakedki mech)" [The Death Throes of a Nation: The Exiled Armenians in Mesopotamia], *Kordz* 3 (1917): 51. Toroyan served as German officer Otto Ölmann's interpreter, accompanying him on a journey from Aleppo to Baghdad. He witnessed the plight of the deportees in the camps along the Euphrates in 1915–1916. Toroyan's account was recorded by Armenian writer Zabel Yesayan and published in Baku in 1917. The same account, almost in its entirety, was published in Paris in 1952 in a volume edited by Levon Mesrob. Decades later, Marc Nichanian translated and published the account in French under the title *L'Agonie d'un peuple* (Paris: Classiques Garnier, 2013).
37. NA/RG59/867.4016/77, Jackson to Morgenthau on 5 June 1915, in Sarafian, *United States Official Records*, 57.
38. DE/PA-AA; BoKon/169; A53a, 3451, Rössler to the embassy in Istanbul on 6 June 1915,

in Wolfgang Gust, ed., *The Armenian Genocide: Evidence from the German Foreign Office Archives, 1915–1916* (New York: Berghahn, 2014), 204.

39. See, for example, Council Records, folder 22, 7–8.
40. DE/PA-AA; R14086; A 23232, Rössler to Bethmann Hollweg on 17 July 1915, in Gust, *The Armenian Genocide*, 260.
41. Council Records, folder 38, session 3.
42. Council Records, folder 38, session 17; Council Records, folder 38, session 10.
43. Council Records, folder 38, session 23.
44. The subcommittee included Rev. Aharon Shirajian, Harutiun Terzian, Mardiros [?], Bedros Keshishian, and Hovhannes Karasarkisian; see Council Records, folder 38, session 24. The council ledgers indicate numerous expenses related to cleaning. See, for example, Council Records, folder 22, 6.
45. The council prepared a special donors' book, with an introduction by the Catholicos, appealing to the Aleppo community to come to the assistance of its brethren in this unprecedented moment in the nation's history.
46. Catholicos Papken, *Badmutiun gatoghigosats Giligio* [History of the Giligia Catholicoses] (Antelias, Lebanon: Dbaran Tbrevanouts, 1939), 918. Alongside Sis, the Catholicos used Adana as one of his headquarters. He stayed in Aleppo until he was exiled to Jerusalem a few months later. Believing more could be done, the council decided (24 June) to reach out individually to community members who had not responded to its letters. It also sent official letters to other religious communities, asking them to announce the same in their respective churches. See Council Records, folder 38, session 15. On 8 June, the council appointed two individuals to help collect pledges; see Council Records, folder 38, session 17.
47. Council Records, folder 22, 11; Council Records, folder 38, session 24.
48. Council Records, folder 38, session 25.
49. For a detailed treatment of Armenian property confiscation, see Taner Akçam and Ümit Kurt, *The Spirit of the Laws: The Plunder of Wealth in the Armenian Genocide* (New York: Berghahn, 2015); and Uğur Ümit Üngör and Mehmet Polatel, *Confiscation and Destruction: The Young Turk Seizure of Armenian Property* (New York: Continuum, 2011).
50. Council Records, folder 38, session 30.
51. Rober Koptaş, "Türkler ve Müslümanlar Bu Cinayetlerden Dolayı Kan Ağlıyor," *Agos*, 30 July 2010, http://bianet.org/biamag/bianet/137766-turkler-ve-muslumanlar-bu-cinayetlerden-dolayi-kan-agliyor.
52. NA/RG59/867.4016/77, Consular agent Greg Young to Morgenthau on 20 September 1915, in Sarafian, *United States Official Records*, 297.

53. See, for example, Council Records, folder 22, 18–19.
54. Council Records, folder 38, sessions 2, 4, 15, 18, and 22.
55. Council Records, folder 38, session 6.
56. Council Records, folder 38, session 10.
57. Council Records, folder 38, session 15.
58. There were nineteen orphans from Hajin (nine boys, ten girls), thirty-seven from Dörtyol (twenty-two boys, fifteen girls), and thirty from Hasanbeyli (twelve boys, eighteen girls); see Council Records, folder 38, session 20.
59. Armenian National Council, Records of the Council for Refugees, folder 41.
60. The Dadrians registered a week later. See Vahram Dadrian, *To the Desert: Pages from My Diary* (London: Taderon Press, 2003), 82.
61. Hilmar Kaiser, "Regional Resistance to Central Government Policies: Ahmed Djemal Pasha, the Governors of Aleppo, and Armenian Deportees in the Spring and Summer of 1915," *Journal of Genocide Research* 12, no. 3 (2010): 214.
62. Erik-Jan Zürcher, "Between Death and Desertion: The Experience of the Ottoman Soldier in World War I," *Turcica* 28 (1996): 249.
63. Der Yeghiayan, *My Patriarchal Memoirs*, 91.
64. Council Records, folder 38, session 3.
65. Council Records, folder 38, session 8. During the same session, the council reported the arrival of an additional eight hundred deportees in horrid conditions. Determining that its means were insufficient to attend to their needs, the council resolved to appeal to the municipality for help. In its fourteenth session on 15 June, the council again decided to ask the municipality for oil, this time four cases.
66. Council Records, folder 38, session 6.
67. Council Records, folder 38, session 7.
68. Council Records, folder 38, session 8.
69. Council Records, folder 38, session 11.
70. Council Records, folder 38, session 13.
71. Council Records, folder 38, session 17. Patriarch Der Yeghiayan was spearheading in Istanbul a similar effort to appeal to Ottoman officials, without any tangible results. See Raymond Kévorkian, *The Armenian Genocide: A Complete History* (London: I. B. Tauris, 2011), 534–538.
72. Council Records, folder 38, session 17.
73. Ottoman authorities issued several decrees, the first as early as 31 May 1915, outlining the process of settlement in great detail, including provisions for deportees during transit and the allocation of houses and cultivable land in settlement areas. See *Arşiv Belgeleriyle*

Ermeni Faaliyetleri, 1914–1918 (Cilt VII) [Armenian Activities in the Archive Documents, 1914–1918 (vol. 7)] (Ankara: Genelkurmay Basımevi, 2006), 134–137. See also, Akçam, *The Young Turks' Crime against Humanity*, 264–272.

74. BOA DH.ŞFR 469/117, Celal Bey to the Ministry of the Interior dated 23 May 1915.
75. BOA DH.ŞFR 470/74, Celal Bey to the Ministry of the Interior dated 25 May 1915.
76. BOA DH.ŞFR 471/112, Celal Bey to the Ministry of the Interior dated 6 May 1915.
77. Aram Andonian, *Medz Vojire* [The Great Crime] (Boston: Bahag Publishing, 1921), 27.
78. Ibid.
79. NA/RG59/867.4016/373, Jackson to the secretary of state on 4 March 1918, in Sarafian, *United States Official Records*, 586.
80. Ibid., 585.
81. *Vakit* published Celal's memoirs in three installments (in the issues dated 10–13 December 1918). In the 12 December installment, Celal addresses the circumstances of his removal from Aleppo. See also Akçam, *The Young Turks' Crime against Humanity*, 135–136. The memoirs were reprinted by the Turkish Armenian newspaper *Agos* on 30 July 2010: Koptaş, "Türkler ve Müslümanlar Bu Cinayetlerden Dolayı Kan Ağlıyor."
82. Puzant Yeghiayan, *Zhamanagagagits badmutiun gatoghigosutean hayots Giligio, 1914–1972* [Contemporary History of the Armenian Catholicosate of Cilicia, 1914–1972] (Antelias, Lebanon: Catholicosate of Cilicia, 1975), 47. For references to Celal's assistance to Armenians in Konya, see Charek, *Marzbede*, 1:4–5.
83. Catholicosate of Cilicia Archives, folder 100/1, 299, as cited in Yeghiayan, *Zhamanagagagits badmutiun*, 47.
84. DE/PA-AA; R14087; A23991, report sent by Rössler to the imperial chancellor on 27 July 1915, in Gust, *The Armenian Genocide*, 265.
85. A copy of the telegram is attached to the minutes of the meeting. See Council Records, folder 38, session 17.
86. Council Records, folder 38, session 17.
87. Council Records, folder 38, session 19.
88. Fahrettin Pasha later gained legendary status for his defense of Medina during the city's siege (1916–January 1919). See Martin Strohmeier, "Fakhri (Fahrettin) Paşa and the End of Ottoman Rule in Medina (1916–1919)," *Turkish Historical Review* 4, no. 2 (2013): 192–223.
89. Yeghiayan, *Zhamanagagagits badmutiun*, 50.
90. Soon thereafter, Celal Bey would be removed from his post for resisting deportation orders.
91. From the Catholicos's account of the meeting (Catholicosate of Cilicia Archives, folder 100/1, 4950/95), as cited in Yeghiayan, *Zhamanagagagits badmutiun*, 50.

92. Ibid. For more on these mass murders, see Uğur Ü. Üngör, "A Reign of Terror: CUP Rule in Diyarbekir Province, 1913–1923" (Department of History MA thesis, University of Amsterdam, June 2005).
93. From the Catholicos's report on his meetings with Cemal Pasha in June 1915, as cited in Yeghiayan, *Zhamanagagagits badmutiun*, 51. The gist of the discussions in the meetings between Cemal and the Catholicos is also provided in documents from the German archives. See Kaiser, "Regional Resistance to Central Government Policies," 191–192.
94. Yeghiayan, *Zhamanagagagits badmutiun*, 51.
95. Council Records, folder 38, session 22.
96. BOA DH. ŞFR 54-A/71, telegram from the Interior Ministry's General Security Directorate to Aleppo Province on 22 July 1915.
97. BOA DH. ŞFR 54-A/91, Talaat to Zor district on 24 July 1915.
98. DE/PA-AA; R14087; A24525, Rössler to Bethmann Hollweg on 31 July 1915, in Gust, *The Armenian Genocide*, 275–276. Kaiser notes that Zor governor Ali Suat Bey escorted Father Sahag and pharmacist Sarkis from Ras ul-Ain to Aleppo "thereby assuring their safe return." See Hilmar Kaiser, *The Extermination of Armenians in the Diyarbekir Region* (Istanbul: Bilgi University, 2014), 385.
99. DE/PA-AA; R14087; A24525, from Rössler to Bethmann Hollweg on 31 July 1915, in Gust, *The Armenian Genocide*, 275–276.
100. Council Records, folder 38, session 22.
101. DE/PA-AA; R14087; A 23991, Rössler to Bethmann Hollweg on 27 July 1915, in Gust, *The Armenian Genocide*, 266.
102. Council Records, folder 38, session 22.
103. DE/PA-AA; BoKon/170; A53a, 4217, letter from Catholicos Sahag II to the German ambassador in Istanbul on 30 June 1915, in Gust, *The Armenian Genocide*, 227–228.
104. Ibid.
105. DE/PA-AA; R14089; A36184, Wolff-Meternich, German ambassador in Istanbul, to Bethmann Hollweg on 7 December 1915, and the chancellor's response, in Gust, *The Armenian Genocide*, 490–492.
106. Michael Quentin Morton, *In the Heart of the Desert: The Story of an Exploration Geologist and the Search for Oil in the Middle East* (Aylesford: Green Mountain Press, 2017), 90; Ross Burns, *Aleppo: A History* (New York: Routledge, 2016), 282.
107. See Andonian, *Medz Vojire*, 28; Charles Glass, *Tribes with Flags: A Journey Curtailed* (London: Secker & Warburg, 1990), 95.
108. Glass, *Tribes with Flags*, 95.
109. Journalists Flavia Amabile's and Marco Tosatti's coauthored book is one of the few

studies of the famed hotel to date. Flavia Amabile and Marco Tosatti, *I Baroni di Aleppo* (Rome: La Lepre Edizioni, 2011). The book has also been translated into German and Turkish. For a general history of the hotel, see Toros Toranian, *Badmutiun Halebi Hotel Baroni yev Armen Mazloumiani, Baron Namaganin* [History of Aleppo's Hotel Baron and Armen Mazloumian's (Baron) Letters] (Beirut: Armenian General Benevolent Union, 1987). For a brief history of the Mazloumians and their role during the war, see Charek, *Marzbede*, 2:57–62. For interviews with Mazloumians about the hotel's history decades later, see Glass, *Tribes with Flags*, 90–109.

110. Ohannes Pacha Kouyoumdjian, *Le Liban: À la veille et au début de la guerre. Mémoire d'un Gouverneur, 1913–1915* (Paris: Centre d'histoire arménienne contemporaine, 2003), 171.
111. Taner Akçam, *Killing Orders: Talaat Pasha's Telegrams and the Armenian Genocide* (Cham, Switzerland: Palgrave Macmillan, 2018), 52.
112. Elizabeth F. Thompson, *Justice Interrupted: The Struggle for Constitutional Government in the Middle East* (Cambridge, MA: Harvard University Press, 2013), 118.
113. Charek, *Marzbede*, 2:58–60.
114. Payladzou Captanian, *Tsavag* (New York: Armenia Printing, 1922), 243. A French translation of the memoir appeared three years earlier under the title *Mémoires d'une déportée* (Paris: M. Flinikowski, 1919). The book has also been translated to Romanian (2005) and German (2015).
115. Andonian, *Medz Vojire*, 27–30.
116. For more on the circumstances of exile, see Charek, *Marzbede*, 2:61–62.
117. Taqui Altounyan, *Chimes from a Wooden Bell: A Hundred Years in the Life of a Euro-Armenian Family* (London: I. B. Tauris, 1990), 26.
118. Altounyan, *Chimes from a Wooden Bell*, 12–15; Jeremy Collingwood, *A Lakeland Saga: The Story of the Collingwood and Altounyan Family in Coniston and Aleppo* (Ammanford, Carmarthenshire: Sigma Press, 2012), 80; *Columbia University Alumni Register, 1754–1931, compiled by the Committee on General Catalogue* (New York: Columbia University Press, 1932), 16.
119. Altounyan, *Chimes from a Wooden Bell*, 17–23.
120. Captanian, *Tsavag*, 244; Philip Mansel, *Aleppo: The Rise and Fall of Syria's Great Merchant City* (London: I. B. Tauris, 2016), 48; Collingwood, *A Lakeland Saga*, 91.
121. Council Records, folder 38, session 20.
122. Council Records, folder 38, session 26.
123. Council Records, folder 38, session 27.
124. Text of letter cited in Catholicos Papken, *Badmutiun gatoghigosats Giligio*, 919–920.
125. Ibid.

126. From the Catholicos's report on the meeting, as cited in Yeghiayan, *Zhamanagagagits badmutiun*, 51.
127. Ibid.
128. A report by Jackson puts the number of deportees who had arrived in Aleppo at fifteen thousand. NA/RG59/867.4016/126, Jackson to Morgenthau on 3 August 1915, in Sarafian, *United States Official Records*, 169.
129. Ibid.
130. NA/RG59/867.4016/148, Jackson to Morgenthau on 19 August 1915, in Sarafian, *United States Official Records*, 207.
131. DE/PA-AA; R14087; A 25860, Rössler to Bethmann Hollweg. Another convoy from Adıyaman suffered a similar fate: of the 696, only 321 arrived in Aleppo, 206 men and 57 women were killed, 70 women and girls and 19 boys were kidnapped. The rest were unaccounted for.
132. Yeghiayan, *Zhamanagagagits badmutiun*, 52.
133. NA/RG59/867.4016/219, Jackson to Morgenthau on 29 September 1915, in Sarafian, *United States Official Records*, 307.
134. BOA DH.EUM 2 Şb. 68/76, Bekir Sami to the Ministry of Interior on 5 September 1915. Another telegram sent a month and a half later indicated that there were thirty thousand deportees in Aleppo city alone awaiting redeportation. See BOA DH.EUM 2 Şb. 68/80, telegram from the Ministry of Interior to the Syria Province on 18 October 1915.
135. DE/PA-AA; R14087; R14095 A53a, 3451, Rössler to the imperial chancellor, enclosure 4, on 3 September 1915, in Gust, *The Armenian Genocide*, 350.
136. Charek, *Marzbede*, 2:2.

CHAPTER TWO. Aleppo: Urban Resistance to Redeportation

1. BNu/Andonian, folder 30, The Deportation of Armenians of Aleppo, 54. See also Raymond Kévorkian, "L'Extermination des déportés Arméniens ottomans dans les camps de concentration de Syrie-Mésopotamie (1915–1916)," special issue, *Revue d'histoire arménienne contemporaine* 2 (1998): 126.
2. As noted earlier, a telegram issued by the Ministry of the Interior on 18 October 1915 indicated that there were thirty thousand deportees in Aleppo City alone awaiting redeportation. See BOA DH.EUM 2 Şb. 68/80. Tens of thousands had already been deported to Bab, Mumbuj, and Maarra, or farther to Urfa, Zor, and Mosul. See BOA DH.EUM 2 Şb. 68/76, Bekir Sami to the Ministry of Interior on 5 September 1915.
3. DE/PA-AA; R 14086, Ambassador Wangenheim to Bethmann Hollweg on17 June 1915. As

cited in Taner Akçam, *The Young Turks' Crime against Humanity: The Armenian Genocide and Ethnic Cleansing in the Ottoman Empire* (Princeton, NJ: Princeton University Press, 2012), 133.

4. Khachig Boghosian (1875–1950) was born in Kayseri, studied in Istanbul, and then traveled to Switzerland for his doctoral studies. Upon his return in 1914, he served as a military doctor in Constantinople, and was arrested along with other Armenian intellectuals in 1915. After spending several weeks in prison in Ayaş and Çankırı, he was deported and ended up in Aleppo, where he became active in the humanitarian resistance network. After the war, he stayed in Aleppo, where he continued his medical practice, helped found a maternity hospital, and established the newspaper *Yeprad*.
5. John Halajian, *A Widow's Story: Tales of an Armenian Genocide Survivor* (Mustang, OK: Tate Publishing, 2016). See also Paren Kazanjian, ed., *The Cilician Armenian Ordeal* (Boston: Hye Intentions, 1989), 442–454.
6. Kazanjian, *The Cilician Armenian Ordeal*, 380.
7. Yeranuhi Simonian, *Im Koghkotas* [My Golgotha] (Antelias: Armenian Catholicosate, 1960), 58.
8. Payladzou Captanian, *Tsavag* (New York: Armenia Printing, 1922), 260.
9. DE/PA-AA; R14094; A 31831, report from Rössler to Bethmann Hollweg, on 5 November 1916, in Wolfgang Gust, ed., *The Armenian Genocide: Evidence from the German Foreign Office Archives, 1915–1916* (New York: Berghahn, 2014), 673.
10. Yervant Odian, *Accursed Years: My Exile and Return from Der Zor, 1914–1919*, trans. Ara Stepan Melkonian (London: Gomidas Institute, 2009), 235.
11. NA/RG59/867.4016/373, Jackson to the secretary of state on 4 March 1918, in Ara Sarafian, ed., *United States Official Records on the Armenian Genocide* (London: Gomidas Institute, 2004), 597.
12. Kazanjian, *The Cilician Armenian Ordeal*, 291.
13. Ibid.
14. BOA DH.ŞFR 54-A/167, coded telegram from the IAMM to the Province of Aleppo dated 29 July 1915. In the two months preceding the formation of IAMM, the central authorities paid little attention to deportees arriving in Syria, leaving the process of internment and temporary settlement to the local authorities. By summer 1915, however, it was clear that the situation in the region would spiral out of control as local authorities scrambled for ways to deal with the sudden influx of tens of thousands of people.
15. IAMM was established in early 1914 with the announced mandate of settling nomadic Arab, Turcoman, and Kurdish tribes, as well as providing homes to Muslim refugees flocking to the empire from Russia and the Balkans. For details, see Fuat Dündar, *Crime of*

Numbers: The Role of Statistics in the Armenian Question, 1878–1918 (New Brunswick, NJ: Transaction Publishers, 2010).

16. BOA DH.ŞFR 56/73, Interior Ministry's General Security Directorate to the district governors of Zor and Urfa dated 13 August 1915.
17. BOA DH.ŞFR 55-A/240, Interior Ministry to Aleppo Province on 13 September 1915.
18. BOA DH.ŞFR 57/52, Interior Ministry to Aleppo Province on 17 October 1915.
19. Ohannes Pacha Kouyoumdjian, *Le Liban: À la veille et au début de la guerre. Mémoire d'un Gouverneur, 1913–1915* (Paris: Centre d'histoire arménienne contemporaine, 2003), 171.
20. DE/PA-AA; BoKon/171; A53, 5989, telegram from the Administrator in Aleppo (Hoffmann) to the embassy in Istanbul dated 18 October 1915, in Wolfgang Gust, ed., *The Armenian Genocide: Evidence from the German Foreign Office Archives, 1915–1916* (New York: Berghahn, 2014), 424.
21. Cengiz Atlı, "Türk Siyasi Hayatının Ardında Kalan İsim: Mustafa Abdulhalik Renda" [A Forgotten Name in Turkish Politics: Mustafa Abdulhalik Renda], *Journal of History Studies* 6, no. 5 (September 2014): 33.
22. NA/RG59/867.4016/373, Jackson to the secretary of state on 4 March 1918, in Sarafian, *United States Official Records*, 585.
23. Hans-Lukas Kieser, *Talaat Pasha: Father of Modern Turkey, Architect of Genocide* (Princeton, NJ: Princeton University Press, 2018), 250.
24. Akçam, *The Young Turks' Crime against Humanity*, xxiv–xxv.
25. Erik-Jan Zürcher, "Young Turk Decision Making Patterns, 1913–1915," in *Le génocide des Arméniens: Un siècle de recherche, 1915–2015*, ed. Annette Becker, Hamit Bozarslan, Vincent Duclert, and Raymond Kévorkian (Paris: Armand Colin, 2015), 14.
26. Kazanjian, *The Cilician Armenian Ordeal*, 407. After his escape from prison, Maljian (1886–1976) returned to Marash. In 1921, he emigrated to the United States, where he served the Armenian Catholic community. See also Stanley Elphinstone Kerr, *The Lions of Marash: Personal Experiences with American Near East Relief, 1919–1922* (Albany: SUNY Press, 1973), 61, 138, and 154. For biographical information, see http://pascalmaljian.com/index.html.
27. Kazanjian, *The Cilician Armenian Ordeal*, 407.
28. See Armenian Nation Council, Council Records for Refugees, folder 38, minutes of session held on 24 October 1915.
29. The members of the council were Tavit Jidejian, Diran Piranian, D. Dakessian, Hagop Barsoumian, and M. Sahagian. See Puzant Yeghiayan, *Zhamanagagagits badmutiun gat'oghigosut'ean hayots Giligio, 1914–1972* [Contemporary History of the Armenian Catholicosate of Cilicia, 1914–1972] (Antelias, Lebanon: Catholicosate of Cilicia, 1975),

52. See also Council Records, folder 38, minutes of session held on 24 October 1915. The Council Records also mention the name of another member, Vahan Kovejian, as well as a certain Roupen Ejghojian, although it is unclear whether he was a member of the newly appointed council or an employee. For a biography of Khachadur Boghigian (1851–1920), see Husig Setragian, *Vark Kahanayits Perio Temi, 1850–2005* [The Lives of the Priests of the Aleppo Prelacy, 1850–2005], vol. 1 (Aleppo: Aleppo Prelacy, 2005), 28–33. (I would like to thank Ani Boghikian Kasparian for pointing me to this source.)

30. DE/PA-AA; BoKon/170; A53a, 5779, Rössler to the ambassador in Extraordinary Mission in Istanbul on 27 September 1915, in Gust, *The Armenian Genocide*, 383.
31. BNu/Andonian, folder 30, The Deportation of Armenians of Aleppo, 31, 35, 93–94. Circassian refugees forced out of the Russian Empire in the late 1800s often harbored resentment toward Christians. Settled in Ottoman Syria, they would play a significant role in the destruction of Armenian deportees in summer 1916.
32. Catholicos Papken, *Badmutiun gatoghigosats Giligio* [History of the Giligia Catholicoses] (Antelias, Lebanon: Dbaran Tbrevanouts, 1939), 922. Initially the Ottoman Ministry of Justice (established in 1870), the ministry was later renamed the Ministry of Justice and Religious Sects and granted "all functions concerned with the non-Muslim *millets*." See Stanford J. Shaw and Ezel Kural Shaw, *History of the Ottoman Empire and Modern Turkey*, vol. 2: *Reform, Revolution, and Republic: The Rise of Modern Turkey, 1808–1975* (Cambridge: Cambridge University Press, 1977), 216–217.
33. See Raymond Kévorkian, *The Armenian Genocide: A Complete History* (London: I. B. Tauris, 2011), 535.
34. DE/PA-AA; BoKon/171; A53a 6211, telegram from Rössler to the German embassy in Istanbul dated 29 October 1915. The document is available online at http://www.armenocide.net/armenocide/armgende.nsf/$$AllDocs/1915-10-29-DE-001.
35. Zaven Der Yeghiayan, *My Patriarchal Memoirs* (Barrington, RI: Mayreni Publishing, 2002), 113.
36. Ibid., 112.
37. BOA DH.ŞFR 57/325, coded telegram from the Internal Ministry's General Security Directorate to the province of Aleppo dated 25 October [7 November] 1915; and BOA DH.ŞFR 57/326, coded telegram from the Internal Ministry's General Security Directorate to IAMM Director Şükrü Bey dated 25 October [7 November] 1915.
38. Der Yeghiayan, *My Patriarchal Memoirs*, 112.
39. Khachadryan, a historian, was the principal of the Getronagan School in Istanbul (1913–1915). He survived the Armenian genocide and became a victim of the Stalin purges in Armenia.

40. Ibid.
41. Survivor Vahram Dadrian noted in his 9 September 1915 diary entry that the Catholicos visited the camp at Katma north of Aleppo City, where Dadrian himself was interned briefly before he managed to enter Aleppo. "Two high-ranking priests accompanied Catholicos Sahag, as well as six prominent men from Sis and Adana. His Holiness informed us that they had appealed to the mayor of Aleppo to find a solution to the tragic condition of the Armenians in Katma. Unfortunately, their pleas were ignored." See Vahram Dadrian, *To the Desert: Pages from My Diary* (London: Taderon Press, 2003), 55. It is very likely that the Catholicos also visited other nearby camps on this trip.
42. In his memoir, Armenian Patriarch of Constantinople Zaven Der Yeghiayan recounts how police chiefs told the charge d'affairs of the Patriarchate during an encounter in early January 1916 about the announcement "at a suitable time" of such a decision. See Der Yeghiayan, *My Patriarchal Memoirs*, 119–120. We also have correspondence from May 1916 on this matter between Talaat and Cemal in the months leading up to the August 1916 decree. See, for example, BOA DH.ŞFR 63/136, Talaat to Cemal on 30 May 1916.
43. For details of the shutting down of the Armenian Patriarchate of Constantinople, see Der Yeghiayan, *My Patriarchal Memoirs*, 121–124; Yeghiayan, *Zhamanagagagits badmutiun*, 60. For the Jerusalem Armenian Patriarchate's role in this period, see Vahram L. Shemmassian, "Armenian Genocide Survivors in the Holy Land at the End of World War I," *Journal of the Society for Armenian Studies* 21 (2012): 227–247.
44. Council Records, folder 38, minutes of session held on 30 October 1915.
45. Council Records, folder 38, minutes of session held on 24 October 1915.
46. After 17 July 1915, the council's record book does not have any entries for meetings until 24 October and then 30 October, and then a final entry is recorded on 15 December 1915. See Council Records, folder 38. The bodies of the Armenian Apostolic Church of Aleppo, including the Council for Refugees, resumed taking minutes of their meetings after the war.
47. NA/RG59/867.4016/373, Jackson to the secretary of state on 4 March 1918, in Sarafian, *United States Official Records*, 587. Typhus wreaked havoc among deportees even before their arrival in Ottoman Syria. U.S. consul in Kharpert Leslie A. Davis recounts the difficult conditions under which he and his associates conducted relief work in the province in late 1915 and after, and the precautions they took to avoid contracting the disease. "Most of the people were dirty and covered with vermin. The disease that was most prevalent there and most to be dreaded was typhus. . . . We took precautions against this by sprinkling naphthalene around the office and wearing naphthalene bands around the neck, arms and legs, in order to prevent the lice from crawling on to the body." Leslie

A. Davis, *The Slaughterhouse Province: An American Diplomat's Report on the Armenian Genocide, 1915–1917* (New Rochelle: Aristide D. Caratzas, 1989), 107.

48. Mgrdich Hairabedian's memoir, 6, BNu unpublished memoirs collection. The memoir was submitted to BNu in July 1978. Hairabedian was born in Hamidiye (later renamed Ceyhan) in 1904.
49. DE/PA-AA; R14089; A35045, report from Rössler to Bethmann Hollweg on 8 November 1915, in Gust, *The Armenian Genocide*, 442–444.
50. Order number 1117 of army command. ATASE Archives: BDH.K.3254, E. 717, Y. 1, F. 1–3, as cited in Hikmet Özdemir, *Cemal Paşa ve Ermeni Göçmenler: 4. Ordu'nun İnsani Yardımları* [Cemal Pasha and the Armenian Deportees: The Humanitarian Assistance of the Fourth Army] (Istanbul: Remzi Kitapevi, 2009), 92.
51. Ibid., 127.
52. Ibid., 127–130. For Rössler's report on these measures, see DE/PA-AA; R14089; A35045, Rössler to Bethmann Hollweg on 8 November 1915, in Gust, *The Armenian Genocide*, 442–444.
53. Özdemir, *Cemal Paşa ve Ermeni Göçmenler*, 128.
54. ATASE Archives, Kls. 3253, Ds. 2, Fih. 7A, telegram from the Aleppo Commissariat to Cemal Pasha on 1 November 1915, as cited in M. Talha Çiçek, *War and State Formation in Syria: Cemal Pasha's Governorate during World War I, 1914–1917* (New York: Routledge, 2014), 118.
55. DE/PA-AA; R14089; A36213, Rössler to Bethmann Hollweg on 30 November 1915, in Gust, *The Armenian Genocide*, 488.
56. NA/RG59/867.4016/373, Jackson to the Secretary of State on 4 March 1918, in Sarafian, *United States Official Records*, 587.
57. John Minassian, *Many Hills Yet to Climb* (Santa Barbara, CA: Jim Cook, 1986), 98–99.
58. Levon Mesrob, ed., *Der Zor* (Paris: B. Elegian, 1955), 57–58.
59. BNu/Andonian, folder 30, "The Deportation of Armenians of Aleppo," 47–50.
60. DE/PA-AA; BoKon/97; 10/12, 9442 (enclosure), telegraphic report from the chairman of the Baghdad Railway in Istanbul Franz Johannes Gunther to the chargé d'affaires of the embassy in Istanbul on 1 November 1915, in Gust, *The Armenian Genocide*, 204.
61. NA/RG59/867.4016/373, Jackson to the secretary of state on 4 March 1918, in Sarafian, *United States Official Records*, 588.
62. Mgrdich Hairabedian's memoir, 6.
63. Kerop Bedoukian, *Some of Us Survived: The Story of an Armenian Boy* (New York: Farrar, Straus, Giroux, 1979), 56.
64. Dikran Yeretsian, *Vorperu Pouyne (1915–1921)* [The Nest of Orphans (1915–1921)] (Aleppo:

Ani Publishing, 1934), 3.

65. Minassian, *Many Hills Yet to Climb*, 98–99.
66. Minassian's eulogy of Rev. Eskijian, 26 March 1916, Eskijian Family Personal Archives.
67. See Yevnige Jebejian, "Minchev Mah" [Until Death], *Chanaser* 28, no. 7–8 (1 and 15 April 1965): 169–170. See also, Dikran Jebejian, "Der Zori Sbante," *Hay Anteb* 2, no. 18 (1965): 14–15. Dikran, Araxia's brother, read this testimony at a genocide commemoration event in Aleppo on 24 April 1955. It was published a decade later, after his death.
68. We do not know what the *emanet* was, and it was very likely left unmentioned to avoid the censors. Letter in Armeno-Turkish from Lutfi Sayegh in Der Zor to Gulenia Eskijian, 1 April 1916, Eskijian Family Private Archives.
69. NA/RG59/867.4016/373, Jackson to the secretary of state on 4 March 1918, in Sarafian, *United States Official Records*, 588.
70. Kazanjian, *The Cilician Armenian Ordeal*, 442–454.
71. Ali Fuad Erden, *Birinci Dünya Harbi'nde Suriye Hatıraları* [Memories of Syria during the First World War] (Istanbul: Kültür Publishing, 2003), 151.
72. Hüseyin Kazım Kadri, *Türkiye'nin Çöküşü* (Istanbul: Hikmet Neşriyat, 1992), 205.
73. Aram Andonian, *Medz Vojire* [The Great Crime] (Boston: Bahag Publishing, 1921), 101.
74. Ibid.
75. DE/PA-AA; R14090; A02889, Rössler to Metternich, enclosure 1 (8 November 1915), 3 January 1916, in Gust, *The Armenian Genocide*, 509.
76. NA/RG59/867.4016/243, memorandum by Walter M. Geddes sent by American Consul General George Horton (Smyrna, Turkey) to the secretary of state on 8 November 1915, in Sarafian, *United States Official Records*, 380–383.
77. Martin Niepage, *The Horrors of Aleppo Seen by a German Eyewitness* (1917; repr. New York: New Age Publishers, 1975), 4. For a brief overview of this account's dissemination in the West, see Hans-Lukas Kieser and Margaret Lavinia Anderson, "Introduction: Unhealed Wounds, Perpetuated Patterns," in *End of the Ottomans: The Genocide of 1915 and the Politics of Turkish Nationalism*, ed. Hans-Lukas Kieser, Margaret Lavinia Anderson, Seyhan Bayraktar, and Thomas Schmutz (London: I. B Tauris, 2019), 6.
78. BOA DH.ŞFR 57/51, telegram from Talaat to Şükrü Bey on 17 October 1915. See also *Osmanli Belgelerinde Ermeniler (1915–1920)* [The Armenians in Ottoman Documents, 1915–1920] (Ankara: Ottoman Archives of the Prime Minister's Office, 1995), 106. Talaat sent the same telegram to the Syria governorate on the same day. See BOA DH.ŞFR 57/71, in *Osmanli Belgelerinde Ermeniler*, 105.
79. Der Yeghiayan, *My Patriarchal Memoirs*, 115.
80. DE/PA-AA; R14090; A02889, Rössler to Metternich, ambassador in Extraordinary Mission

in Istanbul, enclosure 1 (8 November 1915), 3 January 1916, in Gust, *The Armenian Genocide*, 505.

81. Another such case is Kütahya, where the district governor Faik Ali Bey refused to deport the local Armenians—and there were no consequences. Historian Feroz Ahmad used this case to argue that the center was not strong enough to impose its will on local officials—and therefore, whatever localized massacres occurred, they were not coordinated from the center. "But Talaat was unable to impose his will on the governor of a provincial town," he wrote. See Feroz Ahmad, *The Young Turks and the Ottoman Nationalities: Armenians, Greeks, Albanians, Jews, and Arabs, 1908–1918* (Salt Lake City: University of Utah Press, 2014), 82. This line of reasoning, which aims at absolving the central authorities of responsibility in the destruction of Armenians, is patently false. As we see repeatedly in this study, the center intervenes and imposes its will as needed, mindful of other considerations on the ground. This demonstrates strength and control, one can argue, more than weakness. Overwhelmingly, dissenting officials were removed and replaced with ones who fell in line.
82. DE/PA-AA; R14090; A04212, report from Rössler to the ambassador in Extraordinary Mission in Istanbul Metternich on 26 January 1916, in Gust, *The Armenian Genocide*, 531.
83. For a discussion on the deportation of Armenians in Istanbul, see Kévorkian, *The Armenian Genocide*, 540–543.
84. DE/PA-AA; R14093; A25739, report from the chargé d'affaires in Aleppo to the embassy in Istanbul on 29 August 1916, in Gust, *The Armenian Genocide*, 618. In an earlier report, Rössler wrote, "Deportation began once again in Aleppo on 19 June, at first under the pretext that all those 'dangerous to the health of others' had to be removed, then that all the 'suspects' could not be allowed to remain, whereby distinctions are not always made between newcomers and those residing in the town." DE/PA-AA; R14093; A25739, report from Rössler to Bethmann Hollweg on 29 June 1916, in Gust, *The Armenian Genocide*, 600.
85. NA/RG59/867.4016/296, Hoffman Philip's report to the secretary of state on 1 September 1916, in Sarafian, *United States Official Records*, 535.
86. BOA DH.ŞFR 74/75, telegram from Talaat to the Aleppo provincial authorities on 8 March 1917.
87. Odian, *Accursed Years*, 235.
88. Andonian, *Medz Vojire*, 15.
89. Hovhannes Toros Doumanian, "My Memoirs," BNu unpublished memoirs collection. Also available online at http://doumanianmemoirs.blogspot.com. Doumanian eventually found a job as an agricultural engineer working for the effort to contain the locust

infestation in Jezire. "We began our anti-locust training. I was one of twenty officers. Three days later in Mumbudj, I was appointed as a military officer in the army. Dressed in an officer's uniform, I was able to return to Bab-El-Faraj Street without fear. This was a street I had never dared to visit because I would have been arrested," he wrote.

90. The magic of the *vesika* in Aleppo also figures in the account of survivor Vasken Tchilinguirian from Erzerum. See Vasken Tchilinguirian, "Le ciel etait noir sur Garine," 48–49, BNu unpublished memoirs collection. Additional references to the *vesika* appear in sections on Bab and Rakka. For the role of economic motivations, including bribes, in saving deportees during the Armenian genocide, see Richard G. Hovannisian, "Intervention and Shades of Altruism during the Armenian Genocide," in *The Armenian Genocide: History, Politics, Ethics*, ed. Richard G. Hovannisian (New York: St. Martin's, 1992), 181–186.
91. NA/RG59/867.4016/373, Jackson to the secretary of state on 4 March 1918, in Sarafian, *United States Official Records*, 593.
92. References to girls and boys escaping their employers' homes abound in survivor accounts. For example, Captanian tells the story of one woman who escaped from her captor's house and hid in a tent in Sebil. Captanian, *Tsavag*, 213–214.
93. This was a common designation in the United States during the Great War and its immediate aftermath. See, for example, Merrill D. Peterson, *"Starving Armenians": America and the Armenian Genocide, 1915–1920 and After* (Charlottesville: University of Virginia Press, 2004).
94. For more extensive studies of relief efforts in the United States, see Peter Balakian, *The Burning Tigris: The Armenian Genocide and America's Response* (New York: HarperCollins, 2003); Suzanne E. Moranian, "The Armenian Genocide and American Missionary Relief Efforts," in *America and the Armenian Genocide of 1915*, ed. Jay Winter (Cambridge: Cambridge University Press, 2003), 185; and Simon Payaslian, *United States Policy toward the Armenian Question and the Armenian Genocide* (New York: Palgrave Macmillan, 2005).
95. Realizing that the sum was nowhere near sufficient, fundraising efforts were multiplied in the United States. The following year, the committee raised a whopping $2,404,000. Donated funds continued to increase, even doubled, during the following few years. See James L. Barton, *Story of Near East Relief* (New York: Macmillan, 1930), 409.
96. Barton, *Story of Near East Relief*, 17.
97. NA/RG59/867.48/199, Morgenthau to secretary of state on 29 November 1915, in Sarafian, *United States Official Records*, 388.
98. Ibid.

99. NA/RG59/756.48/205, Morgenthau to secretary of state on 21 January 1916, in Sarafian, *United States Official Records*, 392.
100. NA/RG59/756.48/205, letter on behalf of the secretary of state to Rev. James L. Barton of the American Board of Commissioners for Foreign Missions on 13 December 1915, in Sarafian, *United States Official Records*, 391. ACASR eventually became Near East Relief.
101. NA/RG59/867.4016/219, Jackson to Morgenthau on 29 September 1915, in Sarafian, *United States Official Records*, 307–308.
102. NA/RG59/867.4016/179, Morgenthau to secretary of state on 22 October 1915, in Sarafian, *United States Official Records*, 231.
103. In 1916, donations exceeded $2,400,000, then almost doubled in 1917, and reached $7 million in 1918. See Moranian, "The Armenian Genocide and American Missionary Relief Efforts," 195.
104. Taner Akçam, *Killing Orders: Talaat Pasha's Telegrams and the Armenian Genocide* (Cham, Switzerland: Palgrave Macmillan, 2018), 155–156.
105. Captanian, *Tsavag*, 242.
106. NA/RG59/867.4016/373, Jackson to secretary of state on 4 March 1918, in Sarafian, *United States Official Records*, 595.
107. See Der Yeghiayan, *My Patriarchal Memoirs*, 110–111.
108. Minassian, *Many Hills Yet to Climb*, 93.
109. Beatrice Rohner, *Die Stunde ist gekommen: Märtyrerbilder aus der Jetztzeit* (Frankfurt am Main: Verlag Orient, circa 1920), 7–14.
110. Yeretsian, *Vorperu Pouynē*, 3.
111. Several memoirs and accounts refer to this institution as Shirajian's orphanage. Although that is not its official name, I follow survivor usage.
112. For the orphanage's location, see Elmas Boyajian, "Hay vorpanotsi gyanken" [From the Life of the Armenian Orphanage], *Chanaser*, 1 October 1964, 415; and Erden, *Birinci Dünya Harbi'nde Suriye Hatıraları*, 152; and Kévorkian, *The Armenian Genocide*, 643. For the embassy's location, see Thomas Philipp and Birgit Schaebler, *The Syrian Land: Processes of Integration and Fragmentation; Bilād Al-Shām from the 18th to the 20th Century* (Stuttgart: Steiner, 1998), 316.
113. Boyajian, "Hay vorpanotsi gyanken," 415.
114. "Nerga hay vorpanotse" [The Current Armenian Orphanage] (interview with orphanage director Aharon Shirajian), *Darakir*, 13 December 1918, 2–3.
115. NA/RG59/867.4016/219, Jackson to Morgenthau on 29 September 1918, in Sarafian, *United States Official Records*, 313.
116. Ibid.

117. Yeretsian, *Vorperu Pouyne*, 3.
118. Boyajian, "Hay vorpanotsi gyanken," 415.
119. *Deghegakir Halebi Haygagan Vorpanotsi* [Report about the Armenian Orphanage of Aleppo] (Aleppo: "Suriagan Mamul" Publishers, 1922), 4.
120. "Nerga hay vorpanotse," 2.
121. Ibid., 6. For the council's support, see, for example, Council Records, folder 38, minutes of meeting held on 24 October 1915.
122. *Deghegakir Halebi Haygagan Vorpanotsi*, 7.
123. "Nerga hay vorpanotse," 2.
124. *Deghegakir Halebi Haygagan Vorpanotsi*, 7.
125. "Nerga hay vorpanotse," 6–7.
126. Ibid., 7. See also Numen, "Badveli Hovh. Eskijian Halebi Mech" [Rev. Hovhannes Eskijian in Aleppo], *Gochnag Hayasdani* 23, no. 6 (10 February 1923): 175; and Taqui Altounyan, *Chimes from a Wooden Bell: A Hundred Years in the Life of a Euro-Armenian Family* (London: I. B. Tauris, 1990), 25–26. Isabel Kaprielian-Churchill, *Sisters of Mercy and Survival: Armenian Nurses, 1900–1930* (Antelias, Lebanon: Armenian Catholicosate of Cilicia, 2012), 328.
127. Daniel B. Silver, *Refuge in Hell: How Berlin's Jewish Hospital Outlasted the Nazis* (Boston: Houghton Mifflin, 2004).
128. Kerr, *The Lions of Marash*, 29.
129. Altounyan, *Chimes from a Wooden Bell*, 25–26.
130. NA/RG59/867.4016/373, Jackson to the secretary of state on 4 March 1918, in Sarafian, *United States Official Records*, 594.
131. Minassian, *Many Hills Yet to Climb*, 91.
132. "Nerga hay vorpanotse," 2.
133. A. A. Shirajian, "Ver. Shirajianin kordzagitsnere" [The Colleagues of Rev. Shirajian], *Chanaser*, 1 October 1964, 405.
134. "Nerga hay vorpanotse" (Part II), *Darakir*, 15 December 1918, 2.
135. NA/RG59/867.4016/373, Jackson to the secretary of state on 4 March 1918, in Sarafian, *United States Official Records*, 594.
136. Boyajian, "Hay vorpanotsi gyanken," 415.
137. "Nerga hay vorpanotse" (Part II), 2.
138. Ghazar Charek, *Marzbede* (*Haji Hiuseyin*), 2 vols. (Beirut: Azad Printing House, 1945), 1:21. For references to Dr. Boghosian's activities in the resistance network, see also ibid., 1:27–28.
139. Kazanjian, *The Cilician Armenian Ordeal*, 448.

140. Khachig Boghosian, "Himnatire azkayin medz tsernargi me" [The Founder of a Major National Initiative], *Chanaser*, 1 October 1964414.
141. NA/RG59/867.4016/373, Jackson to the Secretary of State on 4 March 1918, in Sarafian, *United States Official Records*, 594.
142. Aram Shorvoghlian, "Gark me tvanshanner vorpanotsi gyanken" [Some Figures from Orphanage Life], *Chanaser*, 1 October 1964, 417–418.
143. Ibid., 417.
144. BOA DH.ŞFR 503/91, telegram from Abdülhalik to the Ministry of the Interior dated 10 February 1916.
145. Akçam, *Killing Orders*, 140; NA/RG59/867.4016/373, Jackson to the Secretary of State on 4 March 1918, in Sarafian, *United States Official Records*, 594.
146. "Appendix A-1: The Ottoman-Turkish Original of Naim Efendi's Text," in Akçam, *Killing Orders*, 194–195. For a discussion on telegrams related to the orphanage established by Madam Koch, see ibid., 136–141.
147. See Akçam, *Killing Orders*, 139; Hans-Lukas Kieser, "Beatrice Rohner's Work in the Death Camps of Armenians in 1916," in *Resisting Genocide: The Multiple Forms of Rescue*, ed. Jacques Sémelin, Claire Andrieu, and Sarah Gensburger (New York: Columbia University Press, 2011), 377. For an account of a child survivor of the Antoura orphanage, see Karnig Panian, *Goodbye, Antoura: A Memoir of the Armenian Genocide* (Stanford: Stanford University Press, 2015).
148. Boyajian, "Hay vorpanotsi gyanken," 415.
149. Minassian, *Many Hills Yet to Climb*, 97.
150. NA/RG59/867.4016/373, Jackson to the secretary of state on 4 March 1918, in Sarafian, *United States Official Records*, 594.
151. Cable from ACASR representative in Turkey to ACASR through the State Department on 4 May 1916. James Bryce and Arnold Toynbee, *The Treatment of the Armenians in the Ottoman Empire, 1915–1916: Documents Presented to Viscount Grey of Fallodon by Viscount Bryce*, ed. Ara Sarafian, uncensored edition (London: Gomidas Institute, 2000), document 14, 70.
152. See Armenian National Council, Council Records for Refugees, folder 22, receipts of miscellaneous expenses.
153. Armenian National Council, Council Records for Refugees, folder 22, receipts of miscellaneous expenses.
154. BNu/Andonian, folder 52, "The Massacres of Der Zor," 109–110.
155. Debórah Dwork, *Children with a Star: Jewish Youth in Nazi Europe* (New Haven: Yale University Press, 1991), 253.

156. Nazan Maksudyan, *Orphans and Destitute Children in the Late Ottoman Empire* (Syracuse: Syracuse University Press, 2014), 4.
157. Halide Edib, *Memoirs of Halide Edib* (New York: The Century, 1926), 406.
158. Charek, *Marzbede*, 2:19–21.
159. For an overview of these assassinations, see Marian Mesrobian MacCurdy, *Sacred Justice: The Voices and Legacy of the Armenian Operation Nemesis* (New York: Transaction Publishers, 2015); Eric Bogosian, *Operation Nemesis: The Assassination Plot that Avenged the Armenian Genocide* (New York: Little, Brown, 2015); Rolf Hosfeld, *Operation Nemesis: Die Türkei, Deutschland und der Völkermord an den Armeniern* (Cologne: Kiepenheuer & Witsch, 2005); and Jacques Derogy, *Resistance and Revenge: The Armenian Assassination of the Turkish Leaders Responsible for the 1915 Massacres and Deportations* (New Brunswick, NJ: Transaction Publishers, 1990).
160. Hilmar Kaiser, *The Extermination of Armenians in the Diyarbekir Region* (Istanbul: Bilgi University, 2014), 384. For a detailed treatment of his "regional resistance" thesis, see Kaiser, "Regional Resistance to Central Government Policies: Ahmed Djemal Pasha, the Governors of Aleppo, and Armenian Deportees in the Spring and Summer of 1915," *Journal of Genocide Research* 12, no. 3 (2010): 214. Kévorkian, *The Armenian Genocide*, 681.
161. Kévorkian and Bloxham consider this argument a "possible explanation" for Cemal's policies vis-à-vis Armenians. See Raymond Kévorkian, "Ahmed Djémal pacha et le sort des déportés arméniens de Syrie-Palestine," in *The Armenian Genocide and the Shoah*, ed. Hans-Lukas Kieser and Dominik J. Schaller (Zurich: Chronos Verlag, 2002), 197–212, and Kévorkian, *The Armenian Genocide*, 683–685; and Donald Bloxham, *The Great Game of Genocide: Imperialism, Nationalism, and the Destruction of the Ottoman Armenians* (Oxford: Oxford University Press, 2005), 139. Historian M. Talha Çiçek considers this argument "irrelevant," noting that Cemal's seemingly independent policies in the Fourth Army region must not be confused with readiness to revolt against his fellow leaders. See Çiçek, *War and State Formation in Syria*, 113.
162. Fuat Dündar, *Modern Türkiye'nin Şifresi: İttihat Ve Terakki'nin Etnisite Mühendisliği, 1913–1918* [Modern Turkey's Code: The CUP's Ethnic Engineering, 1913–1918] (Istanbul: İletişim, 2010), 324–328; and Fatma Müge Göçek, *Denial of Violence: Ottoman Past, Turkish Present, and Collective Violence against the Armenians, 1789–2009* (Oxford: Oxford University Press, 2015), 225.
163. Çiçek, *War and State Formation in Syria*, 109 and 113.
164. Ümit Kurt, "A Rescuer, an Enigma and a Génocidaire: Cemal Pasha," in *End of the Ottomans: The Genocide of 1915 and the Politics of Turkish Nationalism*, ed. Hans-Lukas Kieser, Margaret Lavinia Anderson, Seyhan Bayraktar, and Thomas Schmutz (London: I.

B. Tauris, 2019), 224.

165. Cemal briefly discusses his stint at Adana in his memoir, taking pride in overseeing the reconstruction within four months of all Armenian houses destroyed during the Adana massacres of 1909. See Djemal Pasha, *Memories of a Turkish Statesman, 1913–1919* (London: Hutchinson, 1922), 261–262. For more on Cemal in Adana, see Çiçek, *War and State Formation in Syria*, 5–7.
166. Arguing for his innocence in the destruction of the Armenians, Cemal would later cite these "accomplishments" in an article among a list of ten different humanitarian efforts he engaged in to help Armenians. See Cemal Pasha, "Der Orient in Der Presse. Zur Frage der Greuel in Armenien: Eine Rechtfertigungsfrage," *Der Neue Orient* 6, no. 2 (1919): 120–122.
167. Pratt opened his speech at George Mason University in 1892 with the following words: "A great general has said that the only good Indian is a dead one, and that high sanction of his destruction has been an enormous factor in promoting Indian massacres. In a sense, I agree with the sentiment, but only in this: that all the Indian there is in the race should be dead. Kill the Indian in him, and save the man." Pratt's ideas about "civilizing" Native Americans were implemented at the Carlisle Indian School he established in 1879 and served as inspiration to many boarding schools across the United States. The full text of the speech is available at "History Matters: The U.S. Survey Course on the Web," http://historymatters.gmu.edu/d/4929.
168. Kiud Mkhitarian, *Husher Yev Verhishumner, 1918–1935* [Memories and Remembrances, 1918–1935] (Antelias: Cilicia Catholicosate, 1937), 77–78.
169. See, for example, BOA DH.ŞFR 58/59, Ministry of Interior to Aleppo Province on 18 November 1915.
170. See Erden, *Birinci Dünya Harbi'nde Suriye Hatıraları*, 152; DE/PA-AA; R14092; A16612, report from Hardegg to the embassy in Istanbul on 30 May 1916, in Gust, *The Armenian Genocide*, 588; Özdemir, *Cemal Paşa ve Ermeni Göçmenler*, 106; and Taner Akçam, *A Shameful Act: The Armenian Genocide and the Question of Turkish Responsibility* (New York: Metropolitan Books, 2006), 185.
171. German ambassador Metternich noted that he told the Ottoman army's chief of staff Enver Pasha and Cemal Pasha in December 1915 that "wide circles both in allied foreign countries and in Germany were in the grip of unrest and indignation, and that unless these atrocities [against Armenians] were stopped, these circles would end up withdrawing all their sympathies from the Turkish government." See DE/PA-AA; R14089; A 36184, report from Metternich to Bethmann Hollweg on 7 December 1915, in Gust, *The Armenian Genocide*, 565.

172. DE/PA-AA; BoKon 170; A53a, 5779, Rössler to Ambassador in Extraordinary Mission in Istanbul Hohenlohe-Langenburg on 27 September 1915, in Gust, *The Armenian Genocide*, 382.
173. Coded telegram from Jemal Pasha to Governor of Diyarbakir on 14 July 1915. Takvim-I Vekayi #3540 (27 Nisan, 1335) s. 4–14 (Kararname) in Vahakn N. Dadrian and Taner Akçam, *Judgement at Istanbul: The Armenian Genocide Trials* (New York: Berghahn Books, 2011), 277. Dr. Reshid stands out as a key perpetrator of the Armenian genocide in the province of Diyarbakir and a "willing executioner of the CUP" who massacred tens of thousands of Armenians in the areas under his jurisdiction. See Hans-Lukas Kieser, "Dr Mehmed Reshid (1873–1919): A Political Doctor," in Kieser and Schaller. *The Armenian Genocide and the Shoah*, 245–280.
174. DE/PA-AA; R14087; A 27584, Oppenheim to Bethmann Hollweg on 29 August 1915, in Gust, *The Armenian Genocide*, 332.
175. Kévorkian describes Cemal and Talaat as men with "divergent" personalities and objectives. See Kévorkian, "Ahmed Djémal pacha," 202.
176. Cemal noted instead that "he was prepared to accept money for the Armenians through me [Metternich] and to distribute this through Turkish officials." DE/PA-AA; R14091; A 08702, report from Metternich to the imperial chancellor on 29 March 1916, in Gust, *The Armenian Genocide*, 565.
177. BOA DH.ŞFR 485/47, Bekir Sami to Talaat on 24 August 1915.
178. Erden, *Birinci Dünya Harbi'nde Suriye Hatıraları*, 132.
179. Deportees often thought certain measures protecting them from bandit attacks were Cemal's initiatives, when such orders either came from Istanbul or were at least coordinated with the center. See, for example, BOA DH.ŞFR, 2 Şb. 68/1, General Security Directorate to the Zor district on 15 December 1915.
180. Hardegg was referring to Cemal's orders to hang a few gang leaders who had robbed Armenian deportees. See DE/PA-AA; BoKon171; A 53a, 6675; R14089; A33574, Hardegg to the embassy in Istanbul on 17 November 1915, in Gust, *The Armenian Genocide*, 465.
181. Erden, *Birinci Dünya Harbi'nde Suriye Hatıraları*, 152.
182. Özdemir, *Cemal Paşa ve Ermeni Göçmenler*, 15.

CHAPTER THREE. Wartime Civilian Internment: Concentration Camps in Ottoman Syria

1. The idea of reconcentration was first outlined by Weyler's predecessor, Arsenio Martínez-Campos, who never implemented it because he worried about the suffering it would bring about. Andrea Pitzer, *One Long Night: A Global History of Concentration Camps*

(New York: Little, Brown, 2017), 19–20.

2. "The Debate in the Senate," *New York Times*, 21 February 1896, 2. The speech is referenced in Pitzer, *One Long Night*, 25.
3. BNu/Andonian, folder 30, "The Situation in Bab End of 1915," in "Materials for the History of the Deportations and Massacres: Aleppo and its environs," The Deportation of Armenians of Aleppo, 6.
4. Information on the administrative structure, arrival of deportees, internment, further deportation, collaboration, resistance, and other aspects of life in the camps remains scattered in a wealth of survivor diaries, accounts, memoirs, and sketches; some Ottoman records; and Western diplomatic and missionary documents. Chief among the sources I consult are interviews and survivor testimonies gathered by chronicler Aram Andonian in the immediate aftermath of the genocide and housed at the Nubar Library in Paris. Andonian's folders on camps in Syria (Bab, Meskeneh, Rakka, Hamam, Der Zor, and others), sometimes accompanied with sketches and maps, stand as an invaluable source. For a French translation of these accounts, see Raymond Kévorkian, "L'Extermination des déportés Arméniens ottomans dans les camps de concentration de Syrie-Mésopotamie (1915–1916)," special issue, *Revue d'histoire arménienne contemporaine* 2 (1998).
5. Jonathan Hyslop, "The Invention of the Concentration Camp: Cuba, Southern Africa and the Philippines, 1896–1907," *South African Historical Journal* 63, no. 2 (2011): 251–276.
6. See, for example, Klaus Mühlhahn, "The Concentration Camp in Global Historical Perspective," *History Compass* 8, no. 6 (2010): 543–561, who argues that "in the history of the concentration camp, overlays, transfers, and mimesis are discernable at many points."
7. Hyslop, "The Invention of the Concentration Camp," 273.
8. Iain R. Smith and Andreas Stucki stress the differences between these camps and those of the Nazis in their article "The Colonial Development of Concentration Camps (1868–1902)," *Journal of Imperial and Commonwealth History* 39, no. 3 (2011): 417–437.
9. Sibylle Scheipers argues that it would be "misleading" and "short-sighted" to ignore the collective punishment dimension and view these camps as a mere counterinsurgency measure. See Scheipers, "The Use of Camps in Colonial Warfare," *Journal of Imperial and Commonwealth History* 43, no. 4 (2015): 678–698.
10. For a history of the Herero genocide in the context of German military culture, see Isabel V. Hull, *Absolute Destruction: Military Culture and the Practices of War in Imperial Germany* (Ithaca: Cornell University Press, 2005), 5–90.
11. Benjamin Madley, "From Africa to Auschwitz: How German South West Africa Incubated Ideas and Methods Adopted and Developed by the Nazis in Eastern Europe," *European History Quarterly* 35, no. 3 (2005): 429.

12. Thomas Kühne, "Colonialism and the Holocaust: Continuities, Causations, and Complexities," *Journal of Genocide Research* 15, no. 3 (2013): 343.
13. Nikolaus Wachsmann, *KL: A History of the Nazi Concentration Camps* (New York: Farrar, Straus, and Giroux, 2015), 8.
14. Wachsmann acknowledges this, when he writes that the camps in GSWA "diverged from other colonial camps, as they were propelled less by military strategy than a desire for punishment and forced labour." Kühne, in turn, doesn't dwell on the particularities of the German camps. He states that "the broad range of 'new genocide studies' focusing on colonialism has disabled the idea of a particular German genocidal continuity." See Wachsmann, *KL: A History of the Nazi Concentration Camps*, 8; and Kühne, "Colonialism and the Holocaust," 343.
15. For an excellent exploration, see Stefan Manz, Panikos Panayi, and Matthew Stibbe, eds., *Internment during the First World War: A Mass Global Phenomenon* (London: Routledge, 2018).
16. Surprisingly, Mühlhahn barely even addresses the Armenian genocide, noting, in passing, "between 1915 and 1923, more than 1 million Armenians *left* [emphasis mine] Turkish Asia Minor." See Mühlhahn, "The Concentration Camp in Global Historical Perspective," 548. The "new brutality" that he refers to was not new for African colonies, where collective punishment was commonplace and "entirely normal." See Andrea Rosegarten, "'A Most Gruesome Sight': Colonial Warfare, Racial Thought, and the Question of 'Radicalization' during the First World War in German South-West Africa (Namibia)," *History* 101, no. 346 (2016): 425–447.
17. See, for example, Hull, *Absolute Destruction*, chap. 11; Jay Winter, "Under Cover of War: The Armenian Genocide in the Context of Total War," in *The Specter of Genocide: Mass Murder in Historical Perspective*, ed. Robert Gellately and Ben Kiernan (Cambridge: Cambridge University Press, 2003), 189–214. For brief treatments of camps during the Armenian genocide in a global context, see Joël Kotek and Pierre Rigoulot, *Le siècle des camps* (Paris: JC Lattès, 2000) and Pitzer, *One Long Night*, 105–109. Despite a demonstrably genuine effort to incorporate the Armenian case into the narrative of the history of concentration camps, both works stand as testament to the dearth of literature the authors could consult.
18. See Raymond Kévorkian, *The Armenian Genocide: A Complete History* (London: I. B. Tauris, 2011), 647–672.
19. John Keegan, *The First World War* (New York: Alfred A. Knopf, 1998), 8.
20. Ilhan Tekeli, "Osmanlı İmparatorluğu'ndan Günümüze Nüfusun Zorunlu Yer Değiştirmesi Ve İskan Sorunu" [The Issue of Forced Deportation and Settlement of Population from

the Ottoman Period until Today], *Toplum ve Bilim* 50 (summer 1990): 49–71.

21. Nesim Şeker, "Demographic Engineering in the Late Ottoman Empire and the Armenians," *Middle Eastern Studies* 43, no. 3 (2007): 461–474.
22. Erik-Jan Zürcher, "The Late Ottoman Empire as Laboratory of Demographic Engineering," paper delivered at the conference "Le Regioni Multilingui Come Faglia E Motore Della Storia Europea Nel XIX–XX Secolo" in Naples, 6–8 September 2008; available from *Academia*, http://www.academia.edu.
23. Political scientist and demographer Myron Weiner refers to this process as "substitution." See Myron Weiner and Michel S. Teitelbaum, *Political Demography, Demographic Engineering* (Oxford: Berghahn, 2001), 56.
24. "Mathematical accuracy" is the phrase used by Armenian intellectual Dikran Kelegian, himself a victim of the Armenian Genocide. It is often cited by Akçam in the context of the Ottoman demographic policy during the genocide, and particularly the 5 and 10 percent rule employed by the CUP leadership: Armenians exempted from deportation could not surpass the 5 percent threshold in the eastern provinces of the empire (in most of these regions, deportation was in fact near total), and Armenians in designated settlement areas could not constitute more than 10 percent of the local population. See, for instance, Taner Akçam, *The Young Turks' Crime against Humanity: The Armenian Genocide and Ethnic Cleansing in the Ottoman Empire* (Princeton, NJ: Princeton University Press, 2012), xviii and 243. For an in-depth treatment of the CUP's policy, see Akçam, *The Young Turks' Crime against Humanity*; and Fuat Dündar, *Crime of Numbers: The Role of Statistics in the Armenian Question, 1878–1918* (New Brunswick, NJ: Transaction Publishers, 2010).
25. The inaccessibility of key Ottoman documents accounts, in part, for the absence of thorough studies on camp life. We know from available Ottoman documents and Armenian accounts that authorities kept detailed records of deportation convoys and camp populations, yet these documents are not available to researchers. See, for example, article 12 of the fifty-six-article deportation and settlement guideline prepared by IAMM head Muftizâde Şükrü Kaya Bey: BOA DH.EUM 2 Şb. 68/88, Şükrü Kaya to Talaat on 8 October 1915. Armenian deportee Mihran Aghazarian, in an account published immediately after the war, describes his experience accompanying a Turkish scribe and a policeman tasked with preparing lists and gathering statistical information on convoys arriving in Der Zor. See Mihran Aghazarian, *Aksoragani Husher* [Memoirs of an Exile] (Adana: Hay Tsayn Printing House, 1919). For an overview of the fate of Ottoman documents pertaining to this period, and issues related to researcher access, see Akçam, *The Young Turks' Crime against Humanity*, 1–28.

26. By 1916, the death toll in several of these camps was in the tens every day, and in certain cases reached three digits. See Khatchig Mouradian, "The Meskeneh Concentration Camp, 1915–1917: A Case Study of Power, Collaboration, and Humanitarian Resistance during the Armenian Genocide," *Journal of the Society for Armenian Studies* 24 (2015): 48–51. For an overview of the Armenian genocide, including a brief examination of the Der Zor massacres, see Raymond Kévorkían, "Earth, Fire, Water: or How to Make the Armenian Corpses Disappear," in *Destruction and Human Remains: Disposal and Concealment in Genocide and Mass Violence*, ed. Elisabeth Anstett and Jean-Marc Dreyfus (Manchester: Manchester University Press, 2014), 89–116.
27. BOA DH.EUM 2 Şb. 68/88, Şükrü Kaya to Talaat, 8 October 1915. The ordinance listed Aleppo, Katma, Müslimiye, Suruç, and Ras ul-Ain as transit centres (*merkez i tevakkuf*), Rakka, Hauran, and Der Zor as settlement areas, and Deyrul Hafr, Meskeneh, Abuharar, and Hamam as overnight rest areas along the road. Several of these sites we overcrowded with deportees and turned into de facto concentration camps.
28. DE/PA-AA; R14094; A28162, Report from Rössler to Theobald von Bethmann Hollweg, enclosure, 20 September 1916, in Wolfgang Gust, ed., *The Armenian Genocide: Evidence from the German Foreign Office Archives, 1915–1916* (New York: Berghahn, 2014), 652. Rössler transmitted the same report to the American Embassy in Constantinople around the same time. See Ara Sarafian, ed., *United States Official Records on the Armenian Genocide* (London: Gomidas Institute, 2004), 553.
29. Gust, *The Armenian Genocide*, 652.
30. "Found Armenians Starving in Camps: Neutral Eyewitness Describes a Visit to the Euphrates Valley," *New York Times*, 1 January 1917.
31. See, for example, "Armenians Dying in Prison Camps," *New York Times*, 21 August 1916.
32. Mouradian, "The Meskeneh Concentration Camp," 47.
33. Wachsmann, *KL: A History of the Nazi Concentration Camps*, 124.
34. For examples of such instances, see BNu/Andonian, folder 30, "Sefire," in "Materials for the History of the Deportations and Massacres: Aleppo and Its Environs," The Deportation of Armenians of Aleppo, 23; and BNu/Andonian, folder 52b, "On the Road to Meskeneh," 61–64. Locals also received rewards for capturing army deserters. See Erik-Jan Zürcher, "Between Death and Desertion: The Experience of the Ottoman Soldier in World War I," *Turcica* 28 (1996): 247.
35. BNu/Andonian, folder 52b, "On the Road to Meskeneh," 61–64.
36. BNu/Andonian, folder 30, "The Situation in Bab before the Last Sevkiyat in 1916," in "Materials for the History of the Deportations and Massacres: Aleppo and Its Environs," The deportation of Armenians of Aleppo, 3.

37. Report from Rössler to Bethmann Hollweg, 3 January 1916, enclosure 2, in Gust, *The Armenian Genocide*, 526.
38. BNu/Andonian, folder 52, "The Camp Directors of Meskeneh," 74. IAMM would later assign Kör Hüseyin as camp director at Meskeneh in late 1916. There too he distinguished himself by his brutality, raping, torturing, and killing deportees.
39. "Turkish Brutalities in Karlık," *Hai Tsayn*, 13 December 1918.
40. Yeranuhi Simonian, *Im Koghkotas* [My Golgotha] (Antelias: Armenian Catholicosate, 1960), 14.
41. Ibid., 19.
42. Report from Rössler to Bethmann Hollweg, 3 September 1915, in Gust, *The Armenian Genocide*, 345.
43. Report from Rössler to Bethmann Hollweg, enclosure, 20 September 1916, in Gust, *The Armenian Genocide*, 652.
44. BNu/Andonian, folder 59, Deportation of Armenians of Ras ul-Ain, "The Massacres of Ras ul-Ain," 3–4.
45. Paren Kazanjian, ed., *The Cilician Armenian Ordeal* (Boston: Hye Intentions, 1989), 35–36.
46. See, for example, Katharine Derderian, "Common Fate, Different Experience: Gender-Specific Aspects of the Armenian Genocide, 1915–1917," *Holocaust and Genocide Studies* 19, no. 1 (2005): 1–25. For comparative research, see Kristin Bell, "Victims' Voices: Sexual Violence in the Armenian and Rwandan Genocides" (PhD dissertation, Northeastern University, 2014). Elisa von Joeden-Forgey, "The Devil in the Details: 'Life Force Atrocities' and the Assault on the Family in Times of Conflict," *Genocide Studies and Prevention* 5, no. 1 (2010): 1–19. For recent research on sexualized violence in Nazi-occupied Europe during the Second World War, see David Raub Snyder, *Sex Crimes under the Wehrmacht* (Lincoln: University of Nebraska Press, 2007); and various contributions to Dagmar Herzog, ed., *Brutality and Desire: War and Sexuality in Europe's Twentieth Century* (New York: Palgrave Macmillan, 2009).
47. As Henry Theriault argues, "We must also recognize that genocide can be a tool of rape." See Henry Theriault, "Against the Grain: Critical Reflections on the State and Future of Genocide Scholarship," *Genocide Studies and Prevention* 7, no. 1 (2012): 137. Matthias Bjørnlund, too, emphasizes sadism as a factor in "a thoroughly brutalized environment that left room for local initiatives when it came to the methods of killing and humiliation, initiatives that satisfied individual needs, not only for self-gratification but also for variation." See Matthias Bjørnlund, "'A Fate Worse Than Dying': Sexual Violence during the Armenian Genocide," in Herzog, *Brutality and Desire*, 29.
48. Vahakn N. Dadrian, *The History of the Armenian Genocide: Ethnic Conflict from the*

Balkans to Anatolia to the Caucasus (Oxford: Berghahn Books, 1995), 242.

49. Rössler to Bethmann Hollweg, enclosure, 27 September 1916, in Gust, *The Armenian Genocide*, 652.

CHAPTER FOUR. Gateways to the Desert: The Sebil, Karlık, and Bab Camps

1. BNu/Andonian, folder 30, "The Deportation of Armenians of Aleppo," 56.
2. The local authorities had mandated that all deportees arriving in Aleppo had to register their local address with the police. "Posters [were] glued to the walls, announcing that all Armenians must register at their local police station within a week. Those who disobeyed orders will be heavily fined and thrown into prison," wrote Vahram Dadrian, who had taken refuge in the city, in his 23 September 1915 diary entry. The Dadrians registered a week later. See Vahram Dadrian, *To the Desert: Pages from My Diary* (London: Taderon Press, 2003), 82.
3. Paren Kazanjian, ed., *The Cilician Armenian Ordeal* (Boston: Hye Intentions, 1989), 371.
4. BNu/Andonian, folder 30, "The Deportation of Armenians of Aleppo," 47. Bribes only provided temporary respite. Survivor Vahram Dadrian and his family arrived in Aleppo in mid-September and avoided redeportation for several weeks by bribing local officials and policemen and, finally, by registering as Protestants, "only on paper, of course!" Still, it proved impossible to secure a permit allowing them to remain, and the family was redeported in two separate groups. An Armenian intermediary led them to believe they were being sent to Damascus, but their train didn't stop there and instead left them in the desert area of Hauran. They were eventually settled in Jeresh, where conditions were nowhere near ideal, but it was not Der Zor either. See Dadrian, *To the Desert*, 83.
5. Antranig Actanian (Né Kévork B. Soultanian in Eskişehir in 1887), "La Famille Soultanian et Mon Passé," 38–39, BNu unpublished memoirs collection. Marie Boyajian Soultanian translated the memoir, written in 1948, into French. It is interesting to note that the tenant had two sons who were deserters who hid in the same apartment. When the police arrived, they escaped through the roofs of the neighborhood. Eventually, Soultanian found a farming job and left Aleppo for Kasdon (Qastoon), southwest of Idlib.
6. Yeranuhi Simonian, *Im Koghkotas* [My Golgotha] (Antelias: Armenian Catholicosate, 1960), 56–57.
7. Kazanjian, *The Cilician Armenian Ordeal*, 292–293.
8. Ibid., 292.
9. "Appendix A-1: The Ottoman-Turkish Original of Naim Efendi's Text," in Taner Akçam, *Killing Orders: Talaat Pasha's Telegrams and the Armenian Genocide* (Cham, Switzerland:

Palgrave Macmillan, 2018), 181.

10. BOA DH.ŞFR 62/5, Talaat to Aleppo Province on 14 March 1916. Akçam uses this document to argue for the authenticity of Naim's memoirs. See Akçam, *Killing Orders*, 125.
11. Kazanjian, *The Cilician Armenian Ordeal*, 292.
12. For references to the relevant document in the Ottoman archives, see Akçam, *Killing Orders*, 132–133.
13. Hans-Lukas Kieser, *Talaat Pasha: Father of Modern Turkey, Architect of Genocide* (Princeton, NJ: Princeton University Press, 2018), xiii.
14. Elmas Boyajian, "Hay vorpanotsi gyanken" [From the Life of the Armenian Orphanage], *Chanaser*, 1 October 1964, 415.
15. Payladzou Captanian, *Tsavag* (New York: Armenia Printing, 1922), 248.
16. Yervant Odian, *Accursed Years: My Exile and Return from Der Zor, 1914–1919*, trans. Ara Stepan Melkonian (London: Gomidas Institute, 2009), 96.
17. The deportees were generally redeported to the desert. "From there [Sebil] refugees were sent to Deir Zor, the all-consuming desert. Going to Sebil meant walking to inescapable death. Every Armenian who arrived in Aleppo was obsessed with evading that awful destiny and, if it was not possible to stay in Aleppo, with going anywhere at all but to that notorious place," survivor Vahram Dadrian wrote in his 13 September 1915 diary entry. See Dadrian, *To the Desert*, 58.
18. See Aram Andonian, *Medz Vojire* [The Great Crime] (Boston: Bahag Publishing, 1921), 37.
19. NA/RG59/867.4016/373, Jackson to the secretary of state on 4 March 1918, in Ara Sarafian, *United States Official Records on the Armenian Genocide* (London: Gomidas Institute, 2004), 588–589.
20. *Zohrab zhamanagagitsneri husherum yev vgayutyunnerum* [Krikor Zohrab in the Memoirs and Testimonies of Contemporaries] (Yerevan: Yerevan State University, 2006), 334. This particular dossier by Aram Andonian on the circumstances of the murder of Zohrab and Vartkes was first published in *Haratch* newspaper in Paris from 4 September to 13 October (issues 7,460–7,495).
21. NA/RG59/867.4016/373, Jackson to the secretary of state on 4 March 1918, in Sarafian, *United States Official Records*, 588.
22. Captanian, *Tsavag*, 207.
23. Manuel Kasuni, "Ver. Y. S. Kasuniyi azadume hrashkov" [The miraculous survival of Rev. Y. S. Kasuni], *Chanaser* 28, no. 9 (1 May 1965), 199. Many of Aleppo's famous Armenian bakers moved to the city from Sasun decades prior, making reputations for themselves as master bakers of bread and becoming an integral part of the city's economy.

24. Hagop A. Seropian, *Yegherni Husheres* [My Memoir of the Genocide] (Beirut: Photogravure Paklayan, 2005), 78.
25. Levon Mesrob, ed., *Der Zor* (Paris: B. Elegian, 1955), 56–57.
26. DE/PA-AA; R14093; A 21969, Rössler to Bethmann Hollweg on 29 July 1916, in Wolfgang Gust, *The Armenian Genocide: Evidence from the German Foreign Office Archives, 1915–1916* (New York: Berghahn, 2014), 609.
27. NA/RG59/867.4016/373, Jackson to the secretary of state on 4 March 1918, in Sarafian, *United States Official Records*, 589.
28. Captanian, *Tsavag*, 206–207.
29. BNu/Andonian, folder 42, "The Situation in Bab during the Last Sevkiyat in 1916," The Deportation of Armenians of Bab, 6. .
30. Odian, *Accursed Years*, 99.
31. Captanian, *Tsavag*, 210–211 and 216–218.
32. Ibid., 207–208.
33. Odian, *Accursed Years*, 99. See also Captanian, *Tsavag*, 224.
34. "Appendix A-1: The Ottoman-Turkish Original of Naim Efendi's Text," in Akçam, *Killing Orders*, 178.
35. Odian, *Accursed Years*, 154–155.
36. Ibid., 99.
37. BNu/Andonian, folder 52, "The Camp Directors of Meskeneh," 74. IAMM would later assign Kör Hüseyin as camp director at Meskeneh in late 1916. There too he distinguished himself by his brutality, raping, torturing, and killing deportees.
38. Ibid.
39. The girl, Lusntak Baltajian, was a deportee from Sivas whose entire family had perished. She worked as a servant in the house of an Aleppo resident by the name of Iskender Sebbagh. See BNu/Andonian, "Deportation: Those Who Committed Massacres," Aziz Bey.
40. She eventually took refuge with a deportee from Bandırma called Koharik Ekmekjian and survived the genocide. BNu/Andonian, "Deportation: Those Who Committed Massacres," Aziz Bey.
41. BNu/Andonian, "Deportation: Those Who Committed Massacres," Aziz Bey. Andonian provides no further information about Bozouklian.
42. Seropian, *Yegherni Husheres*, 108.
43. Ibid.
44. See BNu/Andonian, "Deportation: Those Who Committed Massacres."
45. Gregory Ketabgian, *Leaving Kayseri: A Journey of One Hundred Years* (Self-published, 2015), 53–54.

46. "A memory from Yervant Odian." See BNu/Andonian, "Deportation: Those Who Committed Massacres." 54. This cry seems to have been common among gendarmes accompanying deportees. In his memoirs, survivor Hagop Arsenian recalled, "August 18–19, 1915. For two days we enjoyed relative peace without hearing the brutal shouts of the soldiers telling us *ghalghen, yeghen, chekhen*, for it was the Sultan's birthday." See Hagop Arsenian, *Towards Golgotha: The Memoirs of Hagop Arsenian, a Genocide Survivor*, trans. Arda Arsenian Ekmekji (Beirut: Haigazian University Press, 2011), 78.
47. NA/RG59/867.4016/373, Jackson to the secretary of state on 4 March 1918, in Sarafian, *United States Official Records*, 589.
48. Most deportees who were in Aleppo were sent to Sebil or Karlık, then to Bab, and were then redeported to camps along the Euphrates. Thousands of others stationed in Aleppo were transported by train to Ras ul-Ain.
49. Fifty-four families from Zeytun arrived in Bab on May 5. A few weeks later, on May 26–27, families from Hasanbeyli arrived. The council records provide a detailed listing of each of these families who arrived in Bab (family name, number of males and females). See Armenian National Council, List of Armenians around Aleppo, folder 41, 14–19.
50. Armenian National Council, List of Armenians around Aleppo, folder 41, 14–19.
51. Armenian National Council, Records of Council for Refugees, folder 38, session 12.
52. Father Etmekjian, originally from Aintab, continued to serve in the Armenian Apostolic Church of Aleppo after the war.
53. Council Records, folder 38, session 6, and Aleppo Armenian Prelacy Archives, Armenian National Council, List of Armenians around Aleppo, folder 41.
54. Council Records, folder 38, session 22.
55. Mardig Madenjian, *Ravished Paradise: Forced March to Nothingness* (Pasadena, CA: Self-published, 2016), 238–239.
56. Catholicos Khabayan visited the camp at Katma north of Aleppo City on 9 September 1915. See Dadrian, *To the Desert*, 55.
57. Armenian National Council, List of Armenians around Aleppo, folder 41, 4.
58. "Brief information on different *kazas* of the Aleppo Province from the perspective of settlement of deportees," Armenian National Council, List of Armenians around Aleppo, folder 41.
59. Armenian National Council, List of Armenians around Aleppo, folder 41.
60. Armenian National Council, List of Armenians around Aleppo, folder 41, 5.
61. Pharmacist Dikran Efendi Dzaghigian, who accompanied Father Khachadur, for example, vaccinated the children in Bab. Council Records, folder 38, session 10.
62. Armenian National Council, Records of the Council for Refugees, Ledgers, folder 22, 5.

Council Records, folder 38, session 15.

63. Council Records, folder 38, session 22.
64. Council Records, Ledgers, folder 22, 10.
65. Council Records, Ledgers, folder 22.
66. Council Records, folder 38, session 23. In this early period, the council made and executed such decisions with relative ease. Yet by fall 1915, its ability to openly provide spiritual and material assistance to camps was severely curtailed.
67. Council Records, folder 38, session 24.
68. Council Records, folder 38, session 3.
69. BNu/Andonian, folder 42, "Bab," 10. See also Kévorkian, "L'Extermination des déportés Arméniens," 79.
70. BNu/Andonian, folder 42, "The Description of Bab," The Deportation of Armenians of Bab, 4.
71. See Seropian, *Yegherni Husheres*, 88.
72. BNu/Andonian, folder 42, "The Description of Bab," The Deportation of Armenians of Bab, 5.
73. BNu/Andonian, folder 30, "The Situation in Bab before the Last Sevkiyat in 1916," in "Materials for the History of the Deportations and Massacres: Aleppo and Its Environs," The Deportation of Armenians of Aleppo, 2.
74. BNu/Andonian, folder 30, "The Situation in Bab before the Last Sevkiyat in 1916," in "Materials for the History of the Deportations and Massacres: Aleppo and Its Environs," The Deportation of Armenians of Aleppo, 2.
75. Mesrob, *Der Zor*, 46.
76. BNu/Andonian, folder 30, "The Situation in Bab before the Last Sevkiyat in 1916," in "Materials for the History of the Deportations and Massacres: Aleppo and Its Environs," The Deportation of Armenians of Aleppo, 3.
77. BNu/Andonian, folder 42, "The Situation in Bab during the Last Sevkiyat in 1916," The Deportation of Armenians of Bab, 13.
78. BNu/Andonian, folder 42, "The Situation in Bab during the Last Sevkiyat in 1916," The Deportation of Armenians of Bab, 13.
79. Arsenian, *Towards Golgotha*, 105, 106–107.
80. See Christopher Browning, *Remembering Survival: Inside a Nazi Slave Labor Camp* (New York: W. W. Norton, 2010), 170.
81. BNu/Andonian, folder 42, The Deportation of Armenians of Bab.
82. BNu/Andonian, folder 42, The Deportation of Armenians of Bab.
83. DE/PA-AA; R14087; R14095, Rössler to Bethmann Hollweg on 3 September 1915, in Gust,

The Armenian Genocide, 344.

84. BNu/Andonian, folder 42, The Deportation of Armenians of Bab.
85. Jivan and his brother Boghos were among the first pharmacists in Kayseri. See Arshag Alboyajian, *Badmutyun Hay Gesario* [History of Armenian Gesaria], vol. 2 (Cairo: Hagop Papazian Press, 1937), 1528.
86. BNu/Andonian, folder 42, The Deportation of Armenians of Bab, 14.
87. BNu/Andonian, folder 42, The Deportation of Armenians of Bab, 15.
88. See BNu/Andonian, folder 52b, "The Demise of Jivan Kaltakjian," 77–84.
89. BNu/Andonian, folder 42, The Deportation of Armenians of Bab, 5.
90. Seropian, *Yegherni Husheres*, 88–89.
91. BNu/Andonian, folder 42, "The Description of Bab," The Deportation of Armenians of Bab, 15–16.
92. BNu/Andonian, folder 42, "The Description of Bab," The Deportation of Armenians of Bab , 16.
93. BNu/Andonian, folder 42, "The Description of Bab," The Deportation of Armenians of Bab , 17. Scholar Lerna Ekmekçioğlu argues that the Ottoman policies created a "climate for abduction wherein Ottoman Muslims were entitled to incorporate Armenians into their homes, businesses, farms, and state institutions." See Lerna Ekmekçioğlu, "A Climate for Abduction, a Climate for Redemption: The Politics of Inclusion during and after the Armenian Genocide," *Comparative Studies in Society and History* 55, no. 3 (2013): 527.
94. References to deportees being forced to give away their children abound in accounts of eyewitnesses and survivors of the Armenian genocide. U.S. consul in Harput Leslie A. Davis writes, "As one walked through the camp [in the Harput Province] mothers held out their children, begging the visitor to take them and care for them or trying to sell them for a few piasters. . . . Many Turkish officers and other Turks visited the camps to select the prettiest girls and had their doctors present to examine them." See Leslie A. Davis, *The Slaughterhouse Province: An American Diplomat's Report on the Armenian Genocide, 1915–1917* (New Rochelle: Aristide D. Caratzas, 1989), 75.
95. Mesrob, *Der Zor*, 46.
96. Ibid.
97. Lawrence Langer, "The Dilemma of Choice in the Death Camps," in *Echoes From The Holocaust: Philosophical Reflections on a Dark Time*, ed. Alan Rosenberg and Gerald E. Myers (Philadelphia: Temple University Press, 1988), 120.
98. See Stanley Elphinstone Kerr, *The Lions of Marash: Personal Experiences with American Near East Relief, 1919–1922* (New York: SUNY Press, 1973), 44–49.
99. BNu/Andonian, folder 30, "The Situation in Bab End of 1915," in "Materials for the

History of the Deportations and Massacres: Aleppo and Its Environs," The Deportation of Armenians of Aleppo, 6.

100. Another eyewitness remembered these buriers yelling "ölüsü olan" (whoever has dead people). Sometimes no sound came because everyone in the tent was dead. BNu/Andonian, folder 30: "The Situation in Bab end of 1915," in "Materials for the History of the Deportations and Massacres: Aleppo and Its Environs," The Deportation of Armenians of Aleppo, 6.
101. BNu/Andonian, folder 30, "The Situation in Bab end of 1915," in "Materials for the History of the Deportations and Massacres: Aleppo and Its Environs," The Deportation of Armenians of Aleppo, 6.
102. BNu/Andonian, folder 42, "The Situation in Bab during the Last Sevkiyat in 1916," The Deportation of Armenians of Bab.
103. DE/PA-AA; R14090; A05498, Rössler to the imperial chancellor on 9 February 1916, in Gust, *The Armenian Genocide*, 542–543. It is unclear whether the figures provided by "the compassionate person" and the *mezarcı-başı* are of the two days, with the permutation of numbers a typographical mistake.
104. BNu/Andonian, folder 30, "The Situation in Bab before the Last Sevkiyat in 1916," in "Materials for the History of the Deportations and Massacres: Aleppo and Its Environs," The Deportation of Armenians of Aleppo, 6.
105. Ibid., 13.
106. BNu/Andonian, folder 30, "The Situation in Bab before the Last Sevkiyat in 1916," in "Materials for the History of the Deportations and Massacres: Aleppo and Its Environs," The Deportation of Armenians of Aleppo, 8.
107. BNu/Andonian, folder 42, "The Description of Bab," The Deportation of Armenians of Bab, 4.
108. BNu/Andonian, folder 30, "The Situation in Bab before the Last Sevkiyat in 1916," in "Materials for the History of the Deportations and Massacres: Aleppo and Its Environs," The Deportation of Armenians of Aleppo, 18.
109. Ketabgian, *Leaving Kayseri*, 56.
110. BNu/Andonian, folder 30, "The Situation in Bab before the Last Sevkiyat in 1916," in "Materials for the History of the Deportations and Massacres: Aleppo and Its Environs," The Deportation of Armenians of Aleppo, 2.
111. BNu/Andonian, folder 42, "The Situation in Bab during the Last Sevkiyat in 1916," The Deportation of Armenians of Bab, 16–17.
112. BNu/Andonian, folder 42, "The Situation in Bab during the Last Sevkiyat in 1916," The Deportation of Armenians of Bab, 7.

113. BNu/Andonian, folder 42, "The Situation in Bab during the Last Sevkiyat in 1916," The Deportation of Armenians of Bab, 7.
114. BNu/Andonian, folder 30, "The Situation in Bab during the Last Sevkiyat in 1916," The Deportation of Armenians of Aleppo, 19.
115. BNu/Andonian, folder 30, "The Situation in Bab during the Last Sevkiyat in 1916," The Deportation of Armenians of Aleppo, 19.
116. BNu/Andonian, folder 42, "The Situation in Bab during the Last Sevkiyat in 1916," The Deportation of Armenians of Bab, 7.
117. Hovsep Der-Vartanian, *Intilli-Ayrani Sbante, 1916* [The Massacre of Intilli-Ayran, 1916] (Jerusalem: St. John's Printing, 1928), 61.
118. BNu/Andonian, folder 30, "Sefire," in "Materials for the History of the Deportations and Massacres: Aleppo and Its Environs," The Deportation of Armenians of Aleppo, 23.
119. BNu/Andonian, folder 30, "Sefire," in "Materials for the History of the Deportations and Massacres: Aleppo and Its Environs," The Deportation of Armenians of Aleppo, 23.
120. BNu/Andonian, folder 30, "Sefire," in "Materials for the History of the Deportations and Massacres: Aleppo and Its Environs," The Deportation of Armenians of Aleppo, 25.
121. DE/PA-AA; R14092; A19989, Ambassador on Extraordinary Mission in Istanbul to Bethmann Hollweg, enclosure, on 22 July 1916, in Gust, *The Armenian Genocide*, 605.

CHAPTER FIVE. Along the Euphrates: The Meskeneh Concentration Camp

1. Zabel Yesayan and Hayg Toroyan, "Zhoghovurti me hokevarke (Aksoryal hayere Michakedki mech)" [The Death Throes of a Nation: The Exiled Armenians in Mesopotamia], *Kordz* 2 (1917): 111. Hayg Toroyan, an Armenian from Aleppo in the Ottoman Army, accompanied, under the guise of a Muslim name, German officer Otto Ölmann as his interpreter on a journey from Aleppo to Baghdad and witnessed the plight of the deportees in the camps along the Euphrates in 1915–1916. For reasons that are unclear, the two went from Baghdad to Iran, where the German officer committed suicide in Kermanshah. Deserting the military, Toroyan escaped to Tehran and then to the Caucasus, where he sounded the alarm about the destruction of the deportees in the Syrian Desert. His testimonies were recorded by the Armenian writer Zabel Yesayan and published in two installments in Baku in 1917. See Zabel Yesayan and Hayg Toroyan, "Zhoghovurti me hokevarke (Aksoryal hayere Michakedki mech)" [The Death Throes of a Nation: The Exiled Armenians in Mesopotamia], *Kordz* 2 and 3 (1917). Several decades later, Toroyan's account, almost in its entirety, was included in a book of testimonies from the genocide published in Paris. See Levon Mesrob, ed., *1915: Aghed yev Veradzenount*

[1915: Disaster and Rebirth] (Paris: Arax Publishing, 1952), 16–175. In 2013, Marc Nichanian translated and published the account in French. See Hayg Toroyan, *L'Agonie d'un peuple*, trans. Marc Nichanian (Paris: Classiques Garnier, 2013).

2. Account number 12 in James Bryce and Arnold Toynbee, *The Treatment of Armenians in the Ottoman Empire, 1915–1916: Documents Presented to Viscount Grey of Fallodon by Viscount Bryce*, ed. Ara Sarafian, uncensored edition (Princeton, NJ: Gomidas Institute, 2000), 66.
3. DE/PA-AA; R14086; A 21483, Wangenheim to Bethmann Hollweg on 9 July 1915, in Wolfgang Gust, *The Armenian Genocide: Evidence from the German Foreign Office Archives, 1915–1916* (New York: Berghahn, 2014), 240.
4. DE/PA-AA; R14086; A 23232, Rössler to Bethmann Hollweg on 17 July 1915, in Gust, *The Armenian Genocide*, 260.
5. DE/PA-AA; R14087; A 23991, Rössler to Bethmann Hollweg on 27 July 1915, in Gust, *The Armenian Genocide*, 265. Papgen Injearabian, deported from Amasia and orphaned during the deportation, witnessed many corpses as his convoy passed through the same area. See Papgen Injearabian, *Medz Yegherni shrchanin hay vorpi me votisagane* [The Odyssey of an Armenian Orphan during the Great Crime] (Paris: Imprimerie H. Turabian, 1951), 44.
6. Eitan Belkind, *So It Was* (Tel Aviv: Ministry of Defense Publishers, 1977), 115–125 as cited in Yair Auron, *The Banality of Indifference: Zionism and the Armenian Genocide* (New Brunswick: Transaction Publishers, 2000), 182.
7. Yesayan and Toroyan, "Zhoghovorti me hokevarke," 111.
8. BNu/Andonian, folder 52b, "The Corpses Brought by the Euphrates," 60.
9. Account number 12 in Bryce and Toynbee, *The Treatment of Armenians in the Ottoman Empire*, 66.
10. BNu/Andonian, folder 52b, "The Corpses Brought by the Euphrates," 60. For Dr. Schacht's account, see DE/PA-AA; R14089; A35047, report from Rössler to Bethmann Hollweg, enclosure, on 16 November 1915, in Gust, *The Armenian Genocide*, 462.
11. BNu/Andonian, folder 52b, "The Corpses Brought by the Euphrates," 60.
12. Coded telegram from Jemal Pasha to governor of Diyarbakir on 14 July 1915. Takvim-I Vekayi #3540 (27 Nisan, 1335) s. 4–14 (Kararname) in Vahakn N. Dadrian and Taner Akçam, *Judgement at Istanbul: The Armenian Genocide Trials* (New York: Berghahn Books, 2011), 277.
13. Coded telegram from governor of Diyarbakir to Jemal Pasha on 16 July 1915. Takvim-i Vekayi #3540 (27 Nisan, 1335) s. 4–14 (Kararname) in Dadrian and Akçam, *Judgement at Istanbul*, 277.

14. References to locals throwing stones at deportee convoys abound in accounts. See, for example, DE/PA-AA; R14089; A35047, report from Rössler to Bethmann Hollweg, enclosure, on 16 November 1915, in Gust, *The Armenian Genocide*, 464; and Harutiun Kalaydjian, *Milionen Mege: Tseghasbanutyan aganades Zeytuntsi badaniyi me hushere* [One in a Million: The Memories of a Teenager from Zeytun Who Witnessed the Genocide] (Beirut: Zartonk Armenian Daily Publishing, 2018), 19.
15. Hagop A. Seropian, *Yegherni Husheres* [My Memories of the Genocide] (Beirut: Photogravure Paklayan, 2005), 106–107. Deportees from Izmit had arrived in Meskeneh in droves. Survivor Hagop Arsenian recounted that "all the families who had come from the Izmit area, and only one from Ovacık [whence Arsenian came] . . . had settled on the banks of the Euphrates." See Hagop Arsenian, *Towards Golgotha: The Memoirs of Hagop Arsenian, a Genocide Survivor*, trans. Arda Arsenian Ekmekji (Beirut: Haigazian University Press, 2011), 109. References to Armenians from Izmit at the camp are also in Toroyan's testimony. See Yesayan and Toroyan, "Zhoghovurti me hokevarke," 67.
16. Seropian, *Yegherni Husheres*, 106–107.
17. Ibid.
18. *Arşiv Belgeleriyle Ermeni Faaliyetleri, 1914–1918* [Armenian Activities in the Archive Documents, 1914–1918], vol. 7 (Ankara: Genelkurmay Basımevi, 2006), 254–256.
19. Paren Kazanjian, ed., *The Cilician Armenian Ordeal* (Boston: Hye Intentions, 1989), 377.
20. Yesayan and Toroyan, "Zhoghovurti me hokevarke," 67.
21. Kazanjian, *The Cilician Armenian Ordeal*, 293.
22. *Arşiv Belgeleriyle Ermeni Faaliyetleri*, 7:257.
23. Kazanjian, *The Cilician Armenian Ordeal*, 293. The construction of the Jerablus–Zor military supply line is intimately connected to the fate of many Armenian deportees.
24. Yesayan and Toroyan, "Zhoghovurti me hokevarke," 67.
25. BNu/Andonian, folder 52b, "The Camp Directors of Meskeneh," 74.
26. Mesrob, *1915: Aghed yev Veradzenount*, 459.
27. Kazanjian, *The Cilician Armenian Ordeal*, 377.
28. BNu/Andonian, folder 52b, "The Camp Directors of Meskeneh," 74.
29. NA/RG59/867.4016/72, Jackson to Morgenthau on 12 May 1915, in Ara Sarafian, ed., *United States Official Records on the Armenian Genocide* (London: Gomidas Institute, 2004), 40.
30. Yesayan and Toroyan, "Zhoghovurti me hokevarke," 67. There were thousands more deportees on the hills farther inland.
31. Ibid.
32. Arsenian, *Towards Golgotha*, 109. Another deportee would call it "an arid bowl of sand."

See Kazanjian, *The Cilician Armenian Ordeal*, 293.

33. Arsenian, *Towards Golgotha*, 109.
34. Litten journeyed from Baghdad to Aleppo in late January–early February 1916 and upon the request of Rössler wrote a detailed report about what he saw. See DE/PA-AA; R14090; A 05498, Rössler to Bethmann Hollweg on 27 September 1916, in Gust, *The Armenian Genocide*, 543–555.
35. Kazanjian, *The Cilician Armenian Ordeal*, 293.
36. Yesayan and Toroyan, "Zhoghovurti me hokevarke," 67.
37. Aram Andonian, *Medz Vojire* [The Great Crime] (Boston: Bahag Publishing, 1921), 19.
38. DE/PA-AA; R14094; A 28162, report from Rössler to Bethmann Hollweg, enclosure, on 27 September 1916, in Gust, *The Armenian Genocide*, 652.
39. Yesayan and Toroyan, "Zhoghovurti me hokevarke," 68.
40. Ibid., 71.
41. Ibid., 72.
42. DE/PA-AA; R14094; A 28162, report from Rössler to Bethmann Hollweg, enclosure, on 27 September 1916, in Gust, *The Armenian Genocide*, 653. The conditions were similar all along the Euphrates. Survivor Armen Anush remembered how in Der Zor "it was impossible to eat anything unperturbed, as packs of boys, five, ten at a time, turned up from nowhere to attack you and grab what you had. For this reason, every time we found some food, we were careful not to eat it in plain view of the people." See Armen Anush, *Passage through Hell, a Memoir* (Studio City, CA: H. and K. Manjikian Publications, 2007), 68.
43. Account of survivor Yeghishe Hazarabedian in Kazanjian, *The Cilician Armenian Ordeal*, 293.
44. Mesrob, *1915: Aghed yev Veradzenount*, 459.
45. Ibid., 460.
46. See Ephraim K. Jernazian, *Judgment unto Truth: Witnessing the Armenian Genocide* (New Brunswick: Transaction Publishers, 1990), 107.
47. Mesrob, *1915: Aghed yev Veradzenount*, 460–461. Tarpinian does not mention the name of the missionary in his account. He admitted that "I was against turning a nation that was being persecuted for their religion and ethnicity to be the plaything of sect members, but did not dare prohibit them, because they were providing bread."
48. Ibid., 461. According to Tarpinian, the woman rejected a donation made by the camp director saying that nothing would come of his money, and that it was God who would take care of the orphans.
49. Ibid.

50. Ibid., 462.
51. Armenians had opened a marketplace in Meskeneh with the permission of a few local officers, and the proceeds went to the orphanage. The market had a short life, shutting down within less than a month. The officers were then investigated for "abuse of authority." *Arşiv Belgeleriyle Ermeni Faaliyetleri*, 7:238–241.
52. Mesrob, *1915: Aghed yev Veradzenount*, 462.
53. DE/PA-AA; R14094; A 28162, Rössler to Bethmann Hollweg, enclosure, on 27 September 1916, in Gust, *The Armenian Genocide*, 654.
54. Seropian, *Yegherni Husheres*, 109.
55. Ibid., 110. On paper, redeportation employees at the camp were instructed to notify those slated for redeportation forty-eight hours ahead of time, and to make the necessary arrangements for transportation. BOA DH.EUM 2 Şb. 68/88, article 44 of the guideline prepared by IAMM director Şükrü Kaya. Such notification was reserved for those who bribed camp officials heftily. Most redeportation proceedings were hasty, last-minute procedures, whereby tents were overturned and deportees were beaten to hasten their preparation and get on the road, often on foot.
56. Arsenian, *Towards Golgotha*, 109.
57. Yervant Odian, *Accursed Years: My Exile and Return from Der Zor, 1914–1919*, trans. Ara Stepan Melkonian (London: Gomidas Institute, 2009), 212.
58. Kazanjian, *The Cilician Armenian Ordeal*, 378–379.
59. BOA DH.ŞFR 64/194, Talaat to Aleppo Governorate on 27 June 1916.
60. Kazanjian, *The Cilician Armenian Ordeal*, 292.
61. Ibid., 292–293. Hazarabedian provided significant details about this intervention in his account. Initially, Talaat telegraphed the Aleppo governor asking him to keep the two families in Aleppo. The governor in turn contacted the district police chief to inquire about the families, and upon his recommendation had them deported to the desert anyway. We do not know, however, whether the telegram from Talaat cited earlier (BOA DH.ŞFR 64/194) is related to a member of these families, or another close relative of Khrlakian.
62. DE/PA-AA; R14094; A 28162, Rössler to Bethmann Hollweg, enclosure, on 27 September 1916, in Gust, *The Armenian Genocide*, 653.
63. Seropian, *Yegherni Husheres*, 109.
64. Ibid.
65. BOA DH.EUM 2 Şb. 68/88, IAMM director Şükrü Kaya to the Ministry of Interior on 8 October 1915.
66. Seropian, *Yegherni Husheres*, 110. The pharmacist died at Meskeneh. Securing a note from

a designated doctor or pharmacist at camps was a way to delay redeportation at other camps as well. When Odian arrived in Hamam, farther downstream from Meskeneh, his friends told him they knew the camp doctor and suggested that he pretend to be sick to avoid immediate redeportation to Der Zor. See Odian, *Accursed Years*, 216.

67. BNu/Andonian, folder 52b, "Handwritten Armenian Flyers in Meskeneh," 86.
68. BNu/Andonian, folder 52b, "Handwritten Armenian Flyers in Meskeneh," 86.
69. Several copies of these flyers have survived thanks to Andonian. They are kept in the Andonian folder at the AGBU Nubarian Library in Paris.
70. BNu/Andonian, folder 52b, "Handwritten Armenian Flyers in Meskeneh," 88.
71. BNu/Andonian, folder 52b, "Handwritten Armenian Flyers in Meskeneh," 89.
72. BNu/Andonian, folder 52b, "Handwritten Armenian Flyers in Meskeneh," 89.
73. See, for example, Vahakn N. Dadrian, "Children as Victims of Genocide: The Armenian Case," *Journal of Genocide Research* 5, no. 3 (2003): 421–437. In this article, Dadrian only focuses on the different means Turkish authorities employed to annihilate Armenian children.
74. BNu/Andonian, folder 52b, "The Camp Directors of Meskeneh," 72. Andonian was unable to uncover the name of the first camp director. The second was a man named Muhtar Bey.
75. BNu/Andonian, folder 52b, "A Tragic Statistic about Meskeneh," 66.
76. BNu/Andonian, folder 52b, "A Tragic Statistic about Meskeneh," 66–67. After the British entered Aleppo, Yeghpayrian asked Andonian to do all he could to help Hüseyin Avni. Evidently, the tables had been turned. It is also through Yeghpayrian's help that Andonian met with Avni in Aleppo and secured from him the statistics about deportee arrival, departure, and death at Meskeneh from April 1915 to April 1916, in return promising that Yeghpayrian would not provide the British with negative testimony about Avni.
77. BNu/Andonian, folder 52b, "The Camp Directors of Meskeneh," 72.
78. This is the same Naim Bey who would provide official documents pertaining to the Armenian genocide to Andonian after the war. The authenticity of these documents continues to be the center of controversy, although they are, by and large, corroborated by other sources and material.
79. BNu/Andonian, folder 52b, "The Camp Directors of Meskeneh," 72. Andonian provided a detailed picture of these escapes from Meskeneh, during which each family brought along with them in their carriage an Armenian intellectual (writers, teachers, and the like), thus saving several such luminaries and educators.
80. BNu/Andonian, folder 52b, "The Camp Directors of Meskeneh," 72–73.
81. This was not unique to Meskeneh. Many survivor accounts describe how gendarmes

fired in the air allegedly to scare away bandits at night and then asked deportees to pay for the bullets. For example, Artin Kitabjian witnessed this phenomenon on the route from Sebil to Bab. Gregory Ketabgian, *Leaving Kayseri: A Journey of One Hundred Years* (Self-published, 2015), 55.

82. DE/PA-AA; R14090; A 05498, Rössler to Bethmann Hollweg, enclosure, on 27 September 1916, in Gust, *The Armenian Genocide*, 553.
83. BNu/Andonian, folder 52b, "The Camp Directors of Meskeneh," 67. According to Hovannesian, the deportation official was receiving a cut from the boat captain in return for the business he provided them.
84. BNu/Andonian, folder 52b, "The Camp Directors of Meskeneh," 70. Another convoy, some fifty families deported from Aintab the same month (August 1915) managed to safely travel down the river to Der Zor by barge. Dikran Jebejian, "Der Zori Sbante," *Hay Anteb* 2, 18 (1965): 11.
85. BNu/Andonian, folder 52b, "The Camp Directors of Meskeneh," 70.
86. BNu/Andonian, folder 52b, "The Camp Directors of Meskeneh," 70. Accounts of attacks on barges leaving Meskeneh abound in Armenian sources. See, for example, Angele Torossian's testimony in Hovhannes Domardzatsi Torossian, *Badmutiun hay Domardzayi* [History of Armenian Tomarza], vol. 3 (Beirut: Central Publishing Committee of Tomarza History, 1969), 2099.
87. Arsenian, *Towards Golgotha*, 109–110.
88. BNu/Andonian, folder 52b, "About the Re-deportation by *Shakhtoors*," 71.
89. BNu/Andonian, folder 52b, "About the Re-deportation by *Shakhtoors*," 71.
90. There are multiple accounts of deportation by barges from both Rakka and Sebka to Der Zor in the early summer of 1916. See, for example, the report by an associate of Beatrice Rohner's, who arrived in Meskeneh on 20 April and returned to Aleppo on 20 June, only to depart again six days later with additional supplies. Although the associate's name is not mentioned, it is likely that it was Garabed, a man who frequently made these trips to distribute aid to deportees, until one day he left for Der Zor and never returned. DE/PA-AA; R14092; A 19989, report from Wolff-Metternich to Bethmann Hollweg on 22 July 1916, enclosure, in Gust, ed., *The Armenian Genocide*, 607.
91. Max Weber, *From Max Weber: Essays in Sociology* (New York: Routledge, 2009), 78.
92. See, for example, Fuat Dündar, *Crime of Numbers: The Role of Statistics in the Armenian Question, 1878–1918* (New Brunswick, NJ: Transaction Publishers, 2010), 77.
93. Denialist historians have produced several documents from the Ottoman archives concerning measures taken by Talaat and other CUP leaders to curb, and in certain cases even punish, attacks by irregulars and bandits in the region under study. See,

for example, Hikmet Özdemir, *Cemal Paşa ve Ermeni Göçmenler: 4. Ordu'nun İnsani Yardımları* [Cemal Pasha and the Armenian Deportees: The Humanitarian Assistance of the Fourth Army] (Istanbul: Remzi Kitapevi, 2009), 156–162. This policy is not inconsistent with the state's policy of destruction—in fact it is very much consistent with it: the state strove for as much control over violence as possible.

94. BNu/Andonian, folder 52b, "About the Re-deportation by *Shakhtoors*," 74.
95. BNu/Andonian, folder 52b, "About the Re-deportation by *Shakhtoors*," 74.
96. BNu/Andonian, folder 52b, "About the Re-deportation by *Shakhtoors*," 74–77.

CHAPTER SIX. Death and Resilience: The Military Supply Line

1. BNu/Andonian, folder 57, "Dipsi," The Deportations of the Armenians of Dipsi, 1.
2. BNu/Andonian, folder 57, "Dipsi," The Deportations of the Armenians of Dipsi, 1–2. In his account, Ankut refers to *hastane* as "the cemetery of Meskeneh."
3. BNu/Andonian, folder 57, "Dipsi," The Deportations of the Armenians of Dipsi, 2.
4. Hagop Arsenian, *Towards Golgotha: The Memoirs of Hagop Arsenian, a Genocide Survivor*, trans. Arda Arsenian Ekmekji (Beirut: Haigazian University Press, 2011), 113.
5. DE/PA-AA; R14090; A 05498, report from Rössler to Bethmann Hollweg, enclosure, on 27 September 1916, in Wolfgang Gust, ed., *The Armenian Genocide: Evidence from the German Foreign Office Archives, 1915–1916* (New York: Berghahn, 2014), 552.
6. Hagop A. Seropian, *Yegherni Husheres* [My Memories of the Genocide] (Beirut: Photogravure Paklayan, 2005), 140. In the final months of the camp's existence, deportees moving from Meskeneh to Der Zor did not rest at Dipsi anymore and journeyed on directly to Abuharar: "The stench of corpses made it impossible to stop there." See Aram Andonian, *Medz Vojire* [The Great Crime] (Boston: Bahag Publishing, 1921), 104n15.
7. Arsenian, *Towards Golgotha*, 114–115.
8. BNu/Andonian, folder 57, "Dipsi," The Deportations of the Armenians of Dipsi, 2.
9. Levon Mesrob, ed., *1915: Aghed yev Veradzenunt* [1915: Disaster and Rebirth] (Paris: Arax Publishing, 1952), 418.
10. Some families of Armenians who continued to serve in the military were exempted from deportation, but most were indeed deported, and there were clear instructions to not allow them to return to their homes without permission. See, for example, BOA DH.ŞFR 58/89, Interior Ministry to all provinces on 22 November 1915.
11. Mesrob, *1915: Aghed yev Veradzenunt*, 418.
12. Andonian, *Medz Vojire*, 105.
13. BNu/Andonian, folder 57, "Dipsi," The Deportations of the Armenians of Dipsi, 3.

14. Ibid.
15. Paren Kazanjian, ed., *The Cilician Armenian Ordeal* (Boston: Hye Intentions, 1989), 294. The situation of children, many of whom were orphaned, was not any less terrible in this camp than it was elsewhere along the Euphrates line. When setting their tents, the Seropians were surrounded by children begging for food. Seropian also witnessed a group of emaciated children gathered around the corpse of a dead mule, tearing it apart and eating its meat. See Seropian, *Yegherni Husheres*, 140.
16. BOA DH.EUM 2 Şb. 68/88, IAMM director Şükrü Kaya to the Ministry of Interior on 8 October 1915. Seropian, *Yegherni Husheres*, 141.
17. BNu/Andonian, "Aleppo," The Situation of Exiles in Abuharar, 5.
18. Arsenian, *Towards Golgotha*, 115.
19. Seropian, *Yegherni Husheres*, 141.
20. Ibid.
21. Arsenian, *Towards Golgotha*, 118.
22. Gregory Ketabgian, *Leaving Kayseri: A Journey of One Hundred Years* (Self-published, 2015), 62.
23. BNu/Andonian, "Aleppo," The Situation of Exiles in Abuharar, 5.
24. Andonian, *Medz Vojire*, 38n12.
25. Seropian, *Yegherni Husheres*, 141.
26. Ibid., 141–142.
27. BNu/Andonian, "Aleppo," The Situation of Exiles in Abuharar, 8.
28. Arsenian, *Towards Golgotha*, 119.
29. Shmavon Der Stepanian, "Azkn ir azke ge gordzane" [The nation destroying itself], *Yeprad*, 10 December 1927, 2. Chronicler Aram Andonian also mentions the abuses of carriage drivers. See, for example, BNu/Andonian, folder 52b, "A Tragic Statistic about Meskeneh," 66.
30. BNu/Andonian, "Aleppo," The Situation of Exiles in Abuharar, 10–11.
31. DE/PA-AA; R14093; A 21969, Rössler to Bethmann Hollweg on 29 July 1916, in Gust, *The Armenian Genocide*, 609.
32. Telegram No. 19 from chief deportation official to Aleppo Directorate of Deportations on 21 August 1916, *Arşiv Belgeleriyle Ermeni Faaliyetleri, 1914–1918* (Cilt VII) [Armenian Activities in the Archive Documents, 1914–1918 (vol. 7)] (Ankara: Genelkurmay Basımevi, 2006), 70.
33. Ibid.
34. During the investigation, Galip was asked about another telegram he had sent ordering the transfer from Zor to Meskeneh of "two families with two children." Ibid., 77.

35. Ibid., 89–90.
36. BNu/Andonian, "Aleppo," The Situation of Exiles in Abuharar, 6.
37. Kazanjian, *The Cilician Armenian Ordeal*, 294.
38. BNu/Andonian, "Aleppo," The Situation of Exiles in Abuharar, 7. Andonian notes that there was early on a resting camp between Abuharar and Hamam, but it was shut down.
39. Garabed Kapigian, *Yeghernabadoum Sepasdio* [The History of the Great Crime in Sepasdia] (Boston: Hairenik Printing, 1924), 527. Kapigian was an Armenian intellectual from Sepasdia/Sivas who spent two years in Rakka and its environs and witnessed the developments along the Euphrates line firsthand.
40. BNu/Andonian, folder 29, "Hamam," 1; and Kazanjian, *The Cilician Armenian Ordeal*, 294. Article 4 of the deportation guideline issued in September 1915 specifies that Hamam is connected to Rakka. BOA DH.EUM 2 Şb. 68/88, IAMM director Şükrü Kaya to the Ministry of Interior on 8 September 1915.
41. Yervant Odian, *Accursed Years: My Exile and Return from Der Zor, 1914–1919*, trans. Ara Stepan Melkonian (London: Gomidas Institute, 2009), 138.
42. Kapigian, *Yeghernabadoum Sepasdio*, 466.
43. Preacher Vartan Geranian estimated one thousand tents in a letter from Hamam to Beatrice Rohner dated 28 June 1916. See DE/PA-AA; R14093; A 21969, Rössler to Bethmann Hollweg, enclosure 4, on 29 July 1916, in Gust, *The Armenian Genocide*, 612.
44. DE/PA-AA; R14090; A 05498, Rössler to Bethmann Hollweg on 27 September 1916, in Gust, *The Armenian Genocide*, 549.
45. See BNu/Andonian, folder 29, "Hamam," 1, and Kapigian, *Yeghernabadoum Sepasdio*, 465–466.
46. "Communications and transport were the Achilles' heel of the Ottoman army," wrote historian Erik-Jan Zürcher. The empire's railway network was a mere 5,700 kilometers long, interrupted by mountain chains, and with railheads several weeks' journey by road from front lines. This necessitated robust labor battalions to load, unload, and transport supplies. See Erik-Jan Zürcher, "Ottoman Labor Battalions in World War I," in *The Armenian Genocide and the Shoah*, ed. Hans-Lukas Kieser and Dominik J. Schaller (Zurich: Chronos Verlag, 2002), 187–195.
47. The testimony of Yeghishe Hazarabedian, in Kazanjian, *The Cilician Armenian Ordeal*, 294.
48. See Kapigian, *Yeghernabadoum Sepasdio*, 527.
49. Kazanjian, *The Cilician Armenian Ordeal*, 295.
50. See, for example, David Fromkin, *A Peace to End All Peace: The Fall of the Ottoman Empire and the Creation of the Modern Middle East* (New York: Henry Holt, 2001), 200–203.

51. BNu/Andonian, folder 29, "Hamam," 1. Kapigian also speaks about the military points along the Euphrates line, operating under the command of Galip Bey, in his memoir *Yeghernabadoum Sepasdio*.
52. This is Zürcher's translation of "*menzil müfettişliği*." See Zürcher, "Ottoman Labor Battalions," 190.
53. BNu/Andonian, folder 29, "Hamam," 2.
54. Kapigian, *Yeghernabadoum Sepasdio*, 465.
55. DE/PA-AA; R14093; A 21969, report from Rössler to Bethmann Hollweg, enclosure 4, on 29 July 1916, in Gust, *The Armenian Genocide*, 612. It is worth noting that in Nazi concentration camps such "absolutely wretched figures, wandering aimlessly" were dubbed "Muselmänner"—German for "Muslims." See, for example, Wolfgang Sofsky, *The Order of Terror: The Concentration Camp* (Princeton, NJ: Princeton University Press, 1997), 199–205.
56. DE/PA-AA; R14094; A 28162, Rössler to Bethmann Hollweg on 20 September 1916, in Gust, *The Armenian Genocide*, 654.
57. Ibid.
58. Authorities not only welcomed the help of some officials from the area, they even mobilized bandits and murderers to accompany convoys as "guards."
59. BNu/Andonian, "Deportation: Those Who Committed Massacres," Kör Fatih.
60. Andonian and Kapigian make numerous references and provide multiple examples of these abuses. See BNu/Andonian, folder 29, "Hamam," and Kapigian, *Yeghernabadoum Sepasdio*, 407–541.
61. BNu/Andonian, "Deportation: Those Who Committed Massacres," Sevk Memuru Resul. Andonian notes that the girl survived the ordeal and was in Aleppo after the war.
62. BOA DH.ŞFR 66/19, Talaat to Zor provincial district.
63. BOA DH.ŞFR 66/94, Talaat to Zor provincial district.
64. DE/PA-AA; R14094; A 28162, Rössler to Bethmann Hollweg, enclosure, on 27 September 1916, in Gust, *The Armenian Genocide*, 654.
65. Kapigian, *Yeghernabadoum Sepasdio*, 420. Note that Toroyan, who passed through Rakka in November 1915, says the town had five hundred to six hundred households. His estimate is most likely far from accurate, as he probably did not factor in entire neighborhoods of the town, separated from it by fields (e.g., the Circassian neighborhood). See Zabel Yesayan and Hayg Toroyan, "Zhoghovourti me hokevarke (Aksoreal hayere michakedki mech)," *Kordz* 2 and 3 (1917): 72. All other villages and towns on the Euphrates line from Meskeneh to Der Zor examined in this and the previous chapter are situated on the southern banks of the Euphrates.

66. For a detailed treatment of the CUP's practices in this context, see Fuat Dündar, *Modern Türkiye'nin Şifresi: İttihat Ve Terakki'nin Etnisite Mühendisliği, 1913–1918* [Modern Turkey's Code: The CUP's Ethnic Engineering, 1913–1918] (Istanbul: Iletişim, 2010). Kapigian, *Yeghernabadoum Sepasdio*, 421. Kapigian provides a detailed description of the town and its inhabitants. See, in particular, 421–429.
67. BOA DH.EUM 2 Şb. 68/88, Şükrü Kaya to the Ministry of Interior on 8 September 1915 (article 3).
68. There were hundreds of deportees in Rakka and surrounding villages prior to September 1915, but they were far from settled. See NA/RG59/867.4016/97, "A brief statement on the present situation of the Armenian exiles in this region, June 20, 1915," in Ara Sarafian ed., *United States Official Records on the Armenian Genocide* (London: Gomidas Institute, 2004), 118.
69. Kapigian, *Yeghernabadoum Sepasdio*, 430. Kapigian lists three villages: Alakilise, Karhad, and Karaboğazı.
70. Ibid., 430–431.
71. Ibid., 431. Most towns Kapigian lists as the origins of these deportees are in either Central Anatolia or the western parts of the empire.
72. Hratch A. Tarbassian, *Erzurum (Garin): Its Armenian History and Traditions* (New York: Garin Compatriotic Union of the United States, 1975), 242.
73. Kapigian, *Yeghernabadoum Sepasdio*, 415–420.
74. Ibid., 417. Around four hundred people were selected for redeportation.
75. Ibid., 438.
76. Ibid., 438–439.
77. Ibid., 464.
78. NA/RG59/867.48/271, Jackson to Morgenthau on 8 February 1916, in Sarafian, *United States Official Records*, 489. This number is much lower than the number of deportees in Der Zor in the same period (300,000), but most deportees in and around Der Zor would perish before the end of the summer.
79. DE/PA-AA; R14094; A 28162, Rössler to Bethmann Hollweg on 27 September 1916, in Gust, *The Armenian Genocide*, 654.
80. Kapigian, *Yeghernabadoum Sepasdio*, 434.
81. Ibid., 471. We know from Ottoman documents that numerous such requests were sent to provinces and districts in the region beginning in July 1916. One such request was sent to Urfa and Mosul administrators from IAMM on 1 July 1915, requesting the number of Armenians, where they were from, etc. See BOA DH.ŞFR 54/271, coded telegram from Interior Ministry's IAMM to Mosul and Urfa. For a closer analysis of the demographic

policy and the use of censuses and statistics during the Armenian genocide, See Taner Akçam, *The Young Turks' Crime against Humanity: The Armenian Genocide and Ethnic Cleansing in the Ottoman Empire* (Princeton, NJ: Princeton University Press, 2012), 227–285.

82. Kapigian, *Yeghernabadoum Sepasdio*, 471–472.
83. The novel, and the 1924 film of the same title, is a satire-turned-prophecy telling the story of an Austrian National Assembly that, spurred by antisemitism, forces all Jews to emigrate. The highly popular policy ends in economic and cultural disaster, compelling leaders to take steps to bring the Jews back. See Hugo Bettauer, *Die Stadt ohne Juden: Ein Roman von übermorgen* [The City without Jews: A Novel of Our Time] (Vienna: Wien Gloriette-Verl, 1922). A former Nazi party member killed Bettauer in 1925.
84. Kapigian, *Yeghernabadoum Sepasdio*, 484–487.
85. Hovhannes Toros Doumanian, "My Memoirs," BNu unpublished memoirs collection.
86. NA/RG59/867.4016/373, Jackson to the secretary of state on 4 March 1918, in Sarafian, *United States Official Records*, 596.
87. BOA DH.EUM 2 Şb. 74/63–1, telegram from Urfa to Ministry of Interior dated 28 May 1917, as cited in Halil Özşavlı, *Urfa Ermenileri (Sosyal-Siyasi ve Kültürel Hayat)* [Urfa Armenians: Socio-Political and Cultural Life] (Ankara: Gazi Kitabevi, 2013), 42.
88. Kapigian, *Yeghernabadoum Sepasdio*, 504. Most of these deportees moved to Aleppo following the war. They included some of the women and children who were taken into Arab tents as wives or slaves. See ibid., 443.
89. Ibid., 432. Kapigian gives the example of a German-Jewish employee of the U.S. consulate in Aleppo who had arrived in Rakka to distribute aid to Armenians. He purchased jewelry and other valuables for a few thousand liras.
90. Ibid., 431.
91. Ibid., 433. Kapigian estimates that every week, two thousand to three thousand liras entered Rakka through transfers of funds to deportees who had relatives elsewhere.
92. Ibid., 440.
93. Ibid., 440–441.
94. William W. Peet, treasurer of the Bible House, reports that "relief work in Aleppo . . . gives bread to families in nine centers including Damascus, Hama, Rakka, Killis and other outside places . . . twenty-two hundred and forty-five pounds Turkish." See NA/RG59/867.48/284, confidential telegram from U.S. Embassy in Istanbul to secretary of state (via Copenhagen) on 4 May 1916, in Sarafian, *United States Official Records*, 497. Swiss missionary Jakob Künzler, stationed in Urfa, distributed five hundred liras to the needy in Rakka on three occasions. See Kapigian, *Yeghernabadoum Sepasdio*, 482.

95. Kapigian, *Yeghernabadoum Sepasdio*, 481.
96. Ibid.
97. BNu/Andonian, folder 58, "Rakka," The Deportation of the Armenians of Rakka, 113. It is evident that Kapigian and Andonian compiled the folder on Rakka together. Having lived in Rakka for two years, Kapigian was deeply knowledgeable on the events in the town, and it is clear that he exchanged notes with Andonian. Pages of Kapigian's *Yeghernabadoum Sepasdio* are at times a verbatim reproduction of the information in the Andonian folder on Rakka, which in turn was quite possibly written by Kapigian. In this chapter, I mostly use Kapigian as my source.
98. BNu/Andonian, folder 58, "Rakka," The Deportation of the Armenians of Rakka, 113–114.
99. Kapigian, *Yeghernabadoum Sepasdio*, 441–442.
100. There was at least one small massacre in Rakka in early October 1916, during which thirty Armenians were murdered. See DE/PA-AA; R14094; A 31831, Rössler to Bethmann Hollweg on 5 November 1916, in Gust, *The Armenian Genocide*, 673. Kapigian, in turn, speaks of another small massacre during which eighteen to twenty deportees were massacred by Arab bandits in late 1917. See Kapigian, *Yeghernabadoum Sepasdio*, 493.
101. Another curious case is Urfa. Months after its Armenian population was massacred and deported, Urfa felt the need for skilled labor and requested regional authorities to send hundreds of deportee laborers to Urfa.

CHAPTER SEVEN. Zor: That Immense Graveyard of Our Martyrs

1. For a brief treatment of these factors, see Fuat Dündar, *Crime of Numbers: The Role of Statistics in the Armenian Question, 1878–1918* (New Brunswick, NJ: Transaction Publishers, 2010), 77–78. For population statistics, see Kemal H. Karpat, *Ottoman Population, 1830–1914: Demographic and Social Characteristics* (Madison: University of Wisconsin Press, 1985), 188.
2. Dündar, *Crime of Numbers*, 78–79.
3. Samuel Dolbee, "The Desert at the End of Empire: An Environmental History of the Armenian Genocide," *Past & Present* 247, no. 1 (May 2020): 197–233.
4. DE/PA-AA; R14089; A 35047, report from Rössler to Bethmann Hollweg on 16 November 1915, enclosure, in Wolfgang Gust, ed., *The Armenian Genocide: Evidence from the German Foreign Office Archives, 1915–1916* (New York: Berghahn, 2014), 463. Parts of the region were far from arid during certain times of the year. As Dolbee notes, "Emptiness was a product of time; it depended on when one looked. The land turned 'green like an emerald' in the spring, and with this vegetation came nomads pasturing their flocks. One

native of Lebanon even went so far as to describe land he passed through in spring of 1914 as just like 'green Lebanese land' and its air just as fresh." See Samuel Dolbee, "The Locust and the Starling: People, Insects, and Disease in the Late Ottoman Jazira and After, 1860–1940" (PhD dissertation, New York University, 2017), 9.

5. Levon Mesrob, ed., *Der Zor* (Paris: B. Elegian, 1955), 24.
6. Yervant Odian, *Accursed Years: My Exile and Return from Der Zor, 1914–1919*, trans. Ara Stepan Melkonian (London: Gomidas Institute, 2009), 141. For a detailed description of the geography of Der Zor, see Rami Wahid al-Din Dalali, *Dayr al-Zawr fil-'ahd al-'Uthmani: al-hayat as-siyasiyya wat-tanzimat al-idariyya (1516–1918)* [Der Zor during the Ottoman Period: The Political Life and the Administrative Organization] (Damascus: Dar at-Takwin lil-Ta'lif wat-Tarjama wan-Nashr, 2008), 11–14.
7. DE/PA-AA; R14089; A 35047, Rössler to Bethmann Hollweg on 16 November 1915, enclosure, in Gust, ed., *The Armenian Genocide*, 463.
8. Mesrob, *Der Zor*, 24.
9. BNu/Andonian), folder 52, "The Massacres of Der Zor," Der Zor, 38. There were also sixty-seven Apostolic Armenians, eighteen Greeks, twenty-seven Greek Catholics, one Protestant, one Latin, and two Jews. See Karpat, *Ottoman Population, 1830–1914*, 188.
10. DE/PA-AA; R14086; A 19743, Wangenheim in Istanbul to Bethmann Hollweg on 17 June 1915, in Gust, *The Armenian Genocide*, 211. The arduous journey from Zeytun and the surrounding villages to Der Zor via Marash and Aleppo took more than four weeks. See DE/PA-AA; R14087; A 24658, report from the director of the German Christian Charity-Organization for the Orient Frienrich Schuchardt to the German Foreign Office on 20 August 1915, enclosure 2 (12 July 1915), in Gust, *The Armenian Genocide*, 313.
11. For a detailed treatment of the conditions that precipitated the deportation of Armenians from Zeytun, see Aram Arkun, "Zeytun and the Commencement of the Armenian Genocide," in *A Question of Genocide: Armenians and Turks at the End of the Ottoman Empire*, ed. Ronald Grigor Suny, Fatma Müge Göçek, and Norman M. Naimark (Oxford: Oxford University Press, 2011), 221–243; and Hilmar Kaiser, "Regional Resistance to Central Government Policies: Ahmed Djemal Pasha, the Governors of Aleppo, and Armenian Deportees in the Spring and Summer of 1915," *Journal of Genocide Research* 12, no. 3 (2010): 173–218.
12. Armenian National Council, Records of the Council for Refugees, folder 38, session 4. As the Armenian Apostolic Church did not have a presence there, Der Zor's Armenian Catholic Prelacy served as a local partner, and communication between the two was achieved via telegrams sent from the Armenian Catholic Prelacy in Aleppo to its counterpart in Der Zor.

13. Mihran Aghazarian, *Aksoragani Husher* [Memoirs of an Exile] (Adana: Hay Tsayn Printing House, 1919), 3. For a French translation, see Kévorkian, "L'Extermination des déportés Arméniens," 219–227. Aghazarian was a prominent member of the Hunchakian Party who was exiled to Der Zor in 1915. He accidentally met his mother there a year later, and upon her insistence that Armenian males in the area face a higher danger, he escaped to Nusaybin disguised in women's clothing. There, he worked in the finance section of the Baghdad Railway and helped other deportees find jobs. He married Marie Shekherdemian (from Hajin), who gave birth to their first child, Mitra, in Nusaybin. After the armistice, Aghazarian became a teacher in Marash and published *Aksoragani Husher*, a booklet that presented a detailed account of his time in Der Zor, yet no information whatsoever about the circumstances of his own life in, and eventual escape from, Der Zor. For a biography of Aghazarian, see Mitra Aghazarian, *Mihran Aghazarian* (Yerevan: Hayastan, 1983). See also Sisag Varjabedian, *Hayere Lipanani metch: Hanrakidaran lipananahay kaghouti* [The Armenians in Lebanon: Encyclopedia of the Armenian Community in Lebanon], vol. 5 (Beirut: Hamazkayin,1983), 22–24.
14. DE/PA-AA; R14087; A 24658, Schuchardt to the German Foreign Office on 20 August 1915, enclosure 2 (12 July 1915), in Gust, *The Armenian Genocide*, 313.
15. Dikran Jebejian, "Der Zori Sbante," *Hay Anteb* 2, no. 18 (1965): 12.
16. The committee was headed by *nufus memuru* Abdul Kadir Efendi. Other members included the *serkomiser* (chief inspector) and the director of the local branch of Ziraat Bankası (Agricultural Bank). See Aghazarian, *Aksoragani Husher*, 6.
17. Aghazarian prepared deportee lists. He also mentions the names of several other Armenians who had a similar job in Der Zor. See Aghazarian, *Aksoragani Husher*, 26.
18. Ibid. Aghazarian paid thirty liras. See, for example, DE/PA-AA; R14087; A 24658, Schuchardt to the German Foreign Office on 20 August 1915, enclosure 2 (12 July 1915), in Gust, *The Armenian Genocide*, 313.
19. See Aghazarian, *Aksoragani Husher*, 16.
20. Zachary J. Foster, "The 1915 Locust Attack in Syria and Palestine and Its Role in the Famine during the First World War," *Middle Eastern Studies* 51, no. 3 (2015): 370–394.
21. Dolbee, "The Locust and the Starling."
22. BOA DH.ŞFR 54-A/71, telegram from the Interior Ministry's General Security Directorate to Aleppo Province on 22 July 1915.
23. BOA DH.ŞFR 54-A/91, telegram from Talaat to Zor district on 24 July 1915.
24. DE/PA-AA; R14087; A24525, Rössler to Bethmann Hollweg on 31 July 1915, in Gust, *The Armenian Genocide*, 275–276. Rössler repeated the same figure in another report a month later, at which point it was already dated. See DE/PA-AA; R14087; R14095; A 28019,

Rössler to Bethmann Hollweg on 3 September 1915, enclosure 3, in Gust, *The Armenian Genocide*, 348.

25. See Hilmar Kaiser, *The Extermination of Armenians in the Diyarbekir Region* (Istanbul: Bilgi University, 2014), 385. NA/RG59/867.4016/126, Jackson's report to Morgenthau on 3 August 1915, in Ara Sarafian, ed., *United States Official Records on the Armenian Genocide* (London: Gomidas Institute, 2004), 169.
26. DE/PA-AA; R14087; A24525, Rössler to Bethmann Hollweg on 31 July 1915, in Gust, *The Armenian Genocide*, 275–276. According to the report, "300 died from difficulties along the way, 98 drowned in the Euphrates River."
27. BOA DH.ŞFR 54/413, IAMM to the provinces of Adana, Erzerum, Bitlis, Aleppo, Diyarbakir, Sivas, Mamuretul-Aziz, Urfa, Kayseri, Canik, and Izmit on 12 July 1915.
28. The number is based on an official dispatch from the Mardin *mutasarrıf*. See Aghazarian, *Aksoragani Husher*, 8.
29. See BNu/Andonian, folder 52, "The Massacres of Der Zor," Der Zor, 39. See also Kévorkian, "L'Extermination des déportés Arméniens," 174.
30. Aghazarian, *Aksoragani Husher*, 9–10. Another convoy that left the Kharpert area in the same period was comprised of 2,500 people only 600 of whom arrived in Der Zor. See NA/RG59/867.4016/243, American Consul General George Horton to the secretary of state on 8 November 1915, memorandum, in Sarafian, *United States Official Records*, 385.
31. Aghazarian lists deportees from the cities and towns of Diyarbakir, Sivas, Keghi, Tokat, Amassia, Samson, Erzerum, and Bitlis. Aghazarian, *Aksoragani Husher*, 9–10.
32. The words of Jackson, Rössler, and A. Bernau respectively. NA/RG59/867.4016/373, Jackson to the secretary of state on 4 March 1918, in Sarafian, *United States Official Records*, 590; DE/PA-AA; R14091; A 12911, Rössler to the imperial chancellor on 27 April 1916, in Gust, *The Armenian Genocide*, 580; and DE/PA-AA; R14094; A 28162, Rössler to the imperial chancellor on 27 September 1916, enclosure, in Gust, *The Armenian Genocide*, 655. Not all assessments of Ali Suat Bey were glowing. Historian Mihran Minassian points to one contemporary Armenian source that depicts the *mutasarrıf* in a negative light, recounting instances of him accepting bribes. G Azilian, "Ov E Der Zori Nakhgin Garavarich Ali Suate," *Zhoghovurti Tsayne* 1, 85–176 (10 May 1919): 3, as cited in Mihran Minassian, "Aram Andoniani Andib Krarumnere Der Zori Godoradzneroun Masin" [Aram Andonian's Unpublished Writings about the Der Zor Massacres], *Haigazian Armenological Review* 35 (2015): 714 (fn. 55).
33. Aghazarian, *Aksoragani Husher*, 13.
34. See Kaiser, *The Extermination of Armenians in the Diyarbekir Region*, 385–390.
35. Aghazarian, *Aksoragani Husher*, 6. Mount Abdulaziz, near Hasakeh, is a

three-thousand-foot-high mountain ridge between Der Zor and Ras ul-Ain. Remnants from the Der Zor massacres would also be sent there to die in August 1916. "There is no possibility of their living more than a few weeks," Chargé d'Affaires of the U.S. Embassy in Istanbul Hoffman Philip would report. See NA/RG59/867.4016/296, Philip to the secretary of state on 1 September 1916, in Sarafian, *United States Official Records*, 534.

36. Aghazarian, *Aksoragani Husher*, 13. Ali Suat Bey was often out of town, visiting Aleppo for official business and often staying there for days on end. Jackson notes how he was "highly esteemed by many in Aleppo whose homes he frequented on the occasion of his *numerous* [emphasis mine] visits to our city." See NA/RG59/867.4016/373, Jackson to the secretary of state on 4 March 1918, in Sarafian, *United States Official Records*, 590.
37. Of this figure, 22,100 were Apostolic and 1,200 were Protestant Armenians. See NA/RG59/867.4016/219, Jackson's report to Morgenthau on 29 September 1915, enclosures 2 and 3, in Sarafian, *United States Official Records*, 311–312. There were also Armenian Catholics among the deportees in Der Zor. Ibid., notes in enclosure 4, 315.
38. DE/PA-AA; R14104; A 44066, Director of the Orient and Islam Commission of the German Protestant Mission Board to the German Foreign Office on 19 October 1918, enclosure, in Gust, *The Armenian Genocide*, 580.
39. Aghazarian, *Aksoragani Husher*, 13. NA/RG59/867.4016/373, Jackson to the secretary of state on 4 March 1918, in Sarafian, *United States Official Records*, 590.
40. Aghazarian, *Aksoragani Husher*, 13.
41. BNu/Andonian, folder 52, "The Massacres of Der Zor," Levon Shashian, 35–37.
42. Aghazarian lists convoys from Aintab, Marash, Hajin, Dörtyol, Adana, Darson-Mersin, Konya, Adapazar, Izmit, Broussa (Bursa), and Rodosto (Tekirdağ). See Aghazarian, *Aksoragani Husher*, 14.
43. DE/PA-AA; R14089; A 35047, Rössler to Bethmann Hollweg on 16 November 1915, enclosure, in Gust, *The Armenian Genocide*, 464.
44. Aghazarian, *Aksoragani Husher*, 15.
45. DE/PA-AA; R14089; A 35047, Rössler to Bethmann Hollweg on 16 November 1915, enclosure, in Gust, *The Armenian Genocide*, 464.
46. Erik-Jan Zürcher, "Between Death and Desertion: The Experience of the Ottoman Soldier in World War I," *Turcica* 28 (1996): 244.
47. Paren Kazanjian, ed., *The Cilician Armenian Ordeal* (Boston: Hye Intentions, 1989), 362. Quinine was the most common treatment for malaria until the 1920s. For a discussion of malaria in the late Ottoman period, see Chris Gratien, "The Ottoman Quagmire: Malaria, Swamps, and Settlement in the Late Ottoman Mediterranean," *International Journal of Middle East Studies*, 49 (2017), 583–604. For a historical overview of quinine in malaria

treatment, see Jane Achan et al., "Quinine, an Old Anti-Malarial Drug in a Modern World: Role in the Treatment of Malaria," *Malaria Journal* 10:144 (2011), http://www.malariajournal.com.

48. Aghazarian, *Aksoragani Husher*, 15.
49. DE/PA-AA; R14094; A 28162, Rössler to Bethmann Hollweg on 27 September 1916, in Gust, *The Armenian Genocide*, 655.
50. Aghazarian wrote that the orphanage was opened through "the personal arrangement of Ali Suat Bey." See Aghazarian, *Aksoragani Husher*, 19. BOA DH.ŞFR 59/214, Interior Ministry to Zor district governorate, 5 November 1915. Ottoman officials—most prominently Cemal Pasha—tended to overplay their own role in policies that are perceived by deportees as positive, while laying the blame for unpopular policies upon the center. Without direct knowledge of the correspondence between the center and the peripheries, deportee perception of officials was sometimes influenced by these misrepresentations.
51. Aghazarian, *Aksoragani Husher*, 19.
52. Ibid., 20–21.
53. Ibid., 22.
54. Ibid. It is likely that this information was known to Ali Suat Bey, who in turn conveyed it to Levon Shashian. Another possible source for this information could be Dr. Hovhannes Efendi Magarian from Albistan, whom Ali Suat Bey had designated the deportee health supervisor in Der Zor. Ali Suat Bey was fond of the doctor, and a close relationship had developed between the two. See, for example, Aghazarian, *Aksoragani Husher*, 17. Regardless of Aghazarian's source, the information is likely true, and the events surrounding the ouster of Ali Suat Bey are corroborated by a host of other sources.
55. Ibid., 22.
56. Kapigian recounts seeing four to five Turks "in hunting apparel" in spring 1916 who walked up and down Rakka's streets observing everything closely. "A week later they disappeared; perhaps they went to Der Zor." See Garabed Kapigian, *Yeghernabadoum Sepasdio* [The History of the Great Crime in Sepasdia] (Boston: Hairenik Publishing, 1924), 460–461.
57. Taner Akçam, *The Young Turks' Crime against Humanity: The Armenian Genocide and Ethnic Cleansing in the Ottoman Empire* (Princeton, NJ: Princeton University Press, 2012), 277–278.
58. See Aghazarian, *Aksoragani Husher*, 23.
59. "Philanthropy of the American Consul at Aleppo," *Almuqattam*, 20 March 1919. The English translation is part of a collection of documents provided to this author by

Jennine Jackson, the consul's granddaughter-in-law.

60. Rev. Father Pierre Merjimekian, "A Benefactor," *La Renaissance Arabe*, Aleppo, Syria, 1 June 1919. The English translation is part of a collection of documents provided to this author by Jennine Jackson, the consul's granddaughter-in-law.
61. Beatrice Rohner, *Die Stunde ist gekommen: Märtyrerbilder aus der Jetztzeit* (Frankfurt am Main: Verlag Orient, circa 1920), 7–14.
62. For a treatment of the Berlin–Baghdad Railway project, see Peter H. Christensen, *Germany and the Ottoman Railways: Art, Empire, and Infrastructure* (New Haven: Yale University Press, 2017); and Sean McMeekin, *The Berlin Baghdad Express: The Ottoman Empire and Germany's Bid for World Power* (London: Penguin Books, 2010). For an examination of the railroad project's connection to the Armenian genocide, see Hilmar Kaiser, "The Baghdad Railway and the Armenian Genocide, 1915–1916: A Case Study in German Resistance and Complicity," in *Remembrance and Denial: The Case of the Armenian Genocide*, ed. Richard G. Hovannisian (Detroit: Wayne State University Press, 1999), 67–112.
63. NA/RG59/867.4016/126, Brissel to Morgenthau on 29 August 1915, in Sarafian, *United States Official Records*, 263.
64. DE/PA-AA; R14089; A 35047, Rössler to Bethmann Hollweg on 3 January 1916, enclosure 2, in Gust, *The Armenian Genocide*, 525–526.
65. BOA DH.EUM 2 Şb. 68/88, IAMM director Şükrü Kaya to the Ministry of Interior on 8 October 1915.
66. NA/RG59/867.48/271, Jackson to Morgenthau on 8 February 1916, enclosure (3 February 1916), in Sarafian, *United States Official Records*, 169.
67. Ibid. Armenian sources corroborate the German reports. BNu/Andonian, folder 59, "Deportation of Armenians of Ras ul-Ain," The Situation and the Demise of Ras ul-Ain's Armenian Deportees, 22.
68. James Bryce and Arnold Toynbee, *The Treatment of the Armenians in the Ottoman Empire, 1915–1916: Documents Presented to Viscount Grey of Fallodon by Viscount Bryce*, ed. Ara Sarafian, uncensored edition (London: Gomidas Institute, 2000), document 68, 303.
69. Ibid.
70. There is little research on Muslims who helped Armenians during the genocide. See Richard G. Hovannisian, "Intervention and Shades of Altruism during the Armenian Genocide," in *The Armenian Genocide: History, Politics, Ethics*, ed. Richard G. Hovannisian (New York: St. Martin's, 1992), 173–207. In recent years, public interest in the subject has grown, as indicated by articles in the Turkish and Armenian media and efforts by several organizations (for example, the Raoul Wallenberg Foundation) to compile accounts of

righteous Turks during the Armenian Genocide.

71. Yeranuhi Simonian, *Im Koghkotas* [My Golgotha] (Antelias: Armenian Catholicosate, 1960), 23.
72. Haroutioun Mertchian's memoirs, 56, BNu unpublished memoirs collection. To my knowledge, the memoir is only published in the Breton language. See Haroutioun Mertchian, *Steudad an Ankoù: eñvorennoù un Armenian da vare ar ouennlazhadeg* (Lannion: Hor Yezh, 2005).
73. Kazanjian, *The Cilician Armenian Ordeal*, 6.
74. DE/PA-AA; R14089; A 35047, Rössler to Bethmann Hollweg on 3 January 1916, enclosure 2, in Gust, *The Armenian Genocide*, 526.
75. Simonian, *Im Koghkotas*, 14.
76. Ibid., 19.
77. DE/PA-AA; R14087; A 28019, Rössler to Bethmann Hollweg on 3 September 1915, in Gust, *The Armenian Genocide*, 345.
78. BNu/Andonian, folder 59, "Deportation of Armenians of Ras ul-Ain," The Massacres of Ras ul-Ain, 3–4. See also Kévorkian, "L'Extermination des déportés Arméniens," 108.
79. Kazanjian, *The Cilician Armenian Ordeal*, 36.
80. Ibid., 8. A month later, they were marched to Der Zor anyway.
81. Bryce and Toynbee, *The Treatment of the Armenians in the Ottoman Empire*, document 68, 303.
82. Ibid.
83. BOA DH.ŞFR 60/199, telegram from Talaat to Zor district on 16 February 1915.
84. BOA DH.ŞFR 61/32, telegram from the Interior Ministry's General Security Directorate to several provinces and provincial districts on 13 February 1916.
85. Hovhannes Domardzatsi Torossian, *Badmutiun hay Domardzayi* [History of Armenian Tomarza], vol. 3 (Beirut: Central Publishing Committee of Tomarza History, 1969), 2096.
86. Ibid., 2088.
87. NA/RG59/867.4016/373, Jackson to the secretary of state on 4 March 1918, in Sarafian, *United States Official Records*, 591.
88. DE/PA-AA; R14092; A 18542, Metternich to Bethmann Hollweg on 10 July 1916, in Gust, *The Armenian Genocide*, 601.
89. DE/PA-AA; R14091; A 12911, Rössler to Bethmann Hollweg on 27 April 1916, in Gust, *The Armenian Genocide*, 581–582.
90. See Aghazarian, *Aksoragani Husher*, 25.
91. BNu/Andonian, folder 52, "The Massacres of Der Zor," Notes on Der Zor, 48.
92. NA/RG59/867.4016/373, Jackson to the secretary of state on 4 March 1918, in Sarafian,

United States Official Records, 590.

93. Aghazarian, *Aksoragani Husher*, 25. Entire convoys of Armenians were massacred in the Sheddadiya area in summer 1916. See, for example, Angele Torossian's testimony in Torossian, *Badmutiun hay Domardzayi*, 3:2100.
94. BNu/Andonian, folder 52, "The Massacres of Der Zor," Notes on Der Zor, 50.
95. Aghazarian, *Aksoragani Husher*, 31. Aghazarian seems to have known much of what was going on through an Armenian girl Zeki kept in his house. He refers to her in passing in his book (30). Other Armenian sources also make references to an Armenian woman in Zeki's house who witnessed his actions, as well as his anti-Armenian tantrums as he was preparing the ground for annihilation.
96. DE/PA-AA; R14094; A 28162, Rössler to Bethmann Hollweg on 27 September 1916, in Gust, *The Armenian Genocide*, 651.
97. BNu/Andonian, folder 52, "The Massacres of Der Zor," Notes on Der Zor, 52.
98. DE/PA-AA; R14094; A 28162, Rössler to the imperial chancellor on 27 September 1916, enclosure, in Gust, *The Armenian Genocide*, 655.
99. Jebejian, "Der Zori Sbante," 12.
100. Joseph Tawtal, "The Events of Der Zor during the War," *Al-Mashrek* 20, no. 6 (June 1922): 562–570. The Armenian translation (by Mihran Minassian), appeared in *Aztag Magazine*, April 2004, 53–59.
101. Aghazarian, *Aksoragani Husher*, 26–27.
102. DE/PA-AA; R14094; A 31831, Rössler to Bethmann Hollweg on 5 November 1916, in Gust, *The Armenian Genocide*, 672.
103. Aghazarian, *Aksoragani Husher*, 28. Jezire is the area between the Euphrates and the Tigris Rivers just south of Anatolia.
104. Ibid., 29–31.
105. Armen Anush, *Passage through Hell, a Memoir* (Studio City, CA: H. and K. Manjikian Publications, 2007), 104.
106. Ibid., 30. For names of some of those arrested on that day, see BNu/Andonian, folder 52, "The Massacres of Der Zor," Der Zor, 52–58.
107. DE/PA-AA; R14093; A 21969, Rössler to Bethmann Hollweg, enclosure 1, on 29 July 1916, in Gust, *The Armenian Genocide*, 609. Jebejian, a member of the humanitarian resistance network who had worked closely with Rev. Eskijian, was also arrested, tortured, and killed in the weeks after she sent this letter.
108. BNu/Andonian, folder 52, "The Massacres of Der Zor," Der Zor, 37. According to the account by Mesrob Tashjian of Hussenig, who worked with Shashian, they pulled out his teeth, cut out his eyeballs, ears, nose, and testicles.

109. DE/PA-AA; R14093; A 25739, Hoffmann to embassy in Istanbul on 19 August 1916, in Gust, *The Armenian Genocide*, 617. See also, Jebejian, "Der Zori Sbante," 14–15.
110. BNu/Andonian, folder 52, "The Massacres of Der Zor," Der Zor, 37. Three people survived the ordeal from the group, one of whom, a thirteen-year-old boy, was redeported to Souvar, where he arrived four to five days later.
111. BNu/Andonian, folder 52, "The Massacres of Der Zor," Scenes from the Der Zor Massacres, 99.
112. Aghazarian, *Aksoragani Husher*, 31. Again, Aghazarian's account is corroborated by German documents. In his 5 November report to the imperial chancellor, Rössler writes, "According to a new report now at hand, all the camps south of there [Der Zor], i.e. Meyadin and Ana, were also cleared." See DE/PA-AA; R14094; A 31831, Rössler to Bethmann Hollweg on 5 November 1916, in Gust, *The Armenian Genocide*, 673. Rössler's statement was based, in part, on an account by Hovsep Sarkissian (from Aintab) who survived the Der Zor massacres. He told Sister Beatrice Rohner in his testimony that "in July and August, he [Zeki] had all the deportees from Sabkha, Der-el-Zor, Mejadin [Meyadin], Ana, etc., over 150,000 of them, brought to the village of Merad (Marrat)." Ibid, enclosure 1.
113. NA/RG59/867.4016/296, Hoffman Philip to the secretary of state on 1 September 1916, in Sarafian, *United States Official Records*, 535.
114. NA/RG59/867.4016/373, Jackson to the secretary of state on 4 March 1918, in Sarafian, *United States Official Records*, 590–591.
115. DE/PA-AA; R14093; A 25739, Hoffmann to the embassy in Istanbul on 29 August 1916, in Gust, *The Armenian Genocide*, 617.
116. DE/PA-AA; R14093; A 26116, Hoffmann to the Embassy in Istanbul on 5 September 1916, in Gust, *The Armenian Genocide*, 619.
117. Most of the males, particularly from the eastern provinces of the empire, were already killed. Only a small proportion of the deportees that had made it to Der Zor were men, many of whom were imprisoned prior to the final deportations and massacres.
118. See, for example, Jambazian's account. BNu/Andonian, folder 52, "The Massacres of Der Zor," Scenes from the Der Zor Massacres, 102. Survivor Pepe Karademirjian also provides a similar account. BNu/Andonian, folder 52, "The Massacres of Der Zor," Scenes from the Der Zor Massacres, 106.
119. BNu/Andonian, folder 52, "The Massacres of Der Zor," Scenes from the Der Zor Massacres, 102. In his account, Jambazian expressed surprise about how twenty such cases were exposed in his convoy as they were near Suvar.
120. Ibid. Jambazian told of twenty to thirty men dressed as women who managed to escape.

A few of them survived the desert and made it to Aleppo.

121. BNu/Andonian, folder 52, "The Massacres of Der Zor," The second caravan marched from Der Zor, 96–99. See also Kévorkian, "L'Extermination des déportés Arméniens," 206–207.
122. Jebejian, "Der Zori Sbante," 15.
123. DE/PA-AA; R14093; A 25739, Hoffmann to embassy in Istanbul on 19 August 1916, in Gust, *The Armenian Genocide*, 617.
124. Leslie A. Davis, *The Slaughterhouse Province: An American Diplomat's Report on the Armenian Genocide, 1915–1917* (New Rochelle: Aristide D. Caratzas, 1989), 94.
125. Raymond Kévorkian, "Earth, Fire, Water: or How to Make the Armenian Corpses Disappear," in *Destruction and Human Remains: Disposal and Concealment in Genocide and Mass Violence*, ed. Elisabeth Anstett and Jean-Marc Dreyfus (Manchester: Manchester University Press, 2014), 107.
126. T. H. Greenshielde, "The Settlement of Armenian Refugees in Syria and Lebanon, 1915–1939" (PhD dissertation, University of Durham, 1978), 56. For a study of the fate of the Armenians in the region after 1918, see also Raymond Kévorkian, Lévon Nordiguian, and Vahé Tachjian, *Les Arméniens 1917–1939: La quête d'un refuge* (Beirut: Presses de L'Université Saint-Joseph, 2006); Nicola Migliorino, *(Re)constructing Armenia in Lebanon and Syria: Ethno-Cultural Diversity and the State in the Aftermath of a Refugee Crisis* (Oxford: Berghahn Books, 2008); and Vahé Tachjian, *La France en Cilicie et en Haute-Mésopotamie: Aux confins de la Turquie, de la Syrie et de l'Irak, 1919–1933* (Paris: Éditions Karthala, 2004).

CHAPTER EIGHT. Surviving Talaat: The Network's Legacy

1. Mihran Aghazarian, *Aksoragani Husher* [Memoirs of an Exile] (Adana: Hay Tsayn Printing House, 1919), 17.
2. Aram Andonian, *Medz Vojire* [The Great Crime] (Boston: Bahag Publishing, 1921), 86.
3. Delivering a speech during his visit to Der Zor, Syria on 24 March 2010, Armenia's president Serzh Sargsyan said, "Quite often historians and journalists soundly compare Deir ez Zor with Auschwitz saying that 'Deir ez Zor is the Auschwitz of the Armenians.' I think that the chronology forces us to formulate the facts in a reverse way: 'Auschwitz is the Deir ez Zor of the Jews.'" The full text of the speech is available at https://www.president.am/en/statements-and-messages/item/2010/03/24/news-58/.
4. Taner Akçam, *The Young Turks' Crime against Humanity: The Armenian Genocide and Ethnic Cleansing in the Ottoman Empire* (Princeton, NJ: Princeton University Press, 2012), xxix.

5. Vahakn N. Dadrian, *The History of the Armenian Genocide: Ethnic Conflict from the Balkans to Anatolia to the Caucasus* (Oxford: Berghahn Books, 1995), 241.
6. Often, the movement of convoys were indeed aimless, as deportees were marched from one camp to the other, sometimes back and forth, for no apparent reason other than to exhaust them.
7. For a detailed treatment of the statistical dimension, see Fuat Dündar, *Crime of Numbers: The Role of Statistics in the Armenian Question, 1878–1918* (New Brunswick, NJ: Transaction Publishers, 2010) (113–119 deal with the settlement areas in Syria); and Taner Akçam, *The Young Turks' Crime against Humanity: The Armenian Genocide and Ethnic Cleansing in the Ottoman Empire* (Princeton, NJ: Princeton University Press, 2012), 227–285.
8. Talaat himself did not survive for long. The Armenian Revolutionary Federation (ARF) decided in its 9th Congress held in Yerevan in 1919 to assassinate the perpetrators. By 1922, the ARF had gunned down in Berlin, Rome, and Tiflis Ottoman Turkish leaders implicated in the genocide: Interior Minister Talaat Pasha, Ottoman Grand Vizier Said Halim Pasha; Minister of the Navy Cemal Pasha; Committee of Union and Progress founding member Bahaeddine Shakir; and Trebizond governor Cemal Azmi. The project, dubbed "Operation Nemesis," made headlines around the world and influenced a Polish-Jewish university student named Rafael Lemkin to pursue the task of establishing an international law against attempted annihilation of whole ethnic groups. For an overview of Operation Nemesis, see Marian Mesrobian MacCurdy, *Sacred Justice: The Voices and Legacy of the Armenian Operation Nemesis* (New York: Transaction Publishers, 2015); Eric Bogosian, *Operation Nemesis: The Assassination Plot that Avenged the Armenian Genocide* (New York: Little, Brown, 2015); and Jacques Derogy, *Resistance and Revenge: The Armenian Assassination of the Turkish Leaders Responsible for the 1915 Massacres and Deportations* (New Brunswick, NJ: Transaction Publishers, 1990).
9. The scholarship on the experiences of the Armenians in Syria largely focuses on the 1920s and beyond. For the post-1920 period, see, for example, Keith David Watenpaugh, *Bread from Stones: The Middle East and the Making of Modern Humanitarianism* (Oakland: University of California Press, 2015); Seda Altuğ, "Sectarianism in the Syrian Jazira: Community, Land and Violence in the Memories of World War I and the French Mandate (1915–1939)" (PhD dissertation, Utrecht University, 2011); Nicola Migliorino, *(Re)Constructing Armenia in Lebanon and Syria: Ethno-Cultural Diversity and the State in the Aftermath of a Refugee Crisis* (Oxford: Berghahn Books, 2008); Vahé Tachjian, *La France en Cilicie et en Haute-Mésopotamie: Aux confins de la Turquie, de la Syrie et de l'Irak, 1919–1933* (Paris: Éditions Karthala, 2004); Philip Khoury, *Syria and the French Mandate:*

The Politics of Arab Nationalism, 1920–1945 (Princeton, NJ: Princeton University Press, 1987); and Levon Marashlian, "Finishing the Genocide: Cleansing Turkey of Armenian Survivors, 1920–1923," in *Remembrance and Denial: The Case of the Armenian Genocide*, ed. Richard G. Hovannisian, (Detroit: Wayne State University Press, 1999), 113–145.

10. Paren Kazanjian, ed., *The Cilician Armenian Ordeal* (Boston: Hye Intentions, 1989), 409.
11. Respectively: Description recorded in the minutes of the 15 January 1919 meeting, Minute Book of the PNAA, Aleppo Armenian Prelacy Archives, 20; Daniel Neep, *Occupying Syria under the French Mandate: Insurgency, Space and State Formation* (Cambridge: Cambridge University Press, 2012), 27; Keith Watenpaugh, *Being Modern in the Middle East: Revolution, Nationalism, Colonialism, and the Arab Middle Class* (Princeton, NJ: Princeton University Press, 2012), 124.
12. Hagop S. Der Garabedian, *Jail to Jail, Autobiography of a Survivor of the 1915 Armenian Genocide* (New York: iUniverse, 2004), 104.
13. Minutes of the 15 January 1919 meeting, Minute Book of the PNAA, Aleppo Armenian Prelacy Archives, 19. See also Garabed Kapigian, *Yeghernabadoum Sepasdio* [The History of the Great Crime in Sepasdia] (Boston: Hairenik Publishing, 1924), 541.
14. Der Garabedian, *Jail to Jail*, 105. As we shall see, the British occupying forces cared for the survivors arriving in Aleppo.
15. Kapigian, *Yeghernabadoum Sepasdio*, 553.
16. Different sources put the figure in the forties, fifties, and seventies. For three accounts of the massacre, see V. Mistrih, "Un incident à Alep contre les Arméniens (Février 1919)," *SOC Collectanea* 32 (1999): 277–348. See also Kapigian, *Yeghernabadoum Sepasdio*, 552–555.
17. Jafar Pasha Al-Askari, *A Soldier's Story from Ottoman Rule to Independent Iraq: The Memoirs of Jafar Pasha Al-Askari (1885–1936)* (London: Arabian Publishing, 2003), 162. Al-Askari provides details about the condition of Armenians in Aleppo at the time on 161–164.
18. Watenpaugh, *Bread from Stones*, 98.
19. For more on this repatriation and second exile, see Vahé Tachjian, "Du rapatriement en Cilicie au nouvel exode vers la Syrie et le Liban," *Les Arméniens, 1917–1939: La quête d'un refuge*, ed. Raymond Kévorkian, Lévon Nordiguian, and Vahé Tachjian (Beirut: Presses de L'Université Saint-Joseph, 2006), 39–53.
20. Minutes of PNAA election (17 November 1919), 9–11.
21. Minutes of PNAA (21 June 1919), 85.
22. Minutes of PNAA, 14.
23. Memoirs and accounts refer to this institution as Shirajian's orphanage, after its director

Rev. Aharon Shirajian. Although that is not its official name, I follow survivor usage.

24. Minutes of PNAA, 6.
25. In this period, Shirajian resigned from his post, and Adur Levonian, a leader of the defense of Aintab in 1920, replaced him as director. "Halebi Haygagan Vorpanotse" [The Armenian Orphanage of Aleppo," *Souriagan Mamul*, 17 August 1922, 1.
26. The literature on the efforts to reclaim and reintegrate Armenian women scattered in Muslim households has received significant scholarly attention in recent years. For a detailed account of these efforts in the 1920s, see Watenpaugh, *Bread from Stones*, 124–156; and Vahram L. Shemmassian, "The League of Nations and the Reclamation of Armenian Genocide Survivors," in *Looking Backward, Moving Forward: Confronting the Armenian Genocide*, ed. Richard G. Hovannisian (New Brunswick, NJ: Transaction Press, 2003), 81–111. See also Rebecca Jinks, "'Marks Hard to Erase': The Troubled Reclamation of 'Absorbed' Armenian Women, 1919–1927," *American Historical Review* 123, no. 1 (2018): 86–123; Vahé Tachjian, "Gender, Nationalism, Exclusion: The Reintegration Process of Female Survivors of the Armenian Genocide," *Nations and Nationalism* 15, no. 1 (2009): 60–80; and Lerna Ekmekçioğlu, "A Climate for Abduction, a Climate for Redemption: The Politics of Inclusion during and after the Armenian Genocide," *Comparative Studies in Society and History* 55, no. 3 (2013): 522–553; among others.
27. See, for example, Minutes of PNAA, 24 and 47. The Armenian National Unions were organizations that emerged soon after the end of WWI in various Armenian communities aspiring to coordinate local community affairs.
28. Migliorino, *(Re)constructing Armenia in Lebanon and Syria*, 47.
29. Document provided to this author by Jennine Jackson, the consul's granddaughter-in-law.
30. Rev. Father Pierre Merjimekian, "A Benefactor," *La Renaissance Arabe*, Aleppo, Syria, 1 June 1919.
31. John Minassian, *Many Hills Yet to Climb* (Santa Barbara, CA: Jim Cook, 1986), 199.

Bibliography

BNu Memoir Manuscript Collection

Antranig Actanian (Né Kévork B. Soultanian). "La Famille Soultanian et Mon Passé."

Hovhannes Toros Doumanian. "My Memoirs."

Mgrdich Hairabedian's memoir.

Haroutioun Mertchian's memoirs.

Vasken Tchilinguirian. "Le ciel etait noir sur Garine."

Books and Articles

Aghazarian, Mihran. *Aksoragani Husher* [Memoirs of an Exile]. Adana: Hay Tsayn Printing House, 1919.

Aghazarian, Mitra. *Mihran Aghazarian*. Yerevan: Hayastan, 1983.

Ahmad, Feroz. *The Young Turks and the Ottoman Nationalities: Armenians, Greeks, Albanians, Jews, and Arabs, 1908–1918*. Salt Lake City: University of Utah Press, 2014.

Akçam, Taner. *A Shameful Act: The Armenian Genocide and the Question of Turkish Responsibility*. New York: Metropolitan Books, 2006.

———. *The Young Turks' Crime against Humanity: The Armenian Genocide and Ethnic Cleansing in the Ottoman Empire*. Princeton, NJ: Princeton University Press, 2012.

Akçam, Taner, and Ümit Kurt. *The Spirit of the Laws: The Plunder of Wealth in the Armenian*

Genocide. New York: Berghahn, 2015.

Altounyan, Taqui. *Chimes from a Wooden Bell: A Hundred Years in the Life of a Euro-Armenian Family*. London: I. B. Tauris, 1990.

Andonian, Aram. *Medz Vojire* [The Great Crime]. Boston: Bahag Publishing, 1921.

Anstett, Elisabeth, and Jean-Marc Dreyfus, eds. *Destruction and Human Remains: Disposal and Concealment in Genocide and Mass Violence*. Manchester: Manchester University Press, 2014.

Anush, Armen. *Passage through Hell, a Memoir*. Studio City, CA: H. and K. Manjikian Publications, 2007.

Arsenian, Hagop. *Towards Golgotha: The Memoirs of Hagop Arsenian, a Genocide Survivor*. Translated by Arda Arsenian Ekmekji. Beirut: Haigazian University Press, 2011.

Atlı, Cengiz. "Türk Siyasi Hayatının Ardında Kalan İsim: Mustafa Abdulhalik Renda" [A Forgotten Name in Turkish Politics: Mustafa Abdulhalik Renda]. *History Studies* 6, no. 5 (2014): 31–50.

Auron, Yair. *The Banality of Indifference: Zionism and the Armenian Genocide*. New Brunswick: Transaction Publishers, 2000.

Ayalon, Yaron. *Natural Disasters in the Ottoman Empire: Plague, Famine, and Other Misfortunes*. Cambridge: Cambridge University Press, 2015.

Balakian, Peter. *The Burning Tigris: The Armenian Genocide and America's Response*. New York: HarperCollins, 2003.

Barton, James L. *Story of Near East Relief*. New York: Macmillan, 1930.

Bartrop, Paul. *Resisting the Holocaust: Upstanders, Partisans, and Survivors*. Santa Barbara: ABC-CLIO, 2016.

Baumel, Judith Tydor. "Women's Agency and Survival Strategies during the Holocaust." *Women's Studies International Forum* 22, no. 3 (1999): 329–347.

Becker, Annette, Hamit Bozarslan, Vincent Duclert, and Raymond Kévorkian, eds. *Le génocide des Arméniens: Un siècle de recherche, 1915–2015*. Paris: Armand Colin, 2015.

Bedoukian, Kerop. *Some of Us Survived: The Story of an Armenian Boy*. New York: Farrar, Straus, Giroux, 1979.

Bettauer, Hugo. *Die Stadt ohne Juden: Ein Roman von übermorgen* [The City without Jews: A Novel of Our Time]. Vienna: Wien Gloriette-Verl, 1922.

Bloxham, Donald. *The Great Game of Genocide: Imperialism, Nationalism, and the Destruction of the Ottoman Armenians*. Oxford: Oxford University Press, 2005.

Bogosian, Eric. *Operation Nemesis: The Assassination Plot that Avenged the Armenian Genocide*. New York: Little, Brown, 2015.

Boudjikanian, Aida, ed., *Armenians of Lebanon: From Past Princesses and Refugees to*

Present-Day Community. Beirut: Haigazian University Press, 2009.

Bryce, James, and Arnold Toynbee. *The Treatment of the Armenians in the Ottoman Empire, 1915–1916: Documents Presented to Viscount Grey of Fallodon by Viscount Bryce*. Edited by Ara Sarafian. Uncensored edition. London: Gomidas Institute, 2000.

Burns, Ross. *Aleppo: A History*. New York: Routledge, 2016.

Captanian, Payladzou. *Tsavag*. New York: Armenia Printing, 1922.

Çarık, Ghazar. *Marzbede (Haci Hüseyin)*. 2 vols. Beirut: Azad Printing House, 1945.

Catholicos Papken. *Badmutiun gatoghigosats Giligio* [History of the Giligia Catholicoses]. Antelias, Lebanon: Dbaran Tbrevanouts, 1939.

Christensen, Peter H. *Germany and the Ottoman Railways: Art, Empire, and Infrastructure*. New Haven: Yale University Press, 2017.

Çiçek, M. Talha. *War and State Formation in Syria: Cemal Pasha's Governorate during World War I, 1914–1917*. New York, Routledge, 2014.

Collingwood, Jeremy. *A Lakeland Saga: The Story of the Collingwood and Altounyan Family in Coniston and Aleppo*. Ammanford, Carmarthenshire: Sigma Press, 2012.

Cox, John M. "Jewish Resistance against Nazism." In *The Routledge History of the Holocaust*, edited by Jonathan C. Friedman, 326–336. London: Routledge, 2011.

Dadrian, Vahakn N. "The Armenian Question and the Wartime Fate of the Armenians as Documented by the Officials of the Ottoman Empire's World War I Allies: Germany and Austria-Hungary." *International Journal of Middle East Studies* 34 (2002): 59–85.

———. "Children as Victims of Genocide: The Armenian Case." *Journal of Genocide Research* 5, no. 3 (2003): 421–437.

———. *The History of the Armenian Genocide: Ethnic Conflict from the Balkans to Anatolia to the Caucasus*. Oxford: Berghahn Books, 1995.

———. "The Naim-Andonian Documents on the World War I Destruction of Ottoman Armenians: The Anatomy of a Genocide." *International Journal of Middle East Studies* 18 (1986): 311–360.

Dadrian, Vahakn N., and Taner Akçam. *Judgement at Istanbul: The Armenian Genocide Trials*. New York: Berghahn Books, 2011.

Dadrian, Vahram *To the Desert: Pages from My Diary*. London: Taderon Press, 2003.

Dakessian, Antranig. "Shari deghahanutiwne" [The Deportation of Shar]. *Haigazian Armenological Review* 33 (2015): 645–654.

Davis, Leslie A. *The Slaughterhouse Province: An American Diplomat's Report on the Armenian Genocide, 1915–1917*. New Rochelle: Aristide D. Caratzas, 1989.

Der-Vartanian, Hovsep. *Intilli-Ayrani Sbante, 1916* [The Massacre of Intilli-Ayran, 1916]. Jerusalem: St. John's Printing, 1928.

Der Yeghiayan, Zaven. *My Patriarchal Memoirs*. Barrington, RI: Mayreni Publishing, 2002.

Derderian, Katharine. "Common Fate, Different Experience: Gender-Specific Aspects of the Armenian Genocide, 1915–1917." *Holocaust and Genocide Studies* 19, no. 1 (2005): 1–25.

Derogy, Jacques. *Resistance and Revenge: The Armenian Assassination of Turkish Leaders Responsible for the 1915 Massacres and Deportations*. New Brunswick, NJ: Transaction Publishers, 1990.

Djemal Pasha. *Memories of a Turkish Statesman, 1913–1919*. London: Hutchinson, 1922.

Dolbee, Samuel. "The Desert at the End of Empire: An Environmental History of the Armenian Genocide." *Past & Present* 247, no. 1 (May 2020): 197–233.

Dündar, Fuat. *Crime of Numbers: The Role of Statistics in the Armenian Question, 1878–1918*. New Brunswick, NJ: Transaction Publishers, 2010.

———. *Modern Türkiye'nin Şifresi: İttihat Ve Terakki'nin Etnisite Mühendisliği, 1913–1918* [Modern Turkey's Code: The CUP's Ethnic Engineering, 1913–1918]. Istanbul: İletişim, 2010.

Dwork, Debórah. *Children with a Star: Jewish Youth in Nazi Europe*. New Haven: Yale University Press, 1991.

Edib, Halide. *Memoirs of Halide Edib*. New York: The Century, 1926.

Ekmekçioğlu, Lerna. "A Climate for Abduction, a Climate for Redemption: The Politics of Inclusion during and after the Armenian Genocide." *Comparative Studies in Society and History* 55, no. 3 (2013): 522–553.

Erden, Ali Fuad. *Birinci Dünya Harbi'nde Suriye Hatıraları* [Memories of Syria during the First World War]. Istanbul: Kültür Publishing, 2003.

Evans, Richard J. *The Third Reich in History and Memory*. Oxford: Oxford University Press, 2015.

Foster, Zachary J. "The 1915 Locust Attack in Syria and Palestine and Its Role in the Famine during the First World War." *Middle Eastern Studies* 51, no. 3 (2015): 370–394.

Fromkin, David. *A Peace to End All Peace: The Fall of the Ottoman Empire and the Creation of the Modern Middle East*. New York: Henry Holt, 2001.

Fuccaro, Nelida. "Urban Life and Questions of Violence." In *Violence and the City in the Modern Middle East: Changing Cityscapes in the Transformation from Empire to Nation State*, edited by Nelida Fuccaro, 3–22. Stanford: Stanford University Press, 2016.

Gerçek, Burçin. "Turkish Rescuers." The International Raoul Wallenberg Foundation, available online at http://www.raoulwallenberg.net/wp-content/files_mf/1435335304ReportTurkishrescuerscomplete.pdf.

Ghazarian, Haig. *The Caverns of Gesaria: Pages from My Diary*. Yerevan: Armenian National Academy of Sciences, Institute of History, 2014.

Glass, Charles. *Tribes with Flags: A Journey Curtailed*. London: Secker & Warburg, 1990.

Gust, Wolfgang, ed., *The Armenian Genocide: Evidence from the German Foreign Office Archives,*

1915–1916. New York: Berghahn, 2014.

Herzog, Dagmar, ed. *Brutality and Desire: War and Sexuality in Europe's Twentieth Century*. New York: Palgrave Macmillan, 2009.

Hilberg, Raul. *The Destruction of the European Jews*. Chicago: Quadrangle Books, 1961.

Hovannisian, Richard G., ed. *The Armenian Genocide: History, Politics, Ethics*. New York: St. Martin's, 1992.

———, ed. *Remembrance and Denial: The Case of the Armenian Genocide*. Detroit: Wayne State University Press, 1999.

Hyslop, Jonathan. "The Invention of the Concentration Camp: Cuba, Southern Africa and the Philippines, 1896–1907." *South African Historical Journal* 63, no. 2 (2011): 251–276.

Jernazian, Ephraim K. *Judgment unto Truth: Witnessing the Armenian Genocide*. New Brunswick: Transaction Publishers, 1990.

Kadri, Hüseyin Kazım. *Türkiye'nin Çöküşü*. Istanbul: Hikmet Neşriyat, 1992.

Kaiser, Hilmar. *At the Crossroad of Der Zor: Death, Survival, and Humanitarian Resistance in Aleppo, 1915–1917*. London: Gomidas Institute, 2002.

———. *The Extermination of Armenians in the Diyarbekir Region*. Istanbul: Bilgi University, 2014.

———. "Regional Resistance to Central Government Policies: Ahmed Djemal Pasha, the Governors of Aleppo, and Armenian Deportees in the Spring and Summer of 1915." *Journal of Genocide Research* 12, no. 3 (2010): 173–218.

Kalaydjian, Harutyun. *Milionen Mege: Tseghasbanutyan aganades Zrytuntsi badaniyi me hushere* [One in a Million: The Memories of a Teenager from Zeytun Who Witnessed the Genocide]. Beirut: Zartonk Armenian Daily Publishing, 2018.

Kapigian, Garabed. *Yeghernabadoum Sepasdio* [The History of the Great Crime in Sepasdia]. Boston: Hairenik Publishing, 1924.

Kaprielian-Churchill, Isabel. *Sisters of Mercy and Survival: Armenian Nurses, 1900–1930*. Antelias, Lebanon: Armenian Catholicosate of Cilicia, 2012.

Karpat, Kemal H. *The Extermination of Armenians in the Diyarbekir Region*. Istanbul: Bilgi University, 2014.

———. *Ottoman Population, 1830–1914: Demographic and Social Characteristics*. Madison: University of Wisconsin Press, 1985.

Kazanjian, Paren, ed. *The Cilician Armenian Ordeal*. Boston: Hye Intentions, 1989.

Keegan, John. *The First World War*. New York: Alfred A. Knopf, 1998.

Kerr, Stanley Elphinstone. *The Lions of Marash: Personal Experiences with American Near East Relief, 1919–1922*. New York: SUNY Press, 1973.

Kévorkian, Raymond. "Alep, Centre du dispositif genocidaire et des operations de secours aux deportés." In Vartan Derounian, *Mémoire arménienne: Photographies du camp de réfugiés d'Alep, 1922–1936*, edited by Lévon Nordiguian, 15–23. Beirut: Presse de l'Université Saint Joseph, 2010.

———. *The Armenian Genocide: A Complete History*. London: I. B. Tauris, 2011.

———. "L'Extermination des déportés Arméniens ottomans dans les camps de concentration de Syrie-Mésopotamie (1915–1916)." Special issue, *Revue d'histoire arménienne contemporaine* 2 (1998).

Kieser, Hans-Lukas. "Beatrice Rohner's Work in the Death Camps of Armenians in 1916." In *Resisting Genocide: The Multiple Forms of Rescue*, edited by Jacques Sémelin, Claire Andrieu, and Sarah Gensburger, 367–382. New York: Columbia University Press, 2011.

Kieser, Hans-Lukas, and Dominik J. Schaller, eds. *The Armenian Genocide and the Shoah*. Zurich: Chronos Verlag, 2002.

Kieser, Hans-Lukas, Margaret Lavinia Anderson, Seyhan Bayraktar, and Thomas Schmutz, eds. *End of the Ottomans: The Genocide of 1915 and the Politics of Turkish Nationalism*. London: I. B. Tauris, 2019.

Kouyoumdjian, Ohannes Pacha. *Le Liban: À la veille et au début de la guerre. Mémoire d'un Gouverneur, 1913–1915*. Paris: Centre d'histoire arménienne contemporaine, 2003.

Kühne, Thomas. "Colonialism and the Holocaust: Continuities, Causations, and Complexities." *Journal of Genocide Research* 15, no. 3 (2013): 339–362.

Levene, Mark. *The Crisis of Genocide*, vol. 1: *Devastation: The European Rimlands, 1912–1938*. Oxford: Oxford University Press, 2013.

———. *Genocide in the Age of the Nation State*, vol. 1: *The Meaning of Genocide*. London: I. B. Tauris, 2005.

MacCurdy, Marian Mesrobian. *Sacred Justice: The Voices and Legacy of the Armenian Operation Nemesis*. New York: Transaction Publishers, 2015.

Madenjian, Mardig. *Ravished Paradise: Forced March to Nothingness*. Pasadena, CA: Self-published, 2016.

Maksudyan, Nazan. *Orphans and Destitute Children in the Late Ottoman Empire*. Syracuse: Syracuse University Press, 2014.

Mansel, Philip. *Aleppo: The Rise and Fall of Syria's Great Merchant City*. London: I. B. Tauris, 2016.

Marin, Alexandra, and Barry Wellman. "Social Network Analysis: An Introduction." In *The SAGE Handbook of Social Network Analysis*, edited by John Scott and Peter J. Carrington, 11–25. London: SAGE Publications, 2011.

Mesrob, Levon, ed. *1915: Aghed yev Veradzenount* [1915: Disaster and Rebirth]. Paris: Arax Publishing, 1952.

———, ed. *Der Zor*. Paris: B. Elegian, 1955.

Migliorino, Nicola. *(Re)constructing Armenia in Lebanon and Syria: Ethno-Cultural Diversity and the State in the Aftermath of a Refugee Crisis*. Oxford: Berghahn Books, 2008.

Minassian, John. *Many Hills Yet to Climb*. Santa Barbara, CA: Jim Cook, 1986.

Mihran Minassian, "Aram Andoniani Andib Krarumnere Der Zori Godoradzneroun Masin" [Aram Andonian's Unpublished Writings about the Der Zor Massacres]. *Haigazian Armenological Review* 35 (2015): 685–723.

Mkhitarian, Kiud. *Husher Yev Verhishumner, 1918–1935* [Memories and Remembrances, 1918–1935]. Antelias: Cilicia Catholicosate, 1937.

Morton, Michael Quentin. *In the Heart of the Desert: The Story of an Exploration Geologist and the Search for Oil in the Middle East*. Aylesford: Green Mountain Press, 2017.

Niepage, Martin. *The Horrors of Aleppo Seen by a German Eyewitness*. 1917; repr. New York: New Age Publishers, 1975.

Odian, Yervant. *Accursed Years: My Exile and Return from Der Zor, 1914–1919*. Translated by Ara Stepan Melkonian. London: Gomidas Institute, 2009.

Özdemir, Hikmet. *Cemal Paşa ve Ermeni Göçmenler: 4. Ordu'nun İnsani Yardımları* [Cemal Pasha and the Armenian Deportees: The Humanitarian Assistance of the Fourth Army]. Istanbul: Remzi Kitapevi, 2009.

———. *The Ottoman Army, 1914–1918: Disease and Death on the Battlefield*. Salt Lake City: University of Utah Press, 2008.

Özşavlı, Halil. *Urfa Ermenileri (Sosyal-Siyasi ve Kültürel Hayat)* [Urfa Armenians: Socio-Political and Cultural Life]. Ankara: Gazi Kitabevi, 2013.

Pamboukian, Yervant, ed., *Medz Yegherni Arachin Vaverakroghe' Shavarsh Misakian* [The First Chronicler of the Great Crime: Shavarsh Misakian]. Antelias, Lebanon: Catholicosate of Cilicia, 2017.

Panian, Karnig. *Goodbye, Antoura: A Memoir of the Armenian Genocide*. Stanford: Stanford University Press, 2015.

Payaslian, Simon. *United States Policy toward the Armenian Question and the Armenian Genocide*. New York: Palgrave Macmillan, 2005.

Peterson, Merrill D. *"Starving Armenians": America and the Armenian Genocide, 1915–1920 and After*. Charlottesville: University of Virginia Press, 2004.

Philipp, Thomas, and Birgit Schaebler. *The Syrian Land: Processes of Integration and Fragmentation. Bilād Al-Shām from the 18th to the 20th Century*. Stuttgart: Steiner, 1998.

Pitzer, Andrea. *One Long Night: A Global History of Concentration Camps*. New York: Little, Brown, 2017.

Rohner, Beatrice. *Die Stunde ist gekommen: Märtyrerbilder aus der Jetztzeit*. Frankfurt am Main:

Verlag Orient, circa 1920.

Rosenberg, Alan, and Gerald Mysers, eds. *Echoes from the Holocaust: Philosophical Reflections on a Dark Time*. Philadelphia: Temple University Press, 1988.

Rozett, Robert. "Jewish Resistance." In *The Historiography of the Holocaust*, edited by Dan Stone, 341–363. New York: Palgrave Macmillan, 2004.

Sahag-Mesrob. *Anabadi Yerker (1916–1918)* [Songs of the Desert (1916–1918)]. Istanbul: Ararad Printing, 1919.

Salzmann, Ariel. *Tocqueville in the Ottoman Empire: Rival Paths to the Modern State*. Leiden: Brill, 2004.

Sanjian, Avedis K. *The Armenian Communities in Syria under Ottoman Dominion*. Cambridge, MA: Harvard University Press, 1965.

Sarafian, Ara, ed. *Talat Pasha's Report on the Armenian Genocide, 1917*. London: Gomidas Institute, 2011.

———, ed. *United States Official Records on the Armenian Genocide*. London: Gomidas Institute, 2004.

Şeker, Nesim. "Demographic Engineering in the Late Ottoman Empire and the Armenians." *Middle Eastern Studies* 43, no. 3 (2007): 461–474.

Seropian, Hagop A. *Yegherni Husheres* [My Memories of the Genocide]. Beirut: Photogravure Paklayan, 2005.

Setragian, Husig. *Vark Kahanayits Perio Temi, 1850–2005* [The Lives of the Priests of the Aleppo Prelacy, 1850–2005]. Vol. 1. Aleppo: Aleppo Prelacy, 2005.

Shaw, Stanford J., and Ezel Kural Shaw. *History of the Ottoman Empire and Modern Turkey*, vol. 2: *Reform, Revolution, and Republic: The Rise of Modern Turkey, 1808–1975*. Cambridge: Cambridge University Press, 1977.

Shemmassian, Vahram L. "Armenian Genocide Survivors in the Holy Land at the End of World War I." *Journal of the Society for Armenian Studies* 21 (2012): 227–247.

———. "Humanitarian Intervention by the Armenian Prelacy of Aleppo during the First Months of the Genocide." *Journal of the Society for Armenian Studies* 22 (2013): 127–152.

Shirinian, George N. "Turks Who Saved Armenians: Righteous Muslims during the Armenian Genocide." *Genocide Studies International* 9, no. 2 (2015): 208–227.

Silver, Daniel B. *Refuge in Hell: How Berlin's Jewish Hospital Outlasted the Nazis*. Boston: Houghton Mifflin, 2004.

Simonian, Yeranuhi. *Im Koghkotas* [My Golgotha]. Antelias: Armenian Catholicosate, 1960.

Smith, Iain R., and Andreas Stucki. "The Colonial Development of Concentration Camps (1868–1902)." *Journal of Imperial and Commonwealth History* 39, no. 3 (2011): 417–437.

Sofsky, Wolfgang. *The Order of Terror: The Concentration Camp*. Princeton, NJ: Princeton

University Press, 1997.

Straus, Scott. *Making and Unmaking Nations: The Origins and Dynamics of Genocide in Contemporary Africa*. Ithaca: Cornell University Press, 2015.

Strohmeier, Martin. "Fakhri (Fahrettin) Paşa and the End of Ottoman Rule in Medina (1916–1919)." *Turkish Historical Review* 4, no. 2 (2013): 192–223.

Suny, Ronald Grigor. *"They Can Live in the Desert but Nowhere Else": A History of the Armenian Genocide*. Princeton, NJ: Princeton University Press, 2015.

Suny, Ronald Grigor, Fatma Müge Göçek, and Norman M. Naimark, eds. *A Question of Genocide: Armenians and Turks at the End of the Ottoman Empire*. Oxford: Oxford University Press, 2011.

Tachjian, Vahé. *La France en Cilicie et en Haute-Mésopotamie: Aux confins de la Turquie, de la Syrie et de l'Irak, 1919–1933*. Paris: Éditions Karthala, 2004.

Tarbassian, Hratch A. *Erzurum (Garin): Its Armenian History and Traditions*. New York: Garin Compatriotic Union of the United States, 1975.

Tatoulian, Krikor. *Anteghowadz Kaghdnikner* [Buried Secrets]. Beirut: Atlas Publishing, 1967.

Tekeli, Ilhan. "Osmanlı İmparatorluğu'ndan Günümüze Nüfusun Zorunlu Yer Değiştirmesi Ve İskan Sorunu" [The Issue of Forced Deportation and Settlement of Population from the Ottoman Period until Today]. *Toplum ve Bilim* 50 (summer 1990): 49–71.

Tekeyan, Vahan. *Vahan Tekeyan: Selected Poems*. Translated by Gerald Papasian and John Papasian. Fresno: California State University—Fresno, 2014.

Theriault, Henry. "Against the Grain: Critical Reflections on the State and Future of Genocide Scholarship." *Genocide Studies and Prevention* 7, no. 1 (2012): 123–144.

Theriault, Henry C. "Genocide, Denial, and Domination: Armenian-Turkish Relations from Conflict Resolution to Just Transformation." *Journal of African Conflicts and Peace Studies* 1, no. 2 (2009): 82–96.

Thompson, Elizabeth F. *Justice Interrupted: The Struggle for Constitutional Government in the Middle East*. Cambridge, MA: Harvard University Press, 2013.

Torossian, Hovhannes Domardzatsi. *Badmutiun hay Domardzayi* [History of Armenian Tomarza]. Vol. 3. Beirut: Central Publishing Committee of Tomarza History, 1969.

Üngör, Ugur Ümit. *The Making of Modern Turkey: Nation and State in Eastern Anatolia, 1913–1950*. Oxford: Oxford University Press, 2011.

Üngör, Uğur Ümit, and Mehmet Polatel, *Confiscation and Destruction: The Young Turk Seizure of Armenian Property*. New York: Continuum, 2011.

Varjabedian, Sisag. *Hayere Lipanani metch: Hanrakidaran lipananahay kaghouti* [The Armenians in Lebanon: Encyclopedia of the Armenian Community in Lebanon]. Vol. 5. Beirut: 1983.

Weber, Max. *From Max Weber: Essays in Sociology*. New York: Routledge, 2009.

Weiner, Myron, and Michel S. Teitelbaum. *Political Demography, Demographic Engineering*. Oxford: Berghahn, 2001.

Winter, Jay, ed. *America and the Armenian Genocide of 1915*. Cambridge: Cambridge University Press, 2003.

Yeghiayan, Puzant. *Zhamanagagagits badmut'iwn gat'oghigosut'ean hayots Giligio, 1914–1972* [Contemporary History of the Armenian Catholicosate of Cilicia, 1914–1972]. Antelias, Lebanon: Catholicosate of Cilicia, 1975.

Yeretsian, Dikran. *Vorperu Pouynē (1915–1921)* [The Nest of Orphans (1915–1921)]. Aleppo: Ani Publishing, 1934.

Zürcher, Erik-Jan. "Between Death and Desertion: The Experience of the Ottoman Soldier in World War I." *Turcica* 28 (1996): 235–258.

Index

A

Abdulahad Nuri, 28
Abdülhamid (Sultan). *See* Hamidian Massacres
Adana, xxi, 3, 7, 9, 14, 26, 50, 93, 106
Adıvar, Halide Edib, 49
Aghazarian, Mihran, xxiv, xxv, 123, 125–128, 133, 139, 180 (n. 25), 204–205 (n. 13)
Aghazarian, Stepan G., 65, 131
Aintab, 20, 71, 73, 75, 93, 131, 135–136
Akçam, Taner, 140, 142
Albistan, 124, 208 (n. 54)
Aleppo: deportees escape to, 63, 94, 97, 99, 107, 109–110, 130–131, 135; food prices in, xiv; local authorities in, xx; massacre of 1919, 144–145; survivors return to, 143–144. *See also* Celal Bey
Alexanian, Takouhi, 46
Ali Fuad Erden, 38, 53
Ali Suat Bey, 124–128, 131, 133–134, 142
Altounyan, Asadour Aram, xxiv–xxvi, 18, 20, 39, 45–46, 50, 148
Altounyan, Nora, xxiv, 18, 20, 44–46
Altounyan Hospital, xxiv, 18, 20, 35, 37, 46
American Committee for Armenian and Syrian Relief (ACASR), 43, 48. *See also* Near East Relief (NER)
American Red Cross, 144
Amiralian, Arika, xxiv–xxv, 26–27
Amiralian, Levon, 71
Ananian, Gurji, 63
Andonian, Aram, 18, 41, 69, 73, 75, 81, 88, 99, 109, 125, 139
Angora (Ankara), 74, 129, 136
Ankut, Krikor. *See* Krikor Ankut
Antoura, 48

Arab Revolt, 128
Arabs, 47, 50, 86, 88, 94, 107, 113, 117–118, 128; bandits, 101, 203 (n. 100); nationalism, 82; officials, 75, 91, 146–147
Armenian Apostolic Church, xxi–xxii, xxiv–xxv, 4–6, 33, 45, 48, 77, 147. *See also* Armenian patriarchate of Constantinople; Armenian patriarchate of Jerusalem
Armenian Catholic Church, xxi, xxii, xxv, 4, 6, 23, 122–123, 147; clergy, 30, 129, 143
Armenian Evangelical Church, xxi, xxii, xxv, 4, 23, 45; community, 45, 95
Armenian patriarchate of Constantinople, 21, 31–33, 40, 44, 105, 156 (n. 21), 159 (n. 71), 167 (n. 42)
Armenian patriarchate of Jerusalem, 33
Armenian Relief Committee (ARC), xxii, 42–43. *See also* American Committee for Armenian and Syrian Relief (ACASR)
Armenian Revolutionary Federation (ARF), xix, 150 (n. 12), 214 (n. 8)
Arsenian, Hagop, 82, 93, 97, 100, 108, 109, 186 (n. 46)
Arslanian, Dajad, 36,58, 70, 74, 85–86
Assyrians, xxiv, 122, 125
Ayalon, Yaron, xxi, xxii

B

Baghdad Railway, 22, 73, 130
barges, redeportation by, 100–101
Basmajian, Jirair, 73
Bauer, Yehuda, xx
Bedouins, 27, 65, 131, 132, 154 (n. 44)
Bedoukian, Kerop, 36
Beirut, 13, 145, 147
Bekir Sami, 13, 19, 23, 29, 31, 45–46, 52
Belkind, Eitan, 90
Berlin, 17, 18
Berlin–Baghdad Railway, 22, 73, 130
Bernau, Auguste, 62, 65, 67, 94–97, 113–114, 116, 133–134
Bethmann Hollweg, Theobald von, 16
Beylerian, Mikayel, 74
Boer War, 59–60
Boghigian, Khachadur, xxv,15, 31, 77
Boyajian, Elmas, 45, 47–48, 72
Boyajian, Haig, 75
Bozanti, 35
Bozoghluyan, Setrak, 78
Bozouklian, Mgrdich, 75
bribes, 71, 86–87, 94, 96–97, 99, 106, 108, 110, 123
buriers, 85–87, 97–98, 189 (n. 100)

C

Captanian, Payladzou, 19–20, 27, 72–74
Catholic Armenians. *See* Armenian Catholic Church
Catholicos Sahag Khabayan. *See* Khabayan, Catholicos Sahag, II
Celal Bey, 5, 9, 11–14, 19, 23
Cemal Pasha, 11, 24, 26, 31, 35, 46, 91; interactions with prominent Armenians in Aleppo, 18–20, 46–48; meetings with Catholicos, 14–16, 22; reappraisal of role during the genocide, 49–53
Chaghlasian, Toros, 71
Chaldeans, 122. *See also* Assyrians
Charek, Ghazar, xxvii, 7, 19, 23, 47, 49
cholera. *See* epidemics
Chorbajian, Apraham, 7

Chorbajian Majarian, Loossin, 26, 92–93, 97
Çiçek, M. Talha, 50
Cilicia, 4, 6, 14, 33. *See also* Khabayan, Catholicos Sahag, II
Circassians, 31–32, 44, 75, 92, 98–99, 112, 114, 130–133
collaborators, 75
Committee of Union and Progress (CUP), xix, xx, xxiii, 29, 33, 49–50, 61
concentration camps, xvii, xxvii, 27, 29, 34, 49, 62; genesis of, 57–61; liquidation of, 65–67, 87–88, 93, 101–102, 107–108, 110, 133; movement in and between, 63–64, 92, 98; price gouging in, 94–95
Constantinople. *See* Istanbul
conversion, 117, 131–132
Çorum, 87
Cox, John M., xx
Cuba, 57–59

D

Dadrian, Vahakn N., 66, 152 (n. 30)
Dadrian, Vahram, 10, 167 (n. 41), 183 (n. 2), 183 (n. 4)
Damascus, 51, 53, 70, 75, 129, 138, 143, 145
Danielian Eskijian, Gulenia, xv, 37–38, 148
Davis, Leslie A., 137, 167 (n. 47), 188 (n. 94)
Deir Ez-Zor. *See* Der Zor
denial of genocide, xviii, 66, 140–141
Der Garabedian, Hagop, 144
Der Stepanian, Shmavon, 109
Der Yeghiayan, Zaven, 21, 44. *See also* Armenian patriarchate of Constantinople
Der Zor, xvii, xxi, 67, 73, 84, 90–91, 98, 100; massacres in, xxiv, 24, 37, 96, 101; (re) deportation to, 40, 53, 62, 66, 72, 81, 89, 93, 97; sending aid to, 6, 16, 44, 77
Dipsi, 66, 89, 106–108
Directorate for the Settlement of Tribes and Emigrants (IAMM), 4, 28–29, 32, 38, 99, 102, 142
Dishchekenian, Hagop, 112
Dishchekenian, Hovsep, 71, 97
Diyarbakir, 15, 49, 52, 91, 125, 140, 142
Dörtyol, 3, 6, 10–11, 15, 76
Doumanian, Hovhannes Toros, 41, 117
Drapac, Vesna, xviii
Dündar, Fuat, 50, 122, 141
Dwork, Debórah, 49
dysentery. *See* epidemics

E

Eichmann, Adolf, 46
Enver Pasha, 49–50, 176 (n. 171)
epidemics, xxii, 8, 9, 34, 61, 132, 142; cholera, 91; dysentery, 34, 39, 74, 89, 97; malaria, 127, 207 (n. 47); typhoid fever, xv, 37–38, 97; typhus in Aleppo, 20, 26, 34–39, 46–47, 167 (n. 47), typhus in concentration camps, 63, 77, 81–86, 89, 97, 125, 127, 132
Erzerum, 23, 115–116
Eskijian, Gulenia. *See* Danielian Eskijian, Gulenia
Eskijian, Hovhannes, xv, xxiv, 4, 7, 37, 44, 148
Eskişehir, 70
Etmekjian, Hovhannes, 6, 77, 186 (n. 52)
Evangelical Armenians. *See* Armenian Evangelical Church

F

factories. *See* workshops (deportee labor)
Fahri Bey (Fahrettin Pasha), 14–15, 116, 118
Faisal, Emir (Prince), 41, 143
Fatih (Kör), 113
Fikri Bey, 12
Forty Martyrs Cathedral (Aleppo), 7
Foster, Zachary J., 123

G

Galip Bey, 96, 109–110, 112
Garabed (courier), xxiv, 44, 130, 134
Geddes, Walter M., 39
Germany, 17, 20, 60. *See also* Berlin
Ghazarian, Hagop(os), 109
Ghazarosian, Ghazaros (Marzbed), xxvi–xxvii
Goldhagen, Daniel Jonah, xx
Great Britain, 59, 145
Greeks, 9

H

Hairabedian, Mgrdich, 34, 36
Hajin, 3–4, 6, 10, 41, 69, 75–76, 79, 93, 131
Hakkı Bey, 96, 110, 138
Halide Edib (Adıvar), 49
Hamam, 76, 89, 109–113
Hamidian massacres, xxi
Hardegg, Julius Loytved, 53
Harput (Kharpert), 22–23, 124–125
Hasanbeyli, 6, 10, 76, 78–79
Hauran, 51, 53, 73
Hazarabedian, Melkon, 71
Hazarabedian, Yeghishe, 6, 28, 71, 92, 94–95, 97, 108, 110–111
Herero genocide, 59, 66
Hoffmann, Hermann, 135–137
Holocaust, xvii–xviii, xx, 49, 59, 66–67, 82, 116, 140
Hovannesian, Karekin, 100
Hüseyin Avni Bey, 92–94, 96, 99, 102
Hüseyin Kazım Kadri, 38, 51
Hüseyin, Kör. *See* Kör Hüseyin
Hyslop, Jonathan, 59

I

İbrahim Pirizâde, 31
Idlib, xxi–xxii, 15, 32, 77–78, 129
Ishak Çavuş, 112
İsmail Enver. *See* Enver Pasha
Istanbul: Armenians not deported from, 119; arrests of Armenian leaders in, xxvi, 30, 40; humanitarian efforts in, 156 (n. 21)

J

Jackson, Jesse B.: local opinions about, 45, 129; reports by, 7, 29, 34, 40, 42, 47, 72, 76, 132, 136; role in humanitarian resistance, xxiv, 27, 43, 44, 148
Jambazian, Dikran, 135
Jernazian, Ephraim K., 95
Jerusalem, xxiv, 25, 32–33. *See also* Armenian patriarchate of Jerusalem
Jews, xviii, xx, 9, 46, 51, 79, 90, 116, 148
Jidejian, Tavit, 34, 155 (n. 9), 165 (n. 29)
Jiyerjian, Sarkis, 6, 20, 155 (n. 9)
Juskalian, Hovannes, 48

K

Kaiser, Hilmar, 53, 125, 142
Kaltakjian, Boghos, 188 (n. 85)
Kaltakjian, Jivan, 83, 188 (n. 85)
Kapigian, Garabed, xxiv, 115–118, 144

Karajian, Arakel, 130
Karlık, 38, 64, 69–76, 97, 110
Kasabian, Setrag, 134
Kaselian, Avedis, 75, 93
Kasuni, Manuel, 73
Kayseri, 75, 83, 86
Keegan, John, 60
Kehyeyan, Nechan, 70
Kejejian, Maritza, 130
Kelegian, Dikran, 180 (n. 24)
Kerr, Stanley Elphinstone, 46, 84
Kévorkian, Raymond, 31, 50, 60, 137, 142
Khabayan, Catholicos Sahag, II, 9, 11, 13–17, 21,31, 51, 124. *See also* Armenian Apostolic Church; Jerusalem
Khabur, 133, 135–136
Khachadryan, Asdvadzadur, 32
Khachadurian, Artin, 75
Khachadurian, Onnig, 101
Khacherian, Hovhannes, 80, 83, 86–87
Kharpert (Harput), 22–23, 124–125
Khubeserian, Hayganush, 73
Khrlakian, Hagop Agha, 71, 97
Kilis, 15, 71, 77, 124
Kirazian, Rakel, 95
Kitabjian, Artin, 25, 86
Konya, xix, 13, 83, 92, 96
Koomrian, Makroohie, 127
Koomrian, Nathan, 70
Kör Fatih, 113
Kör Hüseyin, 75, 99, 102
Krikor Ankut, xxiv, 106–107
Kühne, Thomas, 59
Künzler, Jakob, 202 (n. 94)
Kurds, 91, 132
Kurt, Ümit, 50
Kut al Amara, 112
Kütahya, 170 (n. 81)
Kutnerian, Kevork, 97
Kuyumjian, Ohannes, 18, 29

L

Lemkin, Raphael, 67, 214 (n. 8)
Liman von Sanders, Otto, 18
lists: of deportees, xxi, 5, 10, 134, 151 (n. 22), 156 (n. 17), 180 (n. 25), 205 (n. 17); of perpetrators, 75
Litten, Wilhelm, 94, 100, 106, 111
locusts, xxii, 123, 170–171 (n. 89)
Lodge, Henry Cabot, 57
Lustig, Walter, 46

M

Maarra, xxi–xxii, 10, 12, 15, 23, 77–78, 163 (n. 2)
Madley, Benjamin, 59
Mahmud Nedim, 101
malaria. *See* epidemics
Maljian, Pascal Harootune, 30, 143
Mamigonian, Hrant, 75
Marash, 6, 26, 63, 65, 71, 93, 97, 127
Marzbed (Ghazaros Ghazarosian), xxvi–xxvii
Matossian, Setrag G., 64
Mazloumian, Armenag, xxiv, xxvi, 13, 18–19, 39, 45, 50, 133
Mazloumian, Krikor, 18
Mazloumian, Onnig, xxiv, xxvi, 13, 18–19, 39, 45, 50
Mehmed Reşid, 52, 91, 125, 142
Mehmed V Reşâd, 11
Mekhlian, Menend, 46
Meskeneh, 62–63, 66–67, 105–107, 109–110, 112–113

Mesopotamia, 4, 94, 111–112, 122, 140
Metternich, Paul Wolff, 52
Meyadin, 132, 136
Migliorino, Nicola, 147
Miller, Donald E., xviii
Minassian, John, 7, 36–37, 44, 46, 148
Misakian, Shavarsh, xix
missionaries, xvii, xxi–xxiv, 20, 27, 129, 137, 147
Mkhitarian, Kiud, 22, 51
Möhring, Laura, 123
Momjian, Garabed, 75
Moore, Bob, xx
Morgenthau, Henry, 8, 22, 42–43
Mosul, xix, 23, 123, 130, 132–133, 137, 144
Mühlhahn, Klaus, 60
Mumbuj, 10, 15, 23, 77, 80, 99, 101; priests exiled to, 31–33
Musa Dagh, xviii

N

Naim Efendi, 38, 48, 71–72, 74, 99, 107
Nama genocide, 59, 66
Near East Relief (NER), 46, 172 (n. 100)
Niepage, Martin, 39
Niğde, 95
Nordigian, Artin Çavuş, 106

O

Odian, Yervant, 25, 27, 41, 74–75, 97, 122
Oppenheim, Max von, 52
orphanages: in Aleppo, xxv–xxvi, 20, 44–48, 72, 146–147; in Der Zor, 127–128, 137; in Meskeneh, 94–96
Ovacık, 74, 82
Ovajikian, Toros, 35
Özdemir, Hikmet, 53

P

patriarchate, Armenian. *See* Armenian patriarchate of Constantinople; Armenian patriarchate of Jerusalem
Peet, William W., 202 (n. 94)
pharmacists, 15–16, 77–78, 82, 97–98, 108, 117, 124
post offices, xix, 63, 81, 83
Protestant Armenians. *See* Armenian Evangelical Church

R

Rahmeddin (corporal), 108–110
Ras ul-Ain, xvii, xix, 51, 53, 124–125, 138; concentration camp, 61, 64–66; massacres in, 24, 101, 128–133, 140–142
Renda, Mustafa Abdülhalik, 29, 152 (n. 30)
Reşid, Mehmed. *See* Mehmed Reşid
Riha, xxi, 15, 77
Rohner, Beatrice, 88, 112, 135, 148; humanitarian work, xxiv, xxv, 37, 44, 48, 130
Rössler, Walter: reports on deportations and massacres, 8, 35, 52, 64, 74, 90, 124, 134; reports on humanitarian efforts, xxiv, 11, 16–17, 27, 46, 73, 85, 110
Roubian Shirajian, Lucia, 46

S

Sahag, Father, 15, 16, 77–78, 124, 161 (n. 98)
Salih Zeki Bey. *See* Zeki Bey
Santoorian, Elmasd, xxiv, 26, 38, 47
Sasun, 145
Satjian, Harutiun, 134

Schacht (German doctor), 91, 122, 126
Sebil, 36, 72–76, 85
Sebka, 38, 89, 136, 196 (n. 90)
Şeker, Nesim, 61
Seropian, Hagop, 73, 75, 80, 92, 96, 108–109
Setian, Kevork, 78
sexual violence, 64–65, 75
Shabin Karahisar, xviii
shakhtoors. *See* barges
Shashian, Levon, xxiv, 126, 128, 135
Shmavonian, A., 8
Sholakian, Apraham, 88
Simonian, Yeranuhi, 7, 27, 64, 70, 131
Sinanian, Haji, 7
Sinanian, Manug, 7
Sivrihisar, 100
Smyrna, 119, 134
Soultanian, Kevork B., 70
South African War, 59–60
Stamboulian, Peniamin, 83
Şükrü Kaya Bey, 28, 32, 35, 39, 48, 114

T

Talaat Pasha, 50, 52–53, 122, 125, 138, 142; orders, 28–32, 39, 41, 71, 97, 113
Tarpinian, Yetvart, 93, 95–96
Tawtal, Joseph, 134
Tec, Nechama, xx
Tengerian, Verzhin, 81, 84
Toroyan, Hayg, 8, 90–91, 93–95
Touryan Miller, Lorna, xviii
typhoid fever. *See* epidemics
typhus. *See* epidemics

U

United States of America, xxii, 42–44, 57, 60, 63
Urfa, xvii, 23, 28, 62, 95, 115–119, 130

V

vaccinations, 8, 78, 186 (n. 61)
Vahan, Father, 79
Van, xviii, xxi, 15
Varjabedian, Gosdan, 111
Varjabedian, Khoren, 111
vesika, 26, 41–42, 82, 115, 171 (n. 90)

W

Wachsmann, Nikolaus, 59
Wangenheim, Hans Freiherr von, 17
Watenpaugh, Keith David, xxii, xxiii, 145
Weber, Max, 101
Weyler, Valeriano, 57–58
workshops (deportee labor), xxiv, 26–27, 50, 147

Y

Yeghpayrian, Karekin, 99, 195 (n. 76)
Yeretsian, Dikran, 37, 46
Yesayan, Harutiun, xxiv, xxv, 11, 20–21, 30–31, 118

Z

Zahle, xxiv, 19
Zeki Bey, 83, 133–136, 142, 211 (n. 95)
Zekiyan, Mihran, 132
Zeynel Çavuş, 64–65
Zeytun, 6, 15, 76, 79, 123–125, 134, 151 (n. 22)
Zollinger, Emil, xxiv, xxv, 45
Zürcher, Erik-Jan, 29, 61